A TRAVELER'S GUIDE
to the Smoky Mountains Region

D1526921

Balun 84

Ky.

W. VA.

VA.

⑨ Southwestern Virginia

Bristol

Kingsport

① Upper East Tennessee

Cumberland Gap

② Knoxville & Surroundings

Knoxville

④ Great Smoky Mtns. Nat. Park

③ Chattanooga & Surroundings

Chattanooga

North Carolina

⑤ Upper Blue Ridge

The Blue Ridge Parkway

⑥

Asheville

Hendersonville

N.C.

⑦ Lower North Carolina

S.C.

⑧ North Georgia

Dahlonega

GA.

ALA.

TENN.

A TRAVELER'S GUIDE

to the Smoky Mountains Region

Jeff Bradley

THE HARVARD COMMON PRESS
Harvard and Boston, Massachusetts

The Harvard Common Press
535 Albany Street
Boston, Massachusetts 02118

Printed in the United States of America.

Library of Congress Cataloging in Publication Data

Bradley, Jeff, 1952–
  A traveler's guide to the Smoky Mountains region.

  Includes index.
  1. Great Smoky Mountains Region (N.C. and Tenn.)—
Description and travel—Guide-books. 2. Appalachian
Region, Southern—Description and travel—Guide-
books. I. Title.
F443.G7B73   1985   917.68'890453   84–25119
ISBN 0–916782–63–8
ISBN 0–916782–64–6 (pbk.)

Maps by Charles Bahne
Cover design by Laurie Dolphin
Cover photo by Marta Turnbull

10 9 8 7 6 5 4 3 2

To George and Irene Bradley,
for making me a Tennessean

Contents

Preface

My father and uncle are in the excavating business in East Tennessee, and from the time I was a boy I heard them talk about the little towns and back roads of the southern Appalachians. My father would come home talking of places such as Big Stone Gap or High Knob, Virginia. Some of his employees could not read, and I would listen as he would give them directions to a job according to landmarks—landmarks with names such as Wadlow Gap, Bumpass Cove, and Sawmill Hollow.

My family made weekend trips to attractions such as Grandfather Mountain, Tweetsie Railroad, and the Great Smoky Mountains National Park. As I got a little older and joined the Scouts, the region's wilderness was opened up to me. I hiked portions of the Appalachian Trail, camped in places such as Linville Gorge, and paddled a canoe down the Nolichucky River.

As I grew older and took to the roads myself, my girlfriend and I made day trips to places such as Blowing Rock, Spruce Pine, and Little Switzerland, North Carolina. We explored little towns that hitherto had been simply names on a map.

When that girlfriend became my wife, we continued to explore the region by hiking in the mountains, pitching our tent in campgrounds, and staying in old inns. We bicycled on the Blue Ridge Parkway and canoed on mountain lakes. We deliberately sought out the back roads and lesser traveled trails, and sometimes just wandered along for entire weekends.

In 1979 we left the southern Appalachians to live in Massachusetts, and our trips south became limited to two or three a year. As we began to mingle with people who considered themselves well traveled, we were somewhat surprised to learn that few of them had ever been to our former home. Those who had had usually made a beeline for the Great Smoky Mountains National Park, and knew nothing of sights such as the flowering rhododendron on Roan Mountain, Tennessee, the fresco paintings in Jefferson, North Carolina, or Natural Tunnel in Virginia. We found ourselves urging people to make trips to the mountains of the South, and supplying them with what information we had.

Virtually all of them came back with enthusiastic reports. The idea for a book on the region gradually took shape, and as I began pulling together the information I realized I was writing with two distinct audiences in mind. The first consists of those who have never been in the Southern mountains at all—those whose impressions of the region and its inhabitants have often been shaped by TV shows like "The Beverly Hillbillies" or books such as *Deliverance.*

The second group is made up of those who have lived in the region all their lives, or who spend a lot of time there in a second home. These folks often consider themselves pretty knowledgeable about things to do and see. I used to fall in this category myself. Often people like us are surprised to learn that Breaks Interstate Park in Virginia contains the Grand Canyon of the East, or that the Grace Calvary Church of Clarkesville, Georgia, was built in 1842 and still looks the same as when the doors first opened.

Whether you are a newcomer or an old-timer, taking to the road in the southern Appalachians is a most pleasurable thing to do. While in and around the oldest mountains in the country you'll find countless charming examples of nature's handiwork, no matter what season of the year. Delights such as icicles hanging from a roadside bluff in winter, spring wildflowers, cool summer days on mountain peaks, and groves of brilliantly colored autumn trees await the traveler.

But those who concentrate totally on nature are missing the best part of the region: the people. In a society that is increasingly homogenized by Top Forty song lists and the all-pervasive television, Southern Appalachia remains a refreshingly different place. The man on the side of the road giving directions may use phrases and words that date from Shakespeare's time. The woman whose quilts are for sale may have duplicated patterns handed down through her family for generations. And the Free Will Baptist preacher you hear on the radio may sound like nothing you have ever heard before. Best of all, the warm welcome extended to visitors at a small-town museum or festival, or even at a country store, is genuine.

Putting this book together was a labor of love. Driving the roads took me to many of my old haunts, and doing the research taught me a lot about this part of the world that I thought I knew so well. Writing about places such as Gregory Bald in the Great Smoky Mountains National Park or the main street of Highlands, North Carolina, made me want to go there again. If the readers of this book can experience a portion of the joy I have had in knowing all these places, then any trip they make to Southern Appalachia will be well worth their while.

Pulling together the information for this book was made a lot easier by the efforts of several people. I must collectively thank the dozens of chambers of commerces that sent along information from four states. Apologies are in order for the various towns, sights, and events that could not be included for lack of space.

A special note of appreciation goes to those individuals who supplied information and looked over the manuscript for errors. David Harkness, whose knowledge of East Tennessee is encyclopedic, checked out Chapter 2, while John Payne of the Chattanooga Area Convention and Visitors' Center cast an eye over Chapter 3. Pat Miller of the Great Smoky Mountains National Park provided valuable assistance, and Don DeFoe of the park kindly looked over Chapter 4. Susan Wilmoth of the High Country Host helped with Chapter 5, and Steve Beatty of the Blue Ridge Parkway checked the facts for Chapter 6. Don Wick of the Tennessee Department of Tourist Development supplied very useful material.

Linda Ziedrich, my editor, curbed tendencies to wax excessively lyrical. Truman Bradley accompanied me on trips south, Benjamin Waterhouse oversaw various aspects of production, and Mike Durall assisted with proofreading. Finally, thanks must go to Marta Turnbull, my wife, for her help in every stage of this enterprise. Little did she know in 1973, when we were pitching a tent in the dark at a campground on the Blue Ridge Parkway, that all such trips would result in a book.

How to Use This Book

A Traveler's Guide to the Smoky Mountains Region is not the first guidebook written for this area. Like the others, it lists restaurants, out-of-the-way mountain towns, and various and sundry wonders to be seen and photographed. Unlike most of the other books, however, this one backs its listings with old tales, history, and commentary to give the reader a sense of why the southern Appalachians are such a special place.

This book was written for people who want to understand the history and culture of the area they visit. Places like Saltville, Virginia, and Kingsport and Chattanooga, Tennessee, may be more interesting when you know that in colonial days salt from Saltville was shipped from King's Port to Chattanooga. And knowing that the first vacationers in this part of the world were rich plantation owners from South Carolina makes it easy to understand why the oldest inns are in the lower part of North Carolina.

That's why this book is filled with seemingly arcane history and odd matter. The magnitude of some information is instantly recognizable; the wartime Manhattan Project in Oak Ridge, Tennessee, had long-lasting implications for us all. Other, less weighty facts are interesting in a quirky sort of way. You'll find, for example, no marker in Burnsville, North Carolina, to honor the grandfather of Jack Dempsey. He did live there, however, and was such a bruiser that the town passed a law banning him from fighting with his fists.

There is a lot of practical information here, too. As any veteran reader of travel brochures can attest, things often get exaggerated in this field. "Quiet mountain towns" can turn out to be choked with traffic, "rustic inns" are all too frequently cheap motels, and "gourmet meals" are sometimes fresh from a tin can. This book tries to honestly appraise towns, attractions, and restaurants, pointing out things worth seeing as well as those that should be taken in only at sixty miles per hour.

So how should you use this book? If you have a definite destination in mind, you can look up the various towns you will pass on the way and see which ones strike your fancy. The towns are listed alphabetically by region, along with major attractions. If your trip is less structured, you might look for pointers in the section headed "Once You're There" at the beginning of each chapter.

Throughout the book runs the theme of getting off the beaten path—away from the highly visited places to some of the lesser known towns and natural attractions. The Great Smoky Mountains National Park is a wonderful place, but you may be less excited about going there when you consider that people make around nine million visits to the park every year. The Pisgah National Forest, right next door, contains natural wonders that in some cases surpass those of the more popular national park. And Pisgah attracts far fewer people.

An important note: Things change. Inns and restaurants close, festivals are held on different dates, and attractions close for refurbishing or change their hours. If you really must see some sight or attend a particular event, take the time to call ahead and make sure that everything is still there and happening on schedule.

"I offer no apologies for any departures from the usual style of travel-writing that may be charged against me—for I think I have seen with impartial eyes, and I am sure I have written at least honestly, whether wisely or not."

Mark Twain, *The Innocents Abroad*

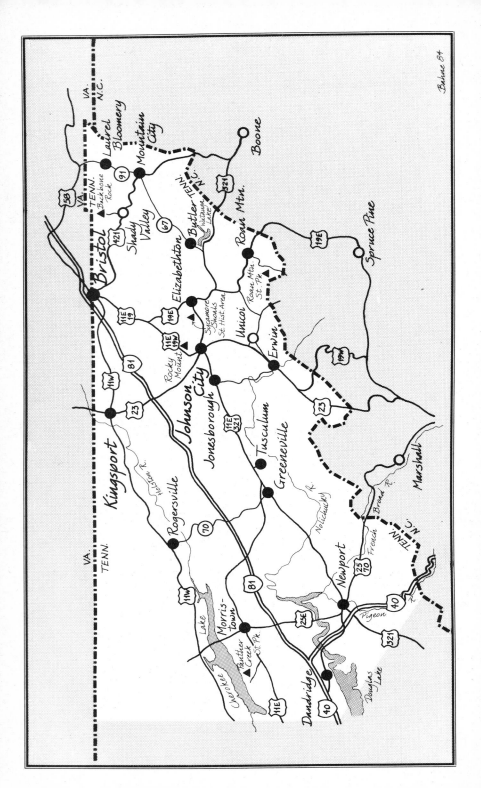

ONE

Upper East Tennessee

THE SHAPE OF TENNESSEE is sometimes compared to that of a ship. Upper Tennessee is the bow of the vessel, steaming toward the Atlantic. The easternmost part of Tennessee is closer to Canada than to Memphis, and the differences between this part of the state and the rest of it are measured in more than miles.

In the beginning this region was populated by the Cherokee Indians, a tribe whose agriculture was as advanced as any in the country, yet who were capable of intense and deadly warfare. The cross-continental Great Warpath ran through here, and the Cherokees knew it well. The white people who settled in the region were a fiercely independent group, who were willing to disobey the orders from their rulers and push into forbidden and forboding territory. Like the Indians with whom they clashed, these people were fighters. They could easily have sat out the Revolutionary War, until an arrogant British officer, Maj. Patrick Ferguson, sent word across the mountains that if they did not halt any and all opposition to the British he would "march his army over the mountains, hang their leaders, and lay their country waste with fire and sword."

Those were fighting words. The call went out, and a thousand men assembled at the Sycamore Shoals of the Watauga River. They elected leaders and set off, on foot and horseback, on a ten-day march that took them into South Carolina. Others joined them on the way, until their force totaled almost eighteen hundred. They found the British camped on the top of Kings Mountain, and crept to within a few yards of the encampment before being discovered. The leader of the pioneers is recorded as yelling, "Here they are, my brave boys. Shout like hell and fight like devils!"

They did just that. A lifetime of squirrel hunting had made them deadly marksmen, and when it was all over Maj. Ferguson and 1,018 of his troops were dead. The mountaineers lost only 28, and Kings Mountain was the beginning of the end of British rule in America.

The settlers' fierce independence—and their willingness to fight if necessary—played a large role in shaping this region. The Indians were subdued, and in an effort to govern themselves instead of being governed by North Carolina, the settlers tried to create a new state, which they named after Benjamin Franklin. With Jonesborough as its capital, the new state was never officially recognized, and the land instead became a territory of the United States. Eventually Tennessee was admitted to the Union in 1796.

There were never many slaves in upper East Tennessee; the farms were too small and the people who owned them too poor. None of the landholdings there could be called plantations. The fiery talk of Southern secession fell on largely unsympathetic ears in the area, and when the Civil War came, the independent people of upper East Tennessee sent more young men to the Union than to the Confederacy.

This political independence was personified in the postwar presidency of Andrew Johnson, and is still characteristic of the area. East Tennessee remains a Republican region of a Democratic state, a situation which hasn't always helped when it comes to parceling out state money.

In the twentieth century industrialists discovered the

area had plenty of natural resources and people who would work hard and seldom listen to union organizers. The people of the rugged hills, for whom poverty had never been a stranger, welcomed with open arms the representatives of national companies such as Eastman Kodak, Mead Paper, and J. P. Stevens. The factories were a mixed blessing, however, for with the needed jobs came belching smokestacks and chemical poisons in the once clear rivers. Much as in other parts of the country, the cities and towns often turned their backs on their older buildings and nineteenth-century storefronts, either tearing them down or covering them up with "modern" facades. Shopping malls devastated formerly vibrant downtowns.

Fortunately, this process has been largely halted. Small towns such as Rogersville, Jonesborough, and Greeneville have begun emphasizing the features that make small-town life so desirable, and the larger cities and industries have begun to reduce or eliminate pollution. There is a renewed interest in Appalachian music and mountain crafts such as quilting. Clogging classes are filled with people who are proud to continue this traditional form of dance, and festivals celebrate the history of even the smallest towns.

What does all this mean for the visitor? The tourism industry came late to upper East Tennessee, and for this reason the traveler will find none of the theme parks or roadside attractions that characterize areas such as Western North Carolina and the vicinity of the Great Smoky Mountains National Park. This can be good and bad—good in that the long lines of crawling cars are missing, and bad in that a wide choice of restaurants and inns is likewise missing.

The old ways persist. It is not at all unusual to see men plowing with a team of horses or mules. These animals are more practical than tractors on the steep hillsides; during the energy crisis of the 1970s they were doubly valued. Women quilt, either singly or in groups, to pass away the long wintertime, although they now take advantage of the high prices that this meticulous handiwork brings. Despite the influence of television the mountain speech is laced with words and expressions that the translators of the King James Bible would find familiar.

Fundamentalist Protestant religion exercises a hold on a large part of the populace. Visitors will see many churches both in the towns and in the country. The area is sometimes called, with both pride and chagrin, the Buckle on the Bible Belt. For urbane visitors, this has one noticeable effect: few restaurants will serve alcoholic beverages, and the ones that do are located in the larger cities. Even in a place such as Kingsport, with a population approaching forty thousand, until 1984 liquor could not be sold by the glass, a fact that was a source of pride to one group of people and a nuisance to a smaller, perhaps more thirsty, population.

The independent spirit that once led men to march to Kings Mountain is now manifesting itself in a way that an increasing number of visitors find appealing. It may surface in a community museum in Erwin that refuses to take state or federal funds, or a pottery in Laurel Bloomery that won't cut corners, or in an entire town—Jonesboro—that confounds cartographers by changing its name back to the old spelling—Jonesborough. However you come into upper East Tennessee, by jet from New York or by the Appalachian Trail, you'll leave with a more profound appreciation of an area and a people with an indomitable way of life.

HOW TO GET THERE

BY AIR. The area's principal airport for passenger service is Tri-Cities Airport, located in the middle of a triangle formed by Kingsport, Johnson City, and Bristol. Service is offered by Piedmont, USAir, and Eastern Airlines, as well as smaller carriers that crisscross Tennessee.

FROM NORTH CAROLINA. There are three main routes from western North Carolina into upper East Tennessee. The first, and the easiest, is from Asheville on I-40. This highway takes the driver through some of the most rugged and remote territory crossed by any interstate in the East. With high mountains on one side and the Pigeon River on the other, it is one of the more twisting interstates anywhere.

Indeed, twistiness characterizes all of the approaches to East Tennessee from North Carolina. History buffs may prefer to follow U.S. 25/70 from Asheville to Newport. This route follows the French Broad River, and was used by drovers and wagon drivers in the 1700s and 1800s on their way to the markets of Charleston, South Carolina. The road is mostly two-laned, although there are sections where one can pass a slow truck or bus. This route takes you near Marshall and Hot Springs (see Chapter 5) and joins I-40 outside of Newport.

U.S. 23 leaves Asheville and heads straight up the side of a mountain toward Erwin. Before I-40 was constructed, this was the prime way of crossing the mountains.

Route 19E from Spruce Pine and U.S. 321 from Boone both lead from North Carolina to Elizabethton, Tennessee. They are similar also in that they offer scenic views and pass small towns like Roan Mountain and Butler, respectively.

U.S. 421, from Boone, North Carolina, is one of Tennessee's Scenic Parkways, but it leads to the least populated section of the state with relatively few things to see.

FROM VIRGINIA. The most obvious road from Virginia, and the one most Easterners use, is I-81. Bristol is the first town they encounter, with Kingsport and Johnson City close by.

Another route from Virginia, one more convenient for travelers coming down I-75 from the Midwest, is U.S. 23. This leads right into Kingsport.

FROM THE REST OF TENNESSEE. Interstate 40 is the most convenient way of getting into upper East Tennessee, although those who wish to avoid the major highway may opt for U.S. 11W or U.S. 11E out of Knoxville. Those taking 11W can visit Rogersville before coming to Kingsport, whereas those who travel 11E can partake of the joys of Jefferson City, Morristown, and Greeneville before hitting Johnson City.

ONCE YOU'RE THERE

There is not an abundance of inns in upper East Tennessee, and most of the restaurants urban dwellers usually prefer are in Kingsport, Johnson City, and Bristol. It may be a good idea to stay in one of these cities and make day trips into the surrounding area.

One good loop, which largely follows officially designated scenic roads, leads from Bristol by U.S. 421 to Mountain City, then by Tennessee 67 to Butler, then by U.S. 321 to Elizabethton and on to Johnson City.

Fanciers of historic small towns might head out of Kingsport on U.S. 11W toward Rogersville, then cut south on Tennessee 70 to Greeneville. From there, U.S. 11E will lead to Jonesborough and then into Johnson City.

The most mountainous route leads from Johnson City to Jonesborough and Erwin on Tennessee 81. Head toward Unicoi on U.S. 23; take Tennessee 107 and then Tennessee 173 to Roan Mountain, which lies on U.S. 19E. A hike to the top of Roan Mountain will cure any stiffness you feel from sitting in the car.

TOWNS AND ATTRACTIONS

BRISTOL. This town straddles Tennessee and Virginia, and the state line is in the middle of—what else?—State Street. Bristol is known to music fans, however, as the birthplace of country music. In 1927 the first country music recording to be distributed nationwide was made here. The artists were the Carter Family, a local trio who recorded such classics as "Will the Circle Be Unbroken" and "Wildwood Flower." Other singers and pickers associated with Bristol include Lester Flatt, Earl Scruggs, Jimmy Rogers, and Tennessee Ernie Ford, who was born here.

Bristol Caverns. An excellent respite from summertime heat, these caverns are well lit and have safe walkways. The formations are well worth seeing, despite the somewhat corny names inflicted on them. The caverns, open all year, are five miles southeast of Bristol on U.S. 421. Call (615) 878-2011.

Bristol International Raceway. One of the National Association for Stock Car Auto Racing tracks, this half-mile oval provides an opportunity to see one of the South's prime spectator sports. Note to novices: Take earplugs, and don't get smart with the people who have large coolers. The Thunder Valley dragway is next door. Eight miles south of Bristol on U.S. 11E.

Grand Guitar. This guitar museum is housed in a building that looks like a seventy-foot-long guitar. It contains a collection of more than two hundred guitars, ukuleles, dobros, banjos, mandolins, autoharps, and violins. Located off I-81, Exit 74A, on U.S. 11W. The building is hard to miss. It is open Tuesday through Saturday from 11:00 to 8:00 and Sundays from 12:00 till 6:00. Closed on Mondays. Closed from January 15 through February 28.

Steele Creek Park. Located outside of Bristol on Tennessee 126, this park sits on one side of a narrow lake. Visitors can rent canoes or paddleboats, and picnicking areas are available.

Train Station Marketplace. Taking a cue from cities such as Knoxville and Chattanooga, Bristol has renovated its turn-of-the-century train station and filled it with a collection of shops and restaurants. Located on the corner of State and Randolph streets.

Dining

Steele Creek Junction. Southern cuisine, including country ham and smoked turkey and beef, is the specialty here. Dinners are served family style, with large platters of food delivered to the table. Beside the restaurant is the Ham House, where you can buy smoked meats to take home. Located on Tennessee 126 south of Bristol.

BUTLER. People in this small town sometimes refer to "old Butler," which was submerged by the construction of Watauga dam and subsequent impoundment of the Watauga River. The citizens simply moved uphill about a quarter mile, and Butler resumed small-town life.

Courtner and Henson Hams. In the days before refrigeration, meat was preserved by coating it with a mixture of salt and sugar and allowing it to cure anywhere from ten months to two years in an outbuilding called a smokehouse. A ham cured in such a fashion is called a country ham, and, sliced and fried, it is the best breakfast meat in the world. The best place in East Tennessee to buy a country ham is Courtner and Henson's in Butler. Housed in two nondescript buildings on the edge of town are thousands of hams that are being cured in the old manner. There are no scheduled tours, but if you catch Howard Courtner on a slow day he may let you take a look at the rows upon rows of white-sacked hams that are aging in the buildings. Hams are shipped from here all over the country, and you can bring home no finer souvenir from the Southern mountains. Courtner and Henson is open Monday through Saturday from 8:00 to 5:00. Phone (615) 768-2744.

CHEROKEE NATIONAL FOREST. Between Virginia and the Smokies the Appalachian Trail runs through portions of the largest national forest in the region. The forest covers 624 thousand acres in ten East Tennessee counties along the Tennessee-North Carolina state line, interrupted only by the Great Smoky Mountains National Park.

The Cherokee National Forest is divided into six ranger districts, three of which lie in upper East Tennessee. (The other three are closer to Chattanooga, and are covered in Chapter 3.) Each is briefly described here. For further information and maps write the Forest Supervisor, 2800 North Ocoee Street, Cleveland, 37311; or call (615) 476-9700.

Nolichucky Ranger District. Located adjacent to the Great Smoky Mountains National Park, this area includes seven campgrounds. For further information write Nolichucky Ranger District, U.S. Forest Service, 504 Justis Drive, Greeneville 37743. Call (615) 638-4109.

Unaka Ranger District. Lying around the mountain town of Erwin, this district includes one natural attraction that shouldn't be missed—the aptly named Beauty Spot. To get to this mountain meadow take Tennessee 230 north from U.S. 23 and follow the signs. There are five campgrounds in the district. For further information write Unaka Ranger District, U.S. Forest Service, 1205 North Main Street, Erwin 37650. Call (615) 743-4452.

Watauga Ranger District. This district contains ten campgrounds, most of which are located near Watauga Lake, a TVA impoundment of the Watauga River. For further information write Watauga Ranger District, U.S. Forest Service, Route 9, Box 352-B, Elizabethton 37643.

CUMBERLAND GAP. "Cumberland Gap is a noted place, / Three kinds of water to wash your face" goes the old bluegrass song. Locals profess to know nothing about the three kinds of water. The town of Cumberland Gap, which grew up at the foot of the break in the mountains, saw plenty of traffic until a new highway bypassed it, and things haven't been the same since. Now there is talk of building a tunnel under the gap, so the local entrepreneurs still have hope.

Iron Furnace. The stone remains of an early nineteenth-century iron furnace are located in one corner of the town. Visitors can step inside and see where the stone walls were glazed by the tremendous heat needed to melt the iron. The furnace is open all the time, and there is no admission fee. To find it drive into Cumberland Gap and follow the signs.

Lodging and Dining

Old Mill Restaurant. Located in downtown Cumberland Gap, this establishment features country dinners in an historic building. It is noted for its hickory-smoked meats.

Note: This book does not venture into Kentucky. Middlesboro, Kentucky—just across the state line from Cumberland Gap—is the largest city in the area and features a reasonable sampling of motels and fast-food emporiums.

DANDRIDGE. Local boosters here have a running battle with their counterparts in Rogersville over which is the second oldest town in Tennessee. Whether second or third, Dandridge is charming. Named after Martha Dandridge Washington, the first First Lady, the town was located on the French Broad River and two important trading routes. Early travelers in the area supported a host of taverns, of which four are still standing.

The seat of Jefferson County, Dandridge is listed in the National Register of Historic Places. The town boasts 36 historic buildings, including the oldest (1845) courthouse still in use in East Tennessee. Frontiersman Davy Crockett was issued a marriage license in Dandridge in 1806, and in 1864 the town witnessed a Civil War skirmish in which Confederate forces routed Union troops and drove them back to Knoxville. The railroad did not come through Dandridge, and the town declined as trade shifted to other places. This decline, however, insured that the old houses and other buildings were not replaced in the name of progress.

After the TVA came into existence, several towns were inundated by newly created lakes. When it looked as if this would happen to Dandridge, the citizens sent up a howl that was heard in the White House. By Executive Order, President Franklin D. Roosevelt brought about the construction of a dike that contained the waters of Douglas Lake and saved Dandridge.

Visitors will find this small town a pedestrian's delight. The houses are well kept, and townsfolk are delighted to have visitors. For a guide to the buildings, get a copy of the Dandridge Landmarks Committee Walking Tour brochure, which describes buildings such as the courthouse, the 1817 Roper Tavern, the 1820 Shepard's Inn, and the 1843 Fain House. Most of the houses listed in the brochure are privately owned and not open to the public. The brochure is available at the courthouse or by mail from Restore Our County, Inc., P.O. Box 329, Dandridge 37725.

Jefferson County Museum. Housed in the 1845 courthouse, this museum contains Indian artifacts, pioneer utensils, Civil War relics, firearms, and documents, letters, and newspapers. The museum is open whenever the courthouse is, and no admission is charged.

Events

Founding Festival. Held in early June, this festival includes mountain music, a re-enactment of a Civil War battle, an antique auto show, booths selling country food, and demonstrations of folk arts and crafts. For further information write Restore Our County, Inc., P.O. Box 329, Dandridge 37725; or call (615) 397-2373.

ELIZABETHTON. Elizabethton's history dates back to the Cherokee Indians, who lived in a village on the Sycamore Shoals of the Watauga River. In 1763 white settlers began trickling into the area, and by 1772 they had set up the Watauga Association—the first permanent American settlement outside the original thirteen colonies. This forerunner of democracy had the first majority-rule system of government on the continent.

The settlers built Fort Watauga, and in 1775 the largest private real estate transaction in U.S. history took place at Sycamore Shoals. A group of land speculators calling themselves the Transylvania Company bought from the Cherokees twenty million acres of land—everything in the Cumberland River watershed and all the land extending to the Kentucky River—for two thousand pounds sterling and goods worth another eight thousand pounds. Twelve hundred Indians reportedly camped at Sycamore Shoals to argue over the deal. Dragging Canoe, a Cherokee warrior, protested this handing over of Indian lands, and when the deal was consummated he made an ominous statement: "You have bought a fair land, but there is a cloud hanging over it. You will find its settlement dark and bloody." In a short time he set about fulfilling his threat, waging war on the whites as they moved further into the land his people had traded away.

John Carter and his son Landon were prominent citizens of the time; Carter County was named after the son. The county seat, Elizabethton, was named after Landon's wife, and it became an important stop for pioneers moving west.

Sycamore Shoals was the gathering point of the "Overmountain Men," a ragtag group of frontiersmen who were not content to sit out the Revolutionary War. They assembled here and marched southeast to Kings Mountain, South Carolina, and thoroughly thrashed the British there in a battle that has been called the turning point of the revolution in the South.

In the twentieth century, German industrialists gathered in Elizabethton to take advantage of the area's timber to manufacture rayon. The American Bemberg Corporation prospered, but the Germans who worked there had to lie low during the world wars.

Carter Mansion. This two-hundred-year-old house, built by John Carter, is perhaps the only relic of the early Watauga Association. Unlike many buildings from that period, it has been preserved rather than restored. Students of early American architecture will note the two over-mantle landscape panels, built-in paintings over the fireplaces. Three rooms have their original wall finishes, and an estimated 90 percent of the home is original building material. It is situated three miles north of the Sycamore Shoals State Historic Area. Take U.S. 321 north past U.S. 19E to Broad Street Extension.

Doe River Covered Bridge. Built in 1882 at a cost of three thousand dollars, this 154-foot structure is one of the oldest covered bridges still in use in the state. It is included in the National Registry of Historic Sites. To get there go to Riverside Avenue.

Sinking Creek Baptist Church. Located on U.S. 321 between Elizabethton and Johnson City, this log building is the oldest church in Tennessee.

Sycamore Shoals State Historic Area. This museum and replica of Fort Watauga lies in the historic area that played such a prominent role in Tennessee history. An informative film is shown throughout the day, and visitors can see native artifacts in the museum. The fort is a good place to take children, and there is a walk along the shoals that gave the place its name. The Visitors' Center is open daily from 8:00 to 4:30, and no admission is charged. The park is open from 8:00 AM until 10:00 PM in the summer and until sundown in the winter. It is located on U.S. 321 on the west end of Elizabethton.

Events

Covered Bridge Celebration. Held in mid-June, this event centers on the century-old covered bridge, and includes arts and crafts as well as live music and plenty to eat. For further information on this and other Elizabethton events call (615) 543-2122.

Peter's Hollow Egg Fight. Every year in April the residents of the region boil dozens of eggs and "fight" each other by gently tapping one egg against another. The one whose egg breaks first loses. Participants feed their chickens secret ingredients in an effort to toughen the eggshells.

Sycamore Shoals Craft Festival. Held in May, this gathering brings together local craftspeople for sales and demonstrations.

ERWIN. This town, nestled in the Unaka Mountains, was named after Dr. J. N. Ervin, but an anonymous clerk in the U.S. Postal Service misspelled the name. Erwin it remained. Near the town is the site of the Greasy Cove Racetrack, where there occurred a telling episode concerning the seventh president of the United States. Young Andrew Jackson owned a race horse, and when he moved to Jonesborough he challenged the owner of the local champion to a race between the two steeds. At the last minute Jackson's jockey got sick, and the future president decided to ride the horse himself. He lost the race, and got into an argument with the winner's owner, who called him "a long, gangling, sorrel-topped soap stick." Only the intervention of friends prevented a duel.

The Greasy Cove Racetrack is no more. Erwin used to be the headquarters of the Clinchfield Railroad, and the extensive rail yards still make up a good portion of the town. They were the scene of one of the more bizarre episodes of Tennessee history. In the early part of this century a circus was visiting Kingsport when an elephant named Mary killed two people. The citizens of Kingsport convened a trial and sentenced the pachyderm to death. Then they had to decide how to dispatch her. Five pistol shots accomplished little, and someone suggested sending the doomed elephant to the railyards in Erwin, where there was a large crane. This was done, and hundreds of people gathered to watch Mary's execution.

Erwin boosters decry any ill feelings directed at their town for this event, and insist that Kingsport should receive all the blame and any notoriety.

Erwin National Fish Hatchery. This is one of only two national fish hatcheries in Tennessee, and well worth a stop. The personnel here extract up to eighteen million rainbow trout eggs per year. These are shipped to other hatcheries around the country, and the fish are stocked in rivers and streams. Children often like to look in the long tanks filled with trout, and the grounds include a picnic area. Adjoining the hatchery is the Unicoi County Heritage Museum and a city park with a swimming pool, tennis courts, ball parks, and a nature trail. The hatchery is located on U.S. 23 and is open to the public seven days a week from 7:30 to 4:00. **Rock Creek Park.** This park, set on a bone-chilling trout stream, is a good place to camp or simply spend some time in the outdoors. It has hiking trails, swimming, 37 tent or trailer camping sites, and several good fishing spots. It is located six miles off Main Street on Forest Road 30. Follow the signs. Call (615) 743-4452. **Unicoi County Heritage Museum.** When the Erwin National Fish Hatchery was built in 1903, a fine home was constructed for the superintendent. Rising heating bills convinced recent superintendents to live elsewhere, and the house became dilapidated. An official of the Reagan administration ordered the house destroyed, but efforts by concerned Erwinians prevented this from happening, and the house became a local museum.

The museum receives no money from the state or the federal government; various civic groups have filled rooms with an eclectic collection of antiques, clothing, and artifacts from Indian days and Civil War battles. Perhaps the best exhibit is "Main Street," a row of small rooms resembling an apothecary; a combination doctor's office, dentist's office, and barbershop; and a combination general store, post office, and bank. There is no mention of the elephant execution. The museum is located on the grounds of the National Fish Hatchery and is open from 1:00 to 5:00 daily from May through October.

GREENEVILLE. This pleasant small town is famous as the home of Andrew Johnson, the president who is most noted for having been impeached. In a celebrated trial in the U.S. Senate, he held his office on the strength of one vote.

A considerable number of industries operate in Greeneville, but none are so big that they dominate the town. Greeneville is a center for the tobacco industry, and the University of Tennessee has a Tobacco Research Center just outside town. In recent years the town has restored old buildings and installed brick sidewalks and old-fashioned light posts in an effort to hold onto the nineteenth century ambiance.

Andrew Johnson National Historic Site. His predecessor in the White House is generally regarded as the president with the humblest beginnings, but Andrew Johnson probably had to work harder to pull himself out of poverty than did Abraham Lincoln. This is evidenced in Greeneville by Johnson's tailor shop, where the future president hired young men to read to him while he sewed. The table on which he worked, and many of his personal affects are in the shop.

Visitors can also tour two houses in which Johnson lived while in Greeneville, and can see his grave in the local cemetery. The first house, which Johnson used from the 1830s until 1851, is across the street from the visitors' center. It is closed to the public, although visitors are invited to peer into the windows to see the furnishings. The second house, which Johnson used from 1851 until he died, is situated one and a half blocks from the visitors' center, and is open to the public. It has been restored to the period following Johnson's presidency.

Greenevillians note with pride that, following his one term and the onerous impeachment, Johnson was re-elected to the U.S. Senate. He died soon afterwards. The cemetery in which he is buried is located one block south of West Main Street.

The three areas of the historic site are open 9:00 to 5:00 every day. Adults pay a small fee to tour the house, but seeing the rest of the park is free. Call (615) 638-3503.

Church with a Cannonball. Not often noted in literature about the town, the Cumberland Presbyterian Church at 201 North Main Street has a Civil War cannonball embedded in the brick about fourteen feet off the ground.

Davy Crockett Birthplace State Park. Davy Crockett is chiefly remembered for managing to die at the Alamo in Texas, but before that he was an author, a three-term congressman, and an all-round character. He and his family lived for a time on the banks of the Nolichucky River, and now visitors can see a replica of their cabin in a park that also boasts camping, picnicking, and swimming facilities. To get there drive east on U.S. 11E and follow the signs. Phone (615) 257-5209.

JOHNSON CITY. Set against the mountains, Johnson City is the most beautiful of the Tri-Cities—from afar. The downtown area, like its counterparts in Kingsport and Bristol, is the victim of the shopping mall, which for Southern cities is this century's equivalent of the Civil War.

The early history of the city centers on David Johnson, who arrived in 1854 and set about creating the town he named after himself. In a one-man effort to make the place boom, he became postmaster, depot agent, merchant, hotel keeper, and magistrate. In 1869 a charter was granted to Johnson City, and Johnson became the first mayor. He must not have done a very good job, for the charter was revoked in 1879. Six years later the state gave Johnson City another charter, and things progressed.

The centerpiece of the city is East Tennessee State University (ETSU), a former teachers' college that has become the largest institution of higher learning in this end of the state. Some ten thousand students study—sometimes—on a 366-acre campus. One of the landmarks is the Memorial Center, an indoor football stadium that can accommodate twelve thousand people.

Perhaps due to the presence of the university and its facilities, Johnson City hosts more rock concerts and other large public events than any Tennessee town east of Knoxville. ETSU is a center of high culture, too, with classical concerts, theater, lectures, and films. To find out what is happening on campus call the Culp University Center at (615) 929-4352.

Carroll Reece Museum. Located on the campus of ETSU, this museum hosts permanent exhibits of paintings,

Appalachian crafts, and history, and various changing displays. Gallery hours are weekdays from 9:00 till 4:00 and weekends from 1:00 till 5:00. Call (615) 929-4392 or 929-4283.

Tipton-Haynes Living Historical Farm. The state of Tennessee owns this combined farm and museum that chronicles the lives of two families who resided on the property. The Tiptons and the Haynes are followed through four periods of history: colonial, Revolutionary War, the War of 1812, and the Civil War. The farm, including the log house, log barn, granary, and several other buildings, has been restored to its appearance of a century ago, complete with antique furniture. A special attraction is the restored Greek Revival law office of one of the former owners. Children like the animals on the farm, and are particularly attracted to a small cave there.

The Tipton-Haynes farm is located just off U.S. 23 at the southern edge of Johnson City. It is open weekdays 10:00 through 6:00, and weekends from 2:00 through 6:00. A small admission fee is charged.

Events

Appalachian Fair. This late-August fair, the largest in upper East Tennessee, features carnival rides, agricultural exhibits, free concerts with Nashville country music stars, and arts and crafts. It is held in the town of Gray, which is between Kingsport and Johnson City. For further information on this and other Johnson City events call (615) 926-2141.

Johnson City Springfest. Held in late April, this event brings together artists and craftspeople, performers, road racers, and participants in the "Crazy Bed Race."

Tipton-Haynes Historical Farm Festival. Held at the historic farm outside of the city, this early-August festival includes demonstrations by artists and craftspeople, sales of their goods, pony rides, and tours of the farm and cave.

Dining

Augustino's. Italian food, cocktails, and live music. 3021 East Oakland Avenue. Phone (615) 282-8255.

Bucwood's Firehouse Bar-b-que. Pork and beef barbecue are sold in a restaurant decorated to look like an early firehouse. 627 West Walnut Street. Phone (615) 929-0502.

Down Home Kitchen. This lively restaurant is the home of hand-picked bluegrass music, and on some Saturday nights it seems as if the roof is going to fly off from the sheer energy put forth by the performers. Located at 300 West Main Street.

JONESBOROUGH. A few years ago Jonesborough was known as Jonesboro, a small town whose inhabitants spent their spare time lusting after Johnson City and other worldly delights. In recent years, however, Tennessee's oldest town has experienced a renaissance of interest in its history and culture. Besides changing to the old way of spelling the name, residents have ripped down aluminum siding, restored historical structures to their original appearance, and otherwise spruced up the town. This activity led Jonesborough in 1969 to be the first entire town placed on the National Register of Historic Places. All of this combines to make Jonesborough a definite stop for history buffs and those who enjoy scenic small towns.

Jonesborough's history dates from 1779, when it was chartered by the North Carolina state legislature. Five years later, showing no gratitude at all, Jonesborough became the capital of the ill-fated State of Franklin. Twenty-one-year-old Andrew Jackson first practiced law here.

Today Jonesborough offers small crafts shops, walking tours, and several festivals that draw thousands of people. The most celebrated is the National Storytelling Festival, which is held in October. During Jonesborough Days, held right before the Fourth of July and at Christmas, several of the historic private homes are decorated and open to the public. For details write to Jonesborough Information, Box 375, Jonesborough 37659.

Antique Bus Tours. You can see the sights in Jonesborough from restored Ford buses of the 1920s and 1930s. Write Jonesborough Transportation Company, Old Town Hall, Main Street, Jonesborough 38759. Call (615) 753-2095.

Lodging and Dining

Jonesborough Accommodations. Jonesborough is one of the few towns in Tennessee to offer bed and breakfast for visitors. Write Jonesborough Accommodations, 144 East Main Street, Jonesborough 37659; or call (615) 753-2095.

The Parson's Table and Widow Brown's. The Parson's Table serves country dinners family-style in an old church, while Widow Brown's serves them in a restored Victorian home next door. Specialties include potatoes baked in pine resin, homemade whole-wheat bread, and a mysterious nonalcoholic punch called the Parson's Brew. Dinners only, except Sundays, when lunch is served too. Reservations are suggested. Located in Parson's Square. Call (615) 753-4322.

KINGSPORT. The center of the fifth most populous county in Tennessee, this industrial city boasts large operations by such companies as Eastman Kodak, Mead Paper, and the Kingsport Press. It is unique among southern cities in that its central area was laid out by a professional city planner. In 1917 Dr. John Nolan's blueprints showed residential sections, business areas, and industrial zones, but they did not anticipate two twentieth century blights, pollution and shopping malls—both of which have had ill effects on "The Model City." Remnants of the plan can be best seen on Broad Street, which has a train station at one end and Church Circle at the other.

Kingsport is noted, too, for sentencing an elephant to death in 1916. This proceeding, unusual even in a state known for the Dayton "Monkey Trial," still causes considerable chagrin to residents of the Model City. It is explained more fully in ERWIN, where the sentence was carried out.

Allendale. Harvey Brooks, a local rags-to-riches success story, built this mansion on a farm where he raised prize-winning horses and Angus cattle. He left the house to the city of Kingsport, which hasn't quite figured out the best use of the old home. Furnished with antiques, it is worth seeing if you are in west Kingsport, but don't make a special trip if you aren't. The house is located on U.S. 11W about four miles west of downtown Kingsport. Open Sundays from 1:00 to 4:30 all year; admission is charged. Call (615) 246-8162.

Bays Mountain Park. Perhaps the finest park owned by a city in Tennessee, if not the whole South, Bays Mountain Park is at once a three-thousand-acre nature preserve, education center, planetarium, and museum. It surrounds a 44-acre reservoir once used for Kingsport's water supply, and visitors can walk around the lake on any of 25 miles of hiking trails. Although this is not a zoo in the usual sense, some indigenous wild animals are kept in cages.

Bays Mountain Park is foremost a nature preserve, so don't bring your volleyball net. This is not a place to go for swimming, boating, or other sports; there are neither concession stands nor soft drink machines. The park is beautiful any season of the year, and is open seven days a week. There is a small charge for parking and for entering the planetarium; everything else is free. This is a great place for all ages. To get to the park head south on U.S. 23 and follow the signs. Access for the handicapped is provided. Call (615) 245-4192.

The Exchange Place. Once a farmhouse lying along the Orebank Road, the Exchange Place is Kingsport's center of traditional Appalachian culture. Concerts, craft fairs, and demonstrations by artisans take place here periodically, and the visitor just stopping by can see the restored house, springhouse, smokehouse, and barn.

Situated at 4812 Orebank Road, The Exchange Place is usually open only on Sunday afternoons, but there are special events on other days. Call (615) 288-6613 or 288-5182 for details of programs.

Long Island. This island in the south fork of the Holston River was for decades a meeting place for the various Cherokee tribes. They caught the short end of the Battle of Island Flats in 1776, and later signed a treaty here which gave up much of their land. The island is now occupied largely by the Tennessee Eastman Company, although a small section on the sourthern end was recently ceded back to the Cherokees. A small park marks this belated acknowledgment of rightful ownership. The best thing about the park is a swinging bridge for pedestrian traffic to the island. Kids of all ages will enjoy it.

The Netherland Inn. George Washington didn't sleep here, but Andrew Jackson did. Overlooking the Holston River, the inn was an important stop for travelers throughout the nineteenth century. Today's visitors can no longer spend the night, but they are invited to tour the inn, with its restored rooms and antiques, walk through a stable, a warehouse, and slave cabins, and see a wharf and flatboat of the kind that was often launched from the old King's Port. Located at 2144 Netherland Inn Road, the inn is open afternoons, Wednesday through Sunday, from May through October, and by appointment. A small fee is charged. Call (615) 246-2662, 247-3211, or 288-5182.

Warrior's Path State Park. Just upstream from Kingsport on the Holston River, Fort Patrick Henry Dam impounds a lake by the same name. Warrior's Path State Park is wrapped around a section of lake. Most of its water comes from the bottom of Boone Lake, the next one upstream, so it is cold, but ideal for boating or waterskiing. This is the best place to camp in the Tri-Cities area, and the park also features swimming, a water slide, miniature golf, and picknicking. The local youth display themselves and their cars every Sunday afternoon during warm weather. This may be fascinating to sociologists, but can get tiresome for everyone else. South of Kingsport on U.S. 37.

Events

Arts and Crafts Festival. Held early in September, this event brings together local craftspeople for sales and demonstrations. For information on this and other Kingsport events write the Kingsport Chamber of Commerce, P.O. Box 1403, Kingsport 37662; or call (615) 246-2010.

Kingsport Fun Fest. This July event offers concerts, arts and crafts demonstrations, sales of handcrafted goods, and activities for everyone from toddlers to the elderly.

Open House Arts and Crafts Show. Held at the Exchange Place, a one-time working farm, this event brings together artists, craftspeople, musicians, and mountain food.

Dining

Chicago Dough Company. A franchise restaurant, Chicago Dough offers deep dish and regular pizza, and other Italian dishes in an atmosphere of old Chicago. Located at 1229 East Stone Drive. Call (615) 247-3184.

Pratt's Barn. This restaurant is no hideaway—you can't miss the 32-foot statue of an Indian standing at attention outside. This larger-than-life folk sculpture, whose loincloth has been known to blow off during storms, stands witness to good food in a country atmosphere. Iced tea is served in Mason jars, and country ham with biscuits is one of the featured items. Pratt's also has one of the better salad bars in east Tennessee. Located at 1225 East Stone Drive (U.S. 11W). Call (615) 246-3711.

Skoby's. This 40-year-old restaurant manages to serve several different cuisines and do a good job with all of them. At Skoby's you can have Chinese food, steaks, seafood, and barbecue, each in a setting that complements the food. Reservations are a good idea. Skoby's is located on Konnarock Road. Call (615) 245-2761.

LAUREL BLOOMERY. Travelers usually have to go through Virginia to get to this Tennessee town, which is the home of Iron Mountain Stoneware, a pottery of exceptionally high quality. Built here to gain access to local clays, the pottery ships dishes, mugs, and bowls all over the world. Visitors are welcome to watch the potters at work, and can buy first- or second-quality goods on the premises. This is not a "crafts center" in the usual sense; pottery is made with modern ovens and equipment. Sales are conducted at Thanksgiving and Mother's Day.

MORRISTOWN. This town has been acclaimed on five occasions as the nation's cleanest. Perhaps to give citizens a better view of their sparkling town, several of the sidewalks are constructed along the second story of buildings in the town's center.

Davy Crockett Tavern and Museum. According to the theme song of the television series starring Fess Parker, Mr. Crockett was "born on a mountaintop in Tennessee," and "killed him a bear when he was only three." The latter may have resulted from his usual activity during his early years, which were spent hanging around his father's tavern. This structure did not survive, but the present museum was constructed of building materials dating from those glorious days near the old site. The museum has little Crockettana, but houses a reasonable collection of everyday pioneer items and handicrafts. Located at 2106 East Main Street, it is open from April through October, 9:00 to 5:00 Monday through Saturday and 2:00 to 5:00 on Sundays. There is a small admission fee.

Panther Creek State Park. This park overlooks Cherokee Lake, whose level fluctuates a great deal in accordance with the flood control needs of the Tennessee Valley Authority (TVA). It is said to be one of the best of the TVA lakes for fishing, and this is a dandy park in which to try your luck. Totalling nineteen hundred acres, it offers a picnic area, 50 campsites, and a bathhouse and visitors' center. The camping area is closed from November through February. Write for information to Panther Creek State Park, Morristown 37814; or call (615) 581-2623.

MOUNTAIN CITY. The county seat of Johnson County is in one of the more remote areas in Tennessee. Lying on U.S. 421, it is often a stopping place for motorists who are passing through from North Carolina to the Tri-Cities.

Backbone Rock. This portion of the Cherokee National Forest centers on a tall ridge of rock which rises abruptly seventy-five feet and runs along for four hundred feet. At one point a tunnel is cut in the rock for cars to drive through. Visitors can walk atop the rock, and there is a campground and picnic area beside it. To get there follow Tennessee 133 north from Shady Valley.

NEWPORT. The seat of Cocke County, this town used to be the center of Tennessee's moonshining country, and it was said that there were more Mason jars sold here than anywhere in the nation. Now it is a big vegetable canning center of the Stokely-Van Camp Company.

ROAN MOUNTAIN. This name applies to both a town and a mountain. The summit of Roan Mountain, said to be the most beautiful spot in Tennessee, is a place free from the hordes who invade the Great Smokies. It is home to the largest natural stand of rhododendron—some six hundred acres of it—in the world. The dense bushes bloom in mid-June, when the top of the 6,313-foot mountain is transformed into a blaze of red, pink, and white. Nearby Bald Mountain is a peak covered with grass, an unusual sight in the southern Appalachians.

Roan Mountain State Park. This new park is a delight. It contains a visitors' center, two campgrounds, an old-fashioned grist mill, a swimming pool, nature trails, hiking trails, and—in winter—cross-country skiing trails. For those who aren't equipped for camping, there are twenty cabins and a restaurant. Reservations for the cabins are advisable. Write the park at Route 1, Box 50, Roan Mountain 37687. Call (615) 772-3303.

Events

Carter County Spring Wildflower Tours. In early May experts and amateurs lead groups of people on hikes and drives through the spring wildflowers. Call (615) 772-3303 for details.

Rhododendron Festival. Each year since 1947 the Roan Mountain Citizens' Club has sponsored this festival at the peak of the blooming period of the rhododendron. The festival always includes a beauty pageant, and often concerts of gospel and bluegrass music. Write for details to the Carter County Chamber of Commerce, Elizabethon 34673.

ROCKY MOUNT. Situated in an area that was considered the "Far West," this log house became in 1770 the capital of the Territory of The United States South of the River Ohio. The house was a showplace of its day, complete with the almost unheard of luxury of glass windows. It now belongs to the state, which has done an excellent job of restoring the house to its 1770 character, complete with period furniture and kitchen. Rocky Mount lies between Bristol and Johnson City on U.S. 11E.

Events

Rocky Mount Festival. Held in mid-July, this event features music and crafts from the frontier era. Call (615) 538-7396 for details.

ROGERSVILLE. Said to be the second oldest town in Tennessee, Rogersville boasts a worthwhile collection of nineteenth century buildings in its historical district. Examples include the Hawkins County Courthouse, circa 1836, the Masonic Temple, circa 1840, and the Kyle House, circa 1839. The small-town atmosphere is very much present here; this is a good place to get out of the car and walk.

Travelers are welcomed to the Hale Springs Inn at 110 West Main Street, which claims to be the oldest continually operated inn in the state. Tennessee's three presidents— Andrew Jackson, James K. Polk, and Andrew Johnson— have slept there.

Like many small towns that are county seats, Rogersville has a courthouse corps, usually old men, who hang around the square making small talk and eyeballing passers-by. In the past some city official took umbrage at this assemblage and installed sharp spikes on the top of a fence to discourage the daily gathering. This nameless bureaucrat underestimated the willpower of the men and the strength of their britches; the iron spikes are now all almost worn away to nothing. *Sic semper tyrannis.*

Lodging

The Hale Springs Inn. Some rooms have fireplaces and sitting areas. These have been recently renovated; other rooms have not. Rates are moderate. 110 West Main Street, Rogersville 37857. Call (615) 272-9967.

TUSCULUM. The name is that of a town and a college, both of which are located east of Greeneville and worth a stop. Tusculum College, a four-year liberal arts institution, is the oldest college west of the Alleghenies and the oldest Presbyterian college in the country. It is the center of cultural life in Greene County, featuring occasional lectures, concerts, and theater. To find out what is happening on campus, call (615) 638-1111.

Samuel W. Doak Homestead. A pioneer minister, the Rev. Samuel Doak sent the men and boys off to fight at Kings Mountain with a shout of "The sword of the Lord and of Gideon." His 1818 Federal-style farmhouse stands on U.S. 11E adjacent to the Tusculum College campus. Inside the restored house is a collection of period furniture and three artists' studios featuring weaving, painting, and pottery. The potter is Lynn Stone, and visitors can watch her spin off cups, bowls, goblets, and other functional objects in terra cotta. The house is open Monday through Saturday from 10:00 to 5:00. No admission is charged.

TWO

Knoxville
and Surroundings

EAST TENNESSEE'S LARGEST CITY was first located on a high
bluff in an effort to head off Indian attacks. Although the
natives chose to attack elsewhere, Knoxville has been fighting off slings and arrows from marauding out-of-town writers ever since.

The earliest was one James Weir, who swung through
town in 1798. He wrote: "It was County Court day when I
came. I saw men jesting, singing, swearing; women yelling
from doorways; half naked Negroes playing on their ban-
joes, while the crowd whooped and danced around them.
Whiskey and peach brandy were cheap. The town was
confused with a promiscuous throng of every denomina-
tion—blanket-clad Indians, leather-shirted woodsmen,
gamblers, hard-eyed and vigilant. My soul shrank back to
hear the horrid oaths and dreadful indignities. . . . There
was what I never did see before, viz., on Sunday, dancing,
singing, and playing cards."

A more recent and more famous commentator was John
Gunther, who in his book *Inside U.S.A.*, published in 1947,
awarded Knoxville the title of ugliest city in America. He

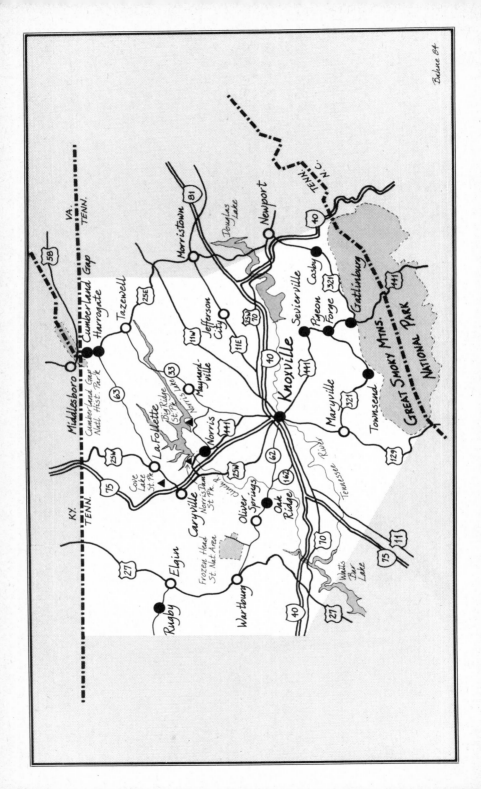

Deluxe 84

adorned this bouquet by further stating that the city possessed "an intense, concentrated, degrading ugliness." It is not recorded whether he ever went back.

Knoxville is familiar throughout most of the country as the host of a world's fair in 1982, and this undertaking brought it in line for more printed abuse; the *Wall Street Journal* took the occasion to call Knoxville "a scruffy little city on the Tennessee River." In spite of such insults from journalists, over eleven million visits were made to the fair. Though some aspects of the fair were disappointing, the turnstiles clicked at a merry rate throughout the summer. The exhibits and events of the fair are now gone, but in their places are enough attractions and doings to occupy most visitors for several days.

History is well represented here. A replica of the original White's Fort is just a few blocks away from what used to be the finest house west of the Appalachians. Knoxville has nine house museums depicting various times in the city's history.

The city began with James White's Fort, a frontier jumping-off point for those who were eagerly cashing in on land offered by North Carolina to Revolutionary War veterans. William Blount, a man whose public service dovetailed neatly with his land dealings, was appointed governor of the Territory South of the River Ohio. He set up his headquarters at White's Fort and promptly suggested that the place be named after General Henry Knox, a man who had never laid eyes on the place; he was, however, Blount's superior. Blount told White to lay out the streets of the new town through the forest, unknowingly giving Knoxville the claim as the first planned city in the West.

The town grew as commerce in the western lands increased, and many of the goods that came through the Cumberland Gap found their way into Knoxville, from where they were shipped by flatboat to New Orleans. When Tennessee was admitted to the Union as the sixteenth state in 1796, Knoxville was the capital. The town's economy was held back by the rapids at Muscle Shoals on the Tennessee River; steamboats *could* travel to the new capital, but it was a perilous journey. When the railroad came to town in 1855 it remedied this situation, but just around the corner was Knoxville's darkest hour—the Civil War.

So many east Tennesseans joined the Union army that the Confederacy considered Knoxville virtually enemy territory, and sent an occupying army in 1861 to keep a lid on things. When this army of about ten thousand was called away on urgent business to Chattanooga in 1863, it was promptly replaced by a Union force twice as big. Three months later the Confederates returned, determined to take up residence again, and laid seige to the city. Rations for the Union soldiers were reduced until each man got only a cracker a day. But they still wouldn't give up. The Confederates heard that a certain Gen. William T. Sherman was headed their way, and in desperation they tried to take the city in a direct attack on Fort Sanders. They were repulsed with great casualties, and left never to return.

After the war Knoxville boomed. The population tripled between 1860 and 1870, for a total of ten thousand, and this figure tripled by the turn of the century. Foundries, marble quarries, machine companies, and cotton and woolen mills were established, and their proprietors built large houses where the Civil War battle had taken place. The University of Tennessee, which was founded as Blount College in 1794, attracted more and more students, who came from a widening area.

The Depression years saw the coming of the Tennessee Valley Authority (TVA), a visionary agency charged with planning and developing an entire region. These were heady times for Knoxvillians, as they witnessed the influx of men and materials. During this time a literary son of Knoxville, James Agee, was writing what was to become his celebrated account of Depression poverty—some say his masterpiece—*Let Us Now Praise Famous Men.*

Then came World War II, and the construction some eighteen miles away of a secret city. Federal officials referred to it in secret memos as the Manhattan Project, but locals called the area Oak Ridge. Over forty-seven thousand construction workers toiled away on a project whose purpose none of them knew. They were followed by an odd assortment of academics, industrial engineers, and military personnel, all of whom were housed in hastily constructed buildings. Many of these people knew little more than did the construction workers. The secret city's population soared to seventy-five thousand, yet the people of Knoxville had no idea of its extent or what when on there.

What was going on at Oak Ridge was announced to the world following the atomic bombing of Hiroshima in August 1945. Still, Oak Ridge was off-limits until 1949 to anyone not cleared for security. Many of the people who had worked on the Manhattan Project stayed on in Tennessee's newest city, and they set about creating a center of high culture in what they considered an intellectual wasteland. For a time Oak Ridge had more Ph.D.'s per capita than any place in America, a phenomenon that drew the attention of Margaret Mead and others who study societies.

Not surprisingly, the people of Oak Ridge have been big proponents of nuclear power and its various uses. Immediately after the war they opened the American Museum of Science and Energy to explain to people what had been and was going on in the secret city. In recent years, with the international concern about nuclear proliferation and calls for a nuclear freeze, the people of the Atomic City have lost some of their enthusiasm about the primary use for the atoms that were split in secret forty years ago.

As the host of the 1982 World's Fair, Knoxville boomed with new construction, renovation, and entrepreneurial activity. There were, however, some unanticipated problems. By 1982 the theme of the fair, energy, was no longer at the forefront of public attention. Because of the recession relatively few countries took part, and those that did spent less money than at earlier fairs. The role of world's fairs is changing, moreover, and Knoxville happened to be the first of the newer, scaled-down expositions. This was lost on some visitors, who commented negatively on what they found. Travelers to Knoxville now will find a surprisingly sophisticated city that is proud of its heritage and eager to please those who come to see its attractions, new and old.

Knoxville and Oak Ridge remain the intellectual centers of East Tennessee, complete with fine restaurants, museums, and bookstores. The University of Tennessee (U.T.) is the hub of cultural activity, hosting a theater program with a national reputation and bringing artists of all types to the area. Visitors from other cities who find themselves weary of overcooked Southern food and longing for urban delights should make a beeline for these two cities.

HOW TO GET THERE

Knoxville is served by more airlines than any other city in the Southern Appalachians. These airlines include Delta, Eastern, Republic, United, and USAir, as well as smaller carriers.

If you are driving, you'll find Knoxville at the intersection of I-40, I-75, and I-81. If you are a fan of blue highways, you can reach Knoxville on U.S. 25 and U.S. 11.

ONCE YOU'RE THERE

IN KNOXVILLE. Most of Knoxville's attractions are downtown or on the University of Tennessee campus; the site of the 1982 World's Fair lies between these two. It makes sense to select a hotel near these areas and thus dispense with parking. Perhaps the ideal place to stay is the Holiday Inn at the corner of Henley Street and Clinch Avenue.

Knoxville has public buses, but most visitors resort to cars to get around outside of the downtown area. Bicyclists will enjoy the World's Fair site and the Third Creek Bike Trail, which goes from Tyson Park, near Cumberland Avenue and U.S. 129, to a shopping plaza about two miles away.

If historic homes are your object, Kingston Pike, leading west from the University of Tennessee area, is a good destination. The Confederate Memorial Hall, the Dulin Gallery of Art, and the Armstrong-Lockett House all lie along this main thoroughfare.

OUTSIDE OF KNOXVILLE. **Oak Ridge** and **Rugby** are both cities that were built by outsiders, the former in secret and the latter with an eager following in two countries. From Knoxville take I-40 west to the Oak Ridge exit. Take Tennessee 162 into Oak Ridge; tour the American Museum of Science and Energy and visit the Graphite Reactor. Catch the best pizza in East Tennessee at Big Ed's, then jump back in the car and take Tennessee 62 out of town. Pass through Oliver Springs and head toward the pleasantly named Wartburg. Turn right on U.S. 27 and proceed north for 21 miles until you come to Elgin. Turn left on Tennessee 52 and go seven miles to Rugby, where you can tour the remaining buildings of what is often called "America's last colony."

Cumberland Gap and **Norris Dam** both mark beginnings. Cumberland Gap opened up Kentucky and the Midwest to pioneers, while Norris Dam marks the beginning of the TVA. Leave Knoxville on I-75 north and get off at the Bethel exit. Get on U.S. 441 and proceed north until you come to the Museum of Appalachia in Norris, the finest collection of mountain artifacts and buildings in the region. Nearby is Norris Dam State Park, the home of the TVA's first dam, still an impressive structure that is almost a half century old.

Leave Norris Dam and go north on U.S. 441 until it reaches I-75 once more. Go north on the interstate to the next exit at Caryville. Follow U.S. 25W to LaFollette, then take Tennessee 63 for 41 miles until it intersects with U.S. 25E. Go north until you come to Harrogate, where the Lincoln Museum can be found on the campus of Lincoln Memorial University. After leaving there, cross the Cumberland Gap and descend to the visitors' center on the Kentucky side. Ample signs mark the way.

On the return trip, retrace your path to Harrogate, follow U.S. 25E to Tazewell, then turn right on Tennessee 33, a scenic parkway, and follow it all the way back to Knoxville.

Those who love the outdoors may want to proceed straight to Cumberland Gap National Historical Park and take one of the trails to the top of Cumberland Mountain. Allow about a half day for the hike; it's a good idea to pack in a lunch to Hensley Settlement or Sand Cave.

TOWNS AND ATTRACTIONS

BIG RIDGE STATE RUSTIC PARK. The TVA originally developed this thirty-six-hundred acre park along the shores of Norris Lake. Now it is run by the state, and facilities include a visitors' center with nature exhibits, 19 cabins, a group camp, and 50 individual camping spots. Swimming, fishing, boating, horseback riding, picnicking, hiking trails, and play areas are also available. The park is located along Tennessee 61 in Maynardville. Write to the park at Maynardville 37807; or call (615) 992-5523.

COSBY. This town is named for Dr. James Cosby, one of the first physicians to practice here. Now it is one of the lesser used entrances to the Great Smoky Mountains National Park.

    Cosby Quilt Shop. Located on Tennessee 32, this shop sells locally made quilts and offers classes in quilting. Call (615) 487-5489.

    Folk Life Center of the Smokies. This organization sponsors festivals and operates a shop for local craftspeople. The shop is located on Tennessee 32 and is open daily. Call (615) 487-5543.

Events

    Cosby Ramp Festival. Held on the first Sunday in May, this festival is in honor of the ramp, a wild cousin of the onion. Veterans of ramp-laden meals describe it as "the gift which keeps on giving;" people who eat a plateful can sometimes smell ramp up to two weeks later. The all-day festival includes gospel, bluegrass, and country music, and a beauty contest. The winning young lady is crowned Maid of Ramps. For further information write the Cosby Ruritan Club, Cosby 37722; or call (615) 623-4313.

Dulcimer and Harp Convention. Each June lovers of mountain music come from all over the country to participate in classes and listen to the sounds of Appalachian dulcimers, hammered dulcimers, autoharps, and Irish harps. Storytelling and events for children are also held. For further information write the Folk Life Center of the Smokies, P.O. Box 8, Cosby 37722; or call (615) 487-5543.

Folk Life Festival of the Smokies. This September gathering features classes in fiddle, banjo, guitar, and saw, and concerts of mountain music. For further information write or call the Folk Life Center in Cosby.

COVE LAKE STATE DAY USE PARK. Right off I-75, this is a good place to camp if you are entering the region. The park has a motel, restaurant, nature trails, and ample areas for swimming, fishing, tent and trailer camping, boating, and picnicking. It is not as big or as scenic as some of the other state parks. In the winter, several hundred Canadian geese make this their feeding ground. Located off I-75 and U.S. 25W. Write to Cove Lake State Day Use Park, Post Office, Caryville 37714; or call (615) 562-8355.

CUMBERLAND GAP NATIONAL HISTORICAL PARK. See Chapter 9.

FROZEN HEAD STATE NATURAL AREA. Named for a peak that remains frozen long after the snow melts around it, this area was recently carved out of some state land holdings that also include Brushy Mountain State Prison. The ten-thousand-acre park is remotely located and never crowded. It offers picnic shelters, toilets, and over fifty miles of trails for overnight and day hikes. Located six miles northeast of Wartburg on Tennessee 62. Write to State Natural Area, Wartburg 37887; or call (615) 346-3318.

GATLINBURG. The mention of this town elicits immediate and varied reactions from people who have been there. The town's location is an entrepreneur's dream; it sits squarely in front of the main entrance to the Great Smoky Mountains National Park, the most visited national park in the country. Local people and out-of-towners make over nine million visits to the park every year, and a good number of them come right through Gatlinburg.

Plenty awaits them. In a stretch less than a mile long, visitors can play Hillbilly Golf, tour the Elvis Hall of Fame, enter the World of the Unexplained Museum, visit the Xanadu Home of the Future, stuff themselves with a hundred varieties of candy, and get outfitted with a stack of T-shirts. And that's just a sampling.

Those who approach Gatlinburg from the Tennessee side, as most travelers do, must drive through Sevierville and Pigeon Forge, both of which subject the visitor to a series of roadside attractions. Gatlinburg, however, is the holy of holies where the tourist dollar is concerned. Hemmed in by the park, it cannot expand its borders. Rents are high, and the competition among merchants is furious. Old motels are replaced by little shopping malls and boutiques; old-style souvenir shops are replaced by more fashionable and more profitable enterprises.

Many people love Gatlinburg. It is jammed with traffic most of the time, and is a popular honeymoon spot. The town can sleep twenty-five thousand people a night without batting an eye. On many weekends a room in Gatlinburg can't be had for love or money. Conventions are held here. Children enjoy the town. The Hot-Rod Club of Darlington, South Carolina, used to love it—until their nocturnal roarings up and down the street became too much for the local constabulary. Old folks like it, and some people are so enthralled with the town that they never make into the national park.

Other people detest the place, and always take the by-pass to enter the park. They see Gatlinburg as the height of commercialism—commercialism that bamboozles the tourists as it plays on the worst stereotypes of mountain people.

Gatlinburg can be exceedingly tacky, but at the end of a day of hiking it is very pleasant to descend into town and be able to eat a good meal without changing your clothes or worrying about your appearance. The town allows al-coholic beverages, but there are no bars in the conventional sense, and the place has a wholesome atmosphere that is rare in a town with so many hotels and people.

Gatlinburg is worth a stop, whether to eagerly line up to see the Ripley's Believe It or Not Museum or to marvel at the extremes to which people will go to make a buck. For more information write the Gatlinburg Chamber of Commerce at P.O. Box 527, Gatlinburg 37738. From out of state call (800) 251-9868; in Tennessee call (615) 436-4178.

Miscellaneous Amusements

American Historical Wax Museum. From Hernando De Soto to Elvis, this place has 130 life-sized figures from American history. Located on the Parkway. Open April through October from 9:00 A.M. until 10:00 P.M. (until 11:00 P.M. during the summer) and November through March from 9:00 until 5:00. Admission is charged.

Christus Gardens. This religiously oriented wax mu-seum has justified the "retreats" of countless church youth groups to fun city. Open all year from 8:00 A.M. to 10:00 P.M., it is located on River Road. Admission is charged.

Ober Gatlinburg Ski Resort. The fastest way to reach this ski resort is to take a gondola that leaves from the center of town. You can also drive to the top of Mount Harrison, where Ober Gatlinburg displays the largest artificial ski turf in the world. Besides skiing, visitors can go ice-skating or Alpine sledding, look at black bears, visit a crafts market, eat in restaurants, dance, or sit in a lounge. The ski resort is open December through March. Write for further details to Ober Gatlinburg, Gatlinburg 37738. Call (615) 436-5423.

Stars Over Gatlinburg Wax Museum. Here's a chance to see representations of Clint Eastwood, Loretta Lynn, Willie Nelson, Elton John, and Katharine Hepburn. Located on the Parkway. Admission is charged.

Xanadu: Home of the Future. This polyurethane structure purports to demonstrate the brave new world of comfortable living. Each room contains the latest in furniture, cookware, and playthings. Located on the Parkway. Admission is charged.

Arts and Crafts

Arrowmont School of Arts and Crafts. The Pi Beta Phi sorority started this school in 1926, when Gatlinburg was a tiny mountain town. Founded to educate mountain children, Arrowmont has evolved into a school of arts and crafts that draws students from all over the country. Their products, as well as those of 55 full-time weavers and 100 other craftspeople, are sold in the **Arrowcraft Shop.** It is located on the Parkway, and is perhaps the only building there surrounded by grass. Prospective students can write to the school at P.O. Box A-567, Gatlinburg 37738. Call (615) 436-4604.

Brass Bell Craft Shop. This shop feature locally handicrafted goods, including Appalachian dulcimers, hammered dulcimers, quilts, baskets, and wood carvings. Located in the Crossroads Mall on U.S. 321 near the intersection of U.S. 441. Call (615) 436-4366.

The Cliff Dwellers. This long-established shop sits above the sidewalk on the Parkway, seemingly above the fray. Inside is an eclectic mix of toys, jewelry, linens, and imported gifts. Call (615) 436-5386.

Davis Dulcimer Shop. Watch dulcimers being made and listen to dulcimer music. Located on Tennessee 73 two miles east of Gatlinburg. Call (615) 436-7461.

Great Smoky Mountain Arts and Crafts Community. Far from the madding crowd in Gatlinburg, this is a collection of some forty artists and craftspeople whose studios, homes, and shops are sprinkled along the Glade Springs Road north of town. To get there go east on U.S. 321 to the Glade Springs Road. Turn left. For further information call (615) 436-4315.

Wood Whittlers. This combined shop and studio features custom-built furniture and wood carvings. On U.S. 321 three miles east of Gatlinburg. Open Monday through Saturday. Phone (615) 436-7187.

Lodging and Dining

Gatlinburg offers over twenty-five thousand motel and hotel rooms. For a complete list, write to the Chamber of Commerce at P.O. Box 527, Gatlinburg 37738.

Buckhorn Inn. Five miles outside of Gatlinburg stands this two-story inn, which has been operating for over forty years. Located on ten acres within a quarter mile of the Great Smoky Mountains National Park, the inn offers a view of Mount LeConte. It is also close to the Glades Road Craft Loop, a gathering of artists and craftspeople.

Guests can stay in one of the five rooms in the main building or in one of the four cottages; all have private baths and working fireplaces, and two of the cottages have kitchenettes. The inn serves breakfast and dinner, specializing in fresh mountain trout and other Southern dishes. The dining room is open to the public by reservation. The Buckhorn Inn is open year-round. For further information write the inn at Route 3, Gatlinburg 37738; or call (615) 436-4668.

Mountain View Hotel. This is the grand old place to stay in Gatlinburg. The hotel has 76 rooms, and the operation includes a motor lodge next door. The hotel's dining room, open all year, serves Southern food family-style. Breakfast, box lunches, and dinner are available. For further information write the hotel at Gatlinburg 37738. Call (615) 436-4132.

Events

For information on any of the festivals listed here, write the Chamber of Commerce at P.O. Box 527, Gatlinburg 37738; or call (615) 436-4178 in Tennessee or (800) 251-9868 from out of state.

Crafts Fairs. As might be expected, crafts are of great interest here. Gatlinburg holds two crafts fairs a year, one in July and one in October.

Great Smoky Mountains Highland Games. Held at Mills Park, this May event brings together aficionados of kilts and cabers for music, dancing, and traditional Scottish athletic events.

Smoky Mountains Music Festival. In May the sounds of banjos and high tenor singing are heard at this annual bluegrass event.

Twelve Days of Christmass. The town is decorated for this December festival, which includes caroling and special events.

Wildflower Pilgrimage. The Great Smoky Mountains National Park is home to a wide variety of wildflowers, to which this event is dedicated. Volunteer naturalists—some of them professors from the University of Tennessee—lead walks to point out the varied species. Held in April.

HARROGATE. Once a fashionable summer resort, this town was named after Harrogate, England, and was the site of a large wooden inn. The resort eventually went bankrupt, and the inn was torn down. Now the chief center of interest in Harrogate is Lincoln Memorial University (LMU).

The school came about because of a conversation between Abraham Lincoln and O. O. Howard, a Civil War general. In discussing the loyalty of the East Tennesseans to the Union, Lincoln is reported to have said, "General, if you come out of this horror and misery alive, and I hope you may, I want you to do something for these people who have been shut out from the world all these years." After the war General Howard founded LMU.

Cudjo Caverns. LMU owns Cudjo Caverns, one of the more unlikely sources of income for a university. The cave was noted by Dr. Thomas Walker on his exploration of the Cumberland Gap in 1750, and it was probably known to the Indians who had traversed the gap before. It lies beneath the juncture of Tennessee, Kentucky, and Virginia. The walkways are safe and the lighting good, and a visit to the cave can be immensely satisfying after a hot day of hiking in the park. One notable feature is the Pillar of Hercules, a formation that is 65 feet high and 35 feet around. Estimates place its age at 85 million years. The cave is open 9:00 to 5:00 daily. Admission is charged.

Lincoln Library and Museum. The third largest collection of "Lincolniana" is housed in a building that was largely paid for by Col. Harland Sanders of Kentucky Fried Chicken fame. Attractively displayed are such items as the cane Lincoln carried to Ford Theatre, a swivel chair he used while practicing law in Springfield, Illinois, and the plaster model for the statue inside the Lincoln Memorial in Washington, D.C.

The museum is open every day during the summer, and Tuesday through Sunday during the spring and fall. During December it is closed to prepare new exhibits, and in January it is open by appointment only. Write to the museum at LMU, Harrogate 37752; or call (615) 869-3611, extension 76 or 77.

KNOXVILLE. This economic, cultural, and educational center of East Tennessee offers a wide array of attractions for visitors. Having hosted a world's fair in 1982, the city is well prepared to take care of travelers. Since there are so many places to visit for their historical interest, I'll list them first.

Armstrong-Lockett House. Sometimes known as Crescent Bend, this house was built in 1834 near the Crescent Bend of the Tennessee River. It contains eighteenth-century American and English furniture and decorative art, and an outstanding collection of English silver. Located at 2728 Kingston Pike, it is open Tuesday through Saturday 10:00 to 4:00, and Sundays from 1:00 to 4:00. A small admission is charged. Call (615) 637-3163.

Blount Mansion. This was the home of William Blount, the governor of the Territory South of the River Ohio. Reputed to be the first frame house west of the Alleghenies, it was erected in 1792, and contrasted greatly with the log cabins that surrounded it. Dignitaries such as Andrew Jackson stayed here, and the house was the social center of early Knoxville. If you want to tour only one historic house, this should be it.

The house is restored to the late eighteenth century style; it is filled with period antiques that include English pottery, American glass, and Shaker chairs. A garden in the back is also typical of the mansion's heyday, and the outbuildings comprise the kitchen, a cooling house, and an office where the state constitution was written.

Listed in the National Register of Historic Landmarks, the mansion is located in downtown Knoxville on Hill Avenue. The visitors' center is in another historic building, the **Craighead-Jackson House**, built in 1818. Both are open Tuesday through Saturday all year, and on Sundays as well from May through October. A small admission is charged. Phone (615) 525-2375.

Confederate Memorial Hall—Bleak House. This antebellum house of fifteen rooms was constructed by slaves who, tradition says, baked the bricks at the site. Confederate Gen. James Longstreet used the house as his headquarters during the siege of Knoxville in 1863, and the number of Minié balls still embedded in the walls attest to his popularity with the Union troops. After the war it was named Bleak House in honor of Charles Dickens's novel, and perhaps to reflect the fortunes of General Longstreet and his followers.

The United Daughters of the Confederacy maintain

the hall as a museum and a memorial to their fallen ancestors. It is filled with period furniture, military uniforms, and Civil War artifacts. Conveniently located at 3148 Kingston Pike, it is open 2:00 to 5:00 Tuesdays through Sundays from April through November; it closes one hour earlier during the rest of the year. It is open Mondays by appointment only. There is a small admission charge. Call (615) 522-2371.

First Presbyterian Church. William Blount and James White lie in the cemetery outside this church in downtown Knoxville. The original structure was built in 1816; the present one dates from 1901. Located at 620 State Street, an easy walk from Blount Mansion.

Marble Springs. John Sevier was a noted Indian fighter, the first governor of Tennessee, and the first member of Congress from a western state. He was given 640 acres as a reward for his service in the Revolutionary War, and because of the ample water supply and deposits of marble on the land he called it Marble Springs. The house, much rougher than Blount Mansion, is more typical of the housing for prominent citizens of the time. In 1941 the state bought the site, and now the house has been restored and filled with period furnishings. Many of the items were used by the Sevier family, including two rocking chairs, Sevier's luggage, and a large cherry wood secretary.

Marble Springs is located six miles south of Knoxville on a marked route via U.S. 441 and the John Sevier Highway, or via U.S. 129 and the John Sevier Highway. Often visitors arrange to see Speedwell Manor and Marble Springs on the same trip. The farm is open 10:00 to 12:00 and 2:00 to 5:00 Tuesday through Saturday, and 2:00 to 5:00 on Sunday. It is closed on Mondays. There is a small admission charge. Call (615) 573-5508.

Ramsey House. Unlike some of his rough-hewn contemporaries, Francis Alexander Ramsey was a man of taste. A surveyor by trade, he was ready when North Carolina passed its 1783 "Land Grab Act," and he acquired nearly two thousand acres of prime acreage. To build his house he brought in an English architect from Charleston—an almost unheard of act—and Ramsey House was the result.

Thomas Hope, the architect, was a great admirer of Sir Christopher Wren. He designed a house with a flat, unbroken facade and large chimneys projecting from the end walls. He used bluestone in combination with pink marble, which sounds garish but doesn't look it. The interior of the house is as elegant as the outside. The rooms are trimmed with a finely moulded chair rail, and the windows have interior paneled shutters.

Ramsey House is privately owned and is listed on the National Register of Historic Places. It is situated east of Knoxville on Thorngate Pike; take I-40 to Tennessee 169, and head south to Thorngate Pike. The house is open April through October, from 10:00 to 5:00 Tuesday through Saturday and from 1:00 to 5:00 on Sunday. You can see the house by appointment November through March. There is a small admission charge. Call (615) 546-0745.

Speedwell Manor. This house was built entirely by slave labor around 1830 in Tazewell, Tennessee, and with its white columns looks like the stereotypical plantation house. It was moved to Knoxville in this century. The carriage entrance sports a Greek Revival facade, and inside the house a window sill bears a legend written by a concealed Confederate soldier who witnessed the Battle of Tazewell. A smokehouse behind the mansion is still used for curing hams. Speedwell Manor is privately owned and open to the public on Tuesday, Thursday, and Sunday from 1:00 to 5:00. Group tours can be arranged by appointment. The house is located outside of the downtown area off U.S. 129 at 2112 Manor Road. Call (615) 577-2757.

James White's Fort. In early Knoxville William Blount had political power, but in times of trouble people turned to James White. His fort preceded the town of

Knoxville and offered protection for the early settlers as well as the travelers passing through. The reconstructed fort now shelters a museum, a smokehouse, and a blacksmith shop. Children usually prefer this fort over the historic houses with their "Do Not Touch" signs. It is located at 205 Hill Avenue, within walking distance of Blount Mansion. There is a small admission charge.

The fort is open from April 15 through October 31 from 9:30 to 5:00 Monday through Saturday and from 1:00 to 5:00 on Sunday. The rest of the year the fort closes one hour earlier. It is closed entirely from December 16 through February 14. Call (615) 525-6514.

Cultural Sites

Beck Cultural Exchange Center. The Beck Center, as it is known in Knoxville, is a museum and resource center focusing on the black culture in East Tennessee. The archives contain black newspapers, photographs, and other historical documents. The exhibits vary from local arts to traveling displays. Located at 1927 Dandridge Avenue, the center is open from 10:00 to 6:00 Tuesday through Saturday, and Sunday by appointment. Call (615) 524-8461.

Dulin Gallery of Art. Located on a bluff overlooking the Tennessee River, this place bills itself as "East Tennessee's Visual Art Center." Typical exhibitions include French contemporary graphics; Hungarian graphics, textiles, and metalsmithing; and holiday art. The house in which the museum resides is on the National Register of Historical Places; it was designed in 1915 by John Russell Pope. The Dulin Gallery is open on Tuesday from noon to 8:00, from Wednesday through Friday from noon to 4:00, and on weekends from 1:00 to 5:00. A small admission fee is charged. The museum is located at 3100 Kingston Pike. Call (615) 525-6101.

East Tennessee Historical Center. The U.S. Customs House, built in 1874, now houses the city library's local history collection as well as the city and county archives. Changing displays include books, paintings, and artifacts relating to Tennessee history. The building is on the National Register of Historic Places, and is located in downtown Knoxville at 800 Market Street. It is open Monday and Tuesday from 9:00 to 8:30, and Wednesday through Friday 9:00 to 5:30. Admission is free. Call (615) 523-0781.

Gem and Mineral Museum of Tennessee. Aside from the usual unusual specimens of gems and minerals, this museum focuses on Tennessee pearls, which are extracted from mussels in the state's rivers. Visitors can also see an amethyst weighing over four hundred pounds. The museum is located at 329 South Central Street, and is open Monday through Friday from 10:00 to 5:30. A moderate admission is charged. Call (615) 535-4215.

Knoxville Academy of Medicine Museum. Seldom visited by tourists, this museum contains a collection of instruments, furniture, pictures, and medical books dating from 1798, all displayed in a replica of an old-time doctor's office. The museum is in the James Park House, on a site where John Sevier started to build a house but never finished. Open by appointment only, the museum is located downtown at 422 Cumberland Avenue. Call (615) 573-3464.

McClung Museum. This museum on the campus of the University of Tennessee houses an eclectic collection of Indian artifacts, geological finds, works of art, and displays of local and natural history. It is also the repository of much of the archeological material of the university. One never knows quite what to expect on entering the door. The museum is located on Circle Park on the campus, and is open Monday through Friday from 9:00 to 5:00. Admission is free. Call (615) 974-2144.

Student's Museum and Akima Planetarium. This museum features natural history, world culture, and student art. There are six special exhibits annually and activities for children during school holidays. Located on the east side of town at 516 Beaman Street, the museum is open Monday through Saturday from 9:00 to 5:00 and on Sunday from 2:00 to 5:00. A small admission is charged. Call (615) 637-1121.

Theater and Film

Lamar-House Bijou Theater. The Lamar House was a hotel built in 1816. Several presidents stayed there. The Bijou Theater, added in 1909, is an old-time opera house with a checkered past. Once the site of high culture, it deteriorated along with downtown Knoxville and for one period was the local porno movie center. While the skinflicks were rolling the theater building was willed to a local church, which found itself in an uncomfortable situation. Luckily the sinners were expelled, and the building is now restored so that respectable people can attend concerts, plays, and ballets. The Bijou is located in downtown Knoxville at 803 Gay Street. Call (615) 522-0832 for ticket information.

Laurel Theatre and Jubilee Center. A product of 1960s political activism, this community-run arts cooperative sponsors lively potpourris of theater, dance, Appalachian music, and other events. You'll never see a Republican fundraiser in this home to the avant-garde Sidewalk Dance Theatre and Play Group. Located in the Fort Sanders community—a pretty good walk from downtown Knoxville—at the corner of Fifteenth Street and Laurel Avenue. Call (615) 523-7641 for the latest word on what's happening.

Tennessee Theatre. Completed in 1928, just at the end of the silent-film era, this is one of the last movie palaces built with a theater organ. The grand old rococo movie theater is worth a trip no matter what film is playing. Especially thrilling is the occasional silent film with organ accompaniment. Located in downtown Knoxville at 604 Gay Street. Call (615) 525-1840.

University Center Film Series. This is a part of the entertainment provided for U.T. students, but outsiders can attend. Sixteen-millimeter second-run films, European imports, and classics are shown several nights a week at the Tennessee Auditorium in the University Center and 35-millimeter films at the Clarence Brown Theater. These films are not always advertised off campus, so call (615) 974-3381.

University of Tennessee Musical Arts Series and University Opera Theater. Sunday afternoon concerts featuring U.T. students and faculty make up the Musical Arts series, while the Opera Theater consists of occasional scenes from opera as well as full-blown productions. These are held at the U.T. Music Hall on Volunteer Avenue, on the campus. Call (615) 974-3241.

University of Tennessee Theaters. The best drama and musicals in the region are at these theaters. Student and professional thespians perform the classics as well as new material.

The **Carousel**, a theater-in-the-round, is the oldest theater on the campus and the scene of several memorable performances, including a staging of *Waiting for Godot* for which several tons of soil were hauled in to simulate the countryside. Special plays for children are often presented here.

The gift of a U.T. alumnus and MGM film director, the **Clarence Brown Theater** is the crown jewel of the U.T. theaters, with facilities that surpass most Broadway houses. The professional actors and actresses of the Clarence Brown Company work their wonders on this stage. The first version of Broadway's successful *Sugar Babies* was performed here.

Theater II is a small experimental theater, located within the Clarence Brown building. It is the scene of student productions, one-act plays, and avant-garde theater productions. Sometimes the best performances are witnessed in this little publicized place.

The U.T. theaters are located on Andy Holt Avenue on the campus. Call (615) 974-5161 for ticket information.

West Knoxville Dinner Theater. This professional company offers comedies, musicals, and drama that can be appreciated while mildly under the influence of alcohol. Located in the western part of the city at 12801 Kingston Pike. Call (615) 966-8769 for details.

Events

Artfest. "Saturday Night on the Town" is the liveliest part of this month-long celebration of the arts, held in September. For further information write the Knoxville Visotors' Bureau, Box 15012, Knoxville 37901; or call (615) 523-7263.

Christmas in the City. The first two weeks in December feature this celebration of yuletide activities.

Dogwood Arts Festival. Held in April, this event celebrates the blooming of the dogwoods. It includes concerts, theater, scenic drives through the city's neighborhoods, parades, arts and crafts exhibits, and music ranging from bluegrass to opera.

Tennessee Valley Agricultural and Industrial Fair. This is the biggest country fair in East Tennessee, complete with agricultural exhibits, arts and crafts, music, and carnival rides. It is held in September.

Miscellaneous Amusements

Knoxville Zoological Park. This is the best zoo in the region, and one of the finer ones in the country. It is a must for children. The zoo made history with the first birth of an African bull elephant in the Western Hemisphere. It houses over a thousand animals, including particularly extensive collections of big cats and reptiles, in environments that are as close to native habitats as possible. Visitors are requested not to bring pets; the animals are not lacking for food.

Located on the east side of town off Rutledge Pike, the park comes complete with a restaurant, The Environment, and a petting zoo for children. The grounds are open daily from 10:00 to 4:30. A moderate admission fee is charged.

Chilhowie Amusement Park. Located next to the Knoxville Zoological Park, this park contains a permanent collection of rides for children and the young at heart. Admission is free, although you must pay to take the rides. There is also a picnic area and a small lagoon. The park is open on weekends only from April through September. Call (615) 637-5840.

Dining

Buddy's Bar-B-Q. The name *Buddy's* has become synonymous with barbecue in Knoxville. The original Buddy's is at 5806 Kingston Pike, but there are three other locations throughout the city. Try the barbecued ribs, but remember to get plenty of napkins. Weekends at Buddy's mean bluegrass. Cold beer, ribs dripping with sauce, and hot hand-picked bluegrass—there's nothing like it!

Cappucino's. Northern Italian cuisine is the specialty here. The pasta is homemade and the wine cellar is extensive. Cocktails are served. 7316 Kingston Pike. Call (615) 584-8521.

Charlie's Place—Regas on 17th. This casual place close to the U.T. campus features plain American food with no flourishes. If you've had it with fettucine and sun-dried tomatoes, this is the place for you. Cocktails are served. 717 Seventeenth Street. Call (615) 525-6141.

Chesapeake's. Offers a wide variety of fresh fish and seafood, including live Maine lobster. Features a raw bar and lounge. Cocktails are served. 500 Henley Street. Call (615) 637-0600.

Copper Cellar. This longtime Knoxville favorite is decorated in copper and leather, but don't let that scare you away. The menu features prime Colorado beef, fresh seafood specialties, and a reasonable wine list. Cocktails are served. Two locations: 1807 Cumberland Avenue (near U.T.), call (615) 522-4300; and 7316 Kingston Pike, call (615) 584-8521.

L & N Fish Market. This restaurant is worth going to just for the setting. Housed in the former Louisville and Nashville train station, it displays stained-glass windows and wooden floors of a pattern not generally seen today. While admiring the windows and floor one can dine on fresh seafood. 401 Henley Street. Call (615) 971-4850.

Lord Lindsey Restaurant. Set in an old yet newly fashionable neighborhood in downtown Knoxville, this restaurant with an Edwardian decor is open for dinner on Fridays and Saturdays and for brunch on Sundays. Cocktails are served. 615 Hill Avenue. Call (615) 522-2178.

The Orangery. Decorated with French antiques, this dimly lit restaurant has an atmosphere of delightful elegance. It offers a French menu and is considered by many people to be the best restaurant in East Tennessee. Check the credit limit on your charge card before going. Cocktails are served. 5412 Kingston Pike (615) 588-2964.

Rathskeller Restaurant. An old Knoxville favorite, this place features prime rib and general American cuisine. Cocktails are served. Kingston Pike at Western Plaza Shopping Center. (615) 588-5264.

Regas Restaurant. This place was serving good meals before the World's Fair was a gleam in the bankers' eyes. American cuisine featuring prime rib, steak, lobster, and homemade bread. Excellent service. Cocktails are served. 318 North Gay Street. (615) 637-9805.

MARYVILLE. This town is the seat of Blount County, which was named after William Blount, the first and only governor of the Territory of the United States South of the River Ohio. Maryville was named after Blount's wife. It is the gateway to the Cades Cove area of the Smokies, an entrance chosen by those who wish to avoid the crowds and commercialism of Gatlinburg.

In 1807 a young boy named Sam Houston moved to the area with his widowed mother and eight brothers. Young Houston ran away from his family and lived for three years with the Cherokees, learning to speak their language and eventually becoming adopted by them. He returned to his family, however, and taught school for a year in a log structure. The school was closed when the one-man faculty took off to fight alongside Andrew Jackson at Horseshoe Bend. Houston was a friend to the Cherokees, and even led a delegation of them to Washington, D.C. Then he headed off to Texas to play an important role in establishing that state. As governor of Texas Houston opposed slavery and refused to join the Confederacy.

Maryville College. This four-year college, founded in 1819 by the Presbyterian Church, is the cultural center of the area. Certain concerts, lectures, and other events are open to the public. For information on campus events, call (615) 982-6412.

Sam Houston Schoolhouse. The man who was to become governor of Texas once taught in this restored log schoolhouse, located five miles from Maryville on Sam Houston Road off U.S. 441. The oldest schoolhouse in Tennessee, it is open all year Monday through Saturday from 10:00 to 5:00 and on Sunday from 1:00 to 5:00. A small visitors' center contains artifacts from Houston's Tennessee life. No admission is charged.

NORRIS. When the fledgling TVA got ready to build its first dam, not enough adequate housing was available for the large work force. Eager to demonstrate all its powers, the TVA decided to build a town and build it right. Norris is the result. The streets were laid out to fit the topography, and modest wood shingled houses of a uniform design were constructed. Large green spaces were left throughout the town. Once owned outright by TVA, Norris was sold to private owners in 1948. Many of the small wooden houses are left, and the citizens of Norris have taken pains to keep their town among the best kept and most attractive in the state.

Museum of Appalachia. If you're going to see one mountain museum in the region, this should be it. The result of the inspiration and perspiration of John Rice Irwin, it contains over two hundred thousand items displayed in 30 buildings on 75 acres. No typical display of artifacts, the Museum of Appalachia often holds demonstrations of activities such as making apple butter, splitting shingles, blacksmithing, and music making. The buildings show how living off the land progressed from dirt floors and rough furniture to hardwood floors with rag rugs.

Many of the buildings were brought from other places in Appalachia to the museum, and one looked so authentic that it was used as the setting for a television series called "Young Dan'l Boone." Children are welcome here, and they can get a glimpse of a time when people their age did not have to change channels to sample adventure.

The privately owned museum is on the outskirts of the town of Norris, one mile off I-75 at Exit 122. It is open during daylight hours every day but Christmas. A moderate admission is charged. Write Museum of Appalachia, Box 359, Norris 37828. Call (615) 494-7680.
Tennessee Fall Homecoming and Fiddle Contest. Held at the Museum of Appalachia, this October event features a music competition, crafts demonstrations, and plenty to eat. For information write the Museum of Appalachia.

NORRIS DAM STATE RESORT PARK. This is one of the better state parks in the area. Covering 2,311 acres, its centerpiece is Norris Dam, the first TVA project. Now almost a half century old, the dam is still an impressive structure. It is 1,860 feet long and 265 feet tall at the highest point. It is named after Nebraska Sen. George Norris, a strong backer of the TVA.

Even without the dam, the park would be a lively place. A grist mill built in 1795 still grinds corn daily and also serves as a gift shop. Beside the mill is a threshing barn and the Lenoir Pioneer Museum. The park offers a restaurant (open June through Labor Day), 45 cabins, an Olympic-size swimming pool, a snack bar, a crafts shop, crafts courses, 2 campgrounds, playgrounds, and summer nature study and recreation programs. There are the usual opportunities for fishing, boating, and hiking. Located on U.S. 441 above the town of Norris. Write the park in Norris 37828, or call (615) 426-7461.

OAK RIDGE. Often called the Atomic City, this place was high-tech before the term was invented. Some of the attractions reflect this.

American Museum of Science and Energy. This is the best museum, overall, in the entire region. Once called the American Museum of Atomic Energy, it served as a mouthpiece for the nuclear industry and encouraged visitors to walk away with radioactive dimes. In these enlightened days, however, atomic energy is no longer touted as a cure for everything, and more emphasis is placed on the other energy sources and energy conservation. Children love this museum; there are plenty of gadgets to manipulate. The museum is located at 300 South Tulane Avenue. Call (615) 576-3200. No admission is charged.

Oak Ridge Community Playhouse. This is amateur theater at its best. Performances of drama and musical comedies are featured year-round, with two popular musicals in the summer. Located in downtown Oak Ridge at Jackson Square. Call (615) 483-1224 for ticket information.

Bull Run Steam Plant. Many people mistakenly think the TVA gets all its electricity from falling water. It is actually the largest user of coal in the Western Hemisphere, and the Bull Run Steam Plant is one of the bigger producers of electricity. A visitors' lobby provides exhibits on how the plant works. If you are feeling particularly puckish, ask about acid rain. The plant is located on the shores of the Clinch River on the Bethel Valley Road, and the visitors' center is open 9:00 to 5:00 Monday through Friday. No admission is charged.

Children's Museum of Oak Ridge. This museum is dedicated "to erasing the hillbilly stereotype," and it does so with exhibits that range from log cabins to contemporary Japanese art. This is a "hands-on" museum— it includes a walk-through coal mine of the type that used ponies to pull the coal cars.

The Children's Museum is open during the school year from 9:00 to 5:00 on weekdays and 1:30 to 4:30 on weekends. June through August it is open weekdays 9:00 to 5:00 (Tuesday nights until 9:00), and Saturdays from 10:00 until 1:00. It is closed on Sundays during the summer. The museum is located at 461 Outer Drive. Write the museum at Box 3066, Oak Ridge 37830; or call (615) 482-1074.

Graphite Reactor. Built in 1943 as a part of the Manhattan Project, this is the world's oldest nuclear reactor and the source of the first gram-size pieces of plutonium. After the war it was used for research and as a source of radioisotopes until nuclear technology surpassed it. Now on the National Register of Historic Places, it is located on the Bethel Valley Road in Oak Ridge. It is open daily 9:00 to 5:00 and Sundays 12:30 to 5:00. There is no admission charge. Write the American Museum of Atomic Energy, Box 117, Oak Ridge 37830; or call (615) 576-3200.

Museum of Fine Arts. This new museum houses a permanent collection of over sixty pieces of modern and contemporary art, as well as changing exhibits. Located at 201 Badger Avenue, it is closed Monday. It is open 1:00 to 9:00 on Tuesday, 9:00 to 5:00 on Wednesday through Friday, and 1:00 to 4:00 on the weekend. Call (615) 482-1441.

University of Tennessee Arboretum. This quiet 250-acre preserve contains one of the Southeast's largest collection of trees and plants from the Appalachian area. If you've been wandering through the forests and wondering what the names of the plants are, here's your place. Over seven hundred species are labeled. Located on Tennessee 62, the arboretum is open from dawn to

dusk. The visitors' center is open daily from 9:00 till
4:30. No admission is charged. Call (615) 483-3571.

Dining

Big Ed's Pizza. An Oak Ridge landmark—the place as
well as the man—Big Ed serves up the best pizza in
east Tennessee. Made entirely of fresh ingredients, it is
a welcome contrast to the francise pizza usually found
in these parts. Located in Jackson Square. Call (615)
482-4885.

The New China Palace. Good Chinese food is rare in east
Tennessee. This is one of the better places to find it.
Located on Melton Lake Drive near the Oak Ridge
Marina.

The Soup Kitchen. Located at 47 East Tennessee Drive,
the lunch-only restaurant offers a choice of seven soups
and chili along with fresh bread baked on the premises.
Open six days a week. Call (615) 482-3525.

PIGEON FORGE. An iron forge on the banks of the Pigeon River
gave this town its name. Pigeon Forge lies between Gatlinburg and Sevierville on U.S. 441, that magic carpet on
which millions of tourists enter the Great Smoky Mountains National Park. Pigeon Forge is dedicated to getting
these out-of-towners to linger for a while.

The lures include an array of small theme parks, water
slides, and various other displays, some of which are truly
amazing in their audacity. For example, one perennial
crowd-pleaser is Porpoise Island, a display of performing
porpoises that has utterly nothing to do with the mountains
or its people. Yet it makes money year after year. H. L.
Mencken said it best: "No one ever went broke underes-
timating the taste of the American public." This statement
should be engraved on the Pigeon Forge town seal.

Ogles Water Park. The epitome of good clean fun, this
roadside park offers travelers a chance to get buffeted
by four-foot-high artificial waves, to ride what is billed
as the largest water slide in the eastern United States,
and to put small children into a pool equipped with

fountains, tunnels, and built-in water pistols. Located on the Parkway, Ogles Water Park is open in May from 11:00 to 6:00, in June and July from 10 A.M. to 10 P.M., and in May, August, and September from 11:00 to 6:00. Admission is charged, and if patrons have forgotten a swimsuit, park concessionaires will cheerfully sell them one.

The Old Mill. Built in 1830, this picturesque mill still produces 13 kinds of meals and flours, all of which are for sale in an adjacent shop. Located east of U.S. 441 on the Little Pigeon River, the mill is open daily from March through mid-November. Admission is charged.

Pigeon Forge Pottery. Pottery is thrown, fired, and sold on the premises. Located off U.S. 441 across the bridge from the Old Mill. The potters work from 8:00 to 4:00 daily, and the shop is open till 6:00. For further information call (615) 453-3883.

Silver Dollar City. Off the beaten track in Pigeon Forge lies Silver Dollar City, a theme park that captures the mountain culture better than any other such park in the region. It comes with a steam train and a collection of carnival rides, but the best reason for coming is to see the craftsmen. Local people make horseshoes, barrels, quilts, and leather harnesses, and are happy to discuss the finer points of their work. Live bluegrass and country music is featured, and the park even has its own festivals. Late June through mid-July marks the **National Mountain Music Festival,** with country, gospel, bluegrass, and traditional music. The **National Crafts Festival** is held in October, and brings together one hundred craftspeople from all over the country for demonstrations and sales.

The park is open daily in the summer months, and several days a week in the spring and fall. The hours vary. For further information call (615) 453-4616.

RUGBY. This little town is all that is left of America's last colony. Thomas Hughes, English author of *Tom Brown's School Days* and other books, decried the system in Britain whereby a landowner's entire estate went to the oldest son. Younger brothers were expected to enter law, medicine, or the clergy, or to "starve like gentlemen." Any form of manual labor was unheard of. Hughes envisioned a place where these young men could toil in dignity, far from the disapproving stares of Victorian society.

He found it in a tract of land on the Cumberland Plateau. The colonists arrived in 1880 and quickly set about constructing a town in the English fashion. These were aristocrats, and one of the first things they built was a tennis court. A library, an Episcopal church, and a hotel soon followed, and at its peak Rugby consisted of 70 buildings and 450 people. The town was carefully followed in the magazines of two continents, and Britons who visited America had to see Rugby to consider their trip complete.

The colonists all had a good time, but economically it was tough going. The first winter proved to be the worst in 25 years. Crops failed. A typhoid epidemic killed seven people in 1881. The rough road leading to the colony was often "barely jackassable." The young men worked hard, but many stopped for tea at four in the afternoon. Eventually the colony failed.

Today Rugby is reviving. There is renewed interest in the buildings and their history, and the new Big South Fork National River and Recreation Area promises to bring more money and visitors to the town. Now explorers can see 17 of the original buildings. Several are private homes that are open only during the annual Rugby Pilgrimage, which is the best time to see the place. The Rugby Pilgrimage is held during the first complete weekend in August, and features lectures, music, and a general celebration of Rugby. For details write the Rugby Restoration Association, Box 8, Rugby 37733; or call (615) 628-2441.

Thomas Hughes Free Public Library. This center of culture for Rugby contains over seven thousand volumes. All of them were published before 1899, and several hundred belonged to Rugby's British colonists. The library is open daily between March 1 and November 15 from 10:00 to 4:30 and Sunday from 12:00 to 4:30.

Christ Church, Episcopal. This is the loveliest building in Rugby, complete with its original hanging lamps and a rosewood reed organ built in 1849.

Kingston Lisle. This was the home of Thomas Hughes, Rugby's founder, and it is fully restored to the condition he left it and furnished with period pieces.

Rugby Colony Craft Cooperative. This shop features work by local craftspeople.

Events

Historic Rugby Pilgrimage of Homes. The best time to see Rugby is during the annual Rugby Pilgrimage, when several private homes are open to the public. Held on the first complete weekend in August, the event features lectures, music, and a general celebration of Rugby. For details write the Rugby Restoration Association, Box 8, Rugby 37733; or call (615) 628-2441.

Spring Music and Crafts Festival. Held in May, this event features folk music of the British Isles and Appalachia, crafts demonstrations and sales, and walking tours of the buildings of Rugby.

Lodging and Dining

Pioneer Cottage. Overnight lodging for singles, couples, or small groups is available year-round at Pioneer Cottage, Rugby's first frame house, built in 1880. The cottage has been restored, modernized, and furnished with period pieces. Call (615) 628-2441 for reservations.

Harrow Road Cafe. Open from March through November, this cafe serves breakfast, lunch, and dinner.

SEVIERVILLE. The seat of Sevier County, Sevierville marks the beginning of the commercial strip leading to the Great Smoky Mountains National Park. It is dominated by an 1896 courthouse of unusual design. Restored in the 1970s, the courthouse is open during business hours Monday through Friday.

Forbidden Caverns. Once used by Indians and later by moonshiners, this large cavern is fun to explore on a rainy or hot day. It is noted for a large display of onyx on one of the walls. The only thing forbidden about the cavern is entering without paying admission. Located on Tennessee 8 between Sevierville and Newport. Open daily from April through November.

TOWNSEND. This small town lies along the Little River and has many vacation homes.

Smoky Mountain Passion Play. Outdoor drama has been performed in Townsend since 1972. The **Smoky Mountain Passion Play**, which portrays the final days of Christ, alternates with **Damascus Road**, the story of the apostle Paul. The amphitheater is accessible for those in wheelchairs, and is located at the Townsend entrance to the national park, off U.S. 321. The plays are performed from early June through August. For further information write the Smoky Mountain Passion Play, Townsend 37882. Call (615) 448-2244.

Tuckaleechee Caverns. The owners of this cavern played in it as boys, and later opened it to the public. Open daily from 9:00 to 6:00 from April through November, the cavern is located off U.S. 321 in Townsend. Admission is charged.

THREE

Chattanooga
and Surroundings

MUCH OF THE AREA described in this chapter is not in the mountains, strictly speaking. Yet it is well worth exploring as one approaches the Great Smokies and the North Carolina mountains from the west

Historically and financially, the area is dominated by Chattanooga. Three interstate highways now converge on this fourth largest city in Tennessee, but Chattanooga has been an important junction of transportation for centuries. The Great Warpath of the Indians came through this area, and the name of the town is an Indian word describing Lookout Mountain, the most prominent geological feature. The city was founded in 1814 by John Ross, who was the principal chief of the Cherokee Nation for 38 years. Initially the town was called Ross's Landing.

As upper East Tennessee was settled, the pioneers would often ship goods by flatboat from Kingsport and other locations toward Chattanooga. An important commodity at one point was salt, which was mined in Virginia, shipped down river, and sold in Chattanooga. In 1838, the year the Cherokees were forced to leave, fifteen hundred barrels of salt came through Chattanooga.

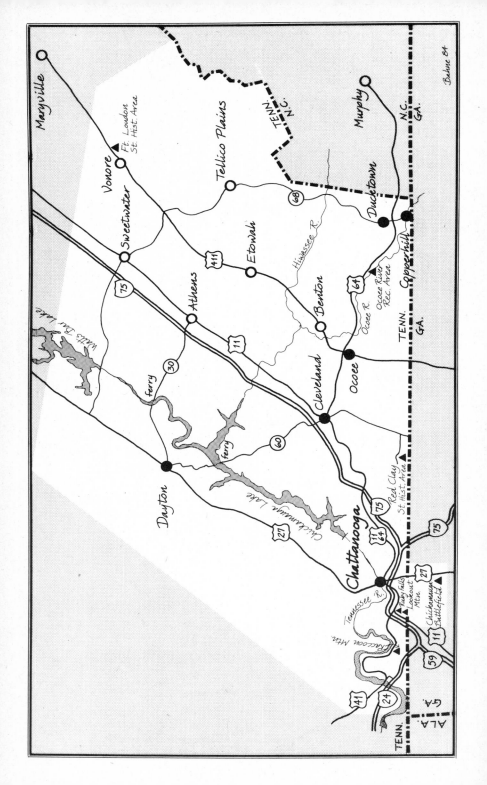

River trade continued to rise, because Chattanooga was, for practical purposes, at the head of navigation on the Tennessee River. Steamboats could go further upstream, but they passed at their peril a navigation hazard called the Suck. For a period Chattanooga rivaled Memphis as a cotton-shipping port. The railroad changed that, and Chattanooga's river traffic slowed, but the junction of the railroads gave the city a new life.

Then came the Civil War. The Union army wanted to split the Confederacy, and Chattanooga was the key to its strategy. Since the town lies in a depression surrounded by hills, the Confederates could not defend it. They abandoned Chattanooga as the Union army advanced in September 1863. The troops clashed south of Chattanooga at the Chickamauga battlefield, and by the time night came one out of four soldiers was dead, a total of 34 thousand were dead, wounded, or missing. The Union forces were pushed back into Chattanooga, and the Confederates, intent on starving them out, took the high ground of Lookout Mountain and Missionary Ridge.

Help came to the Union forces in the form of Gen. Ulysses S. Grant and additional troops from Virginia. On the afternoon of November 24, the Union troops advanced through the fog up the side of Lookout Mountain and engaged the Confederates in what is called the Battle Above the Clouds. The Confederate lines gave way. A young Union officer, Arthur MacArthur, led a Union charge that won him a battlefield promotion, a Congressional Medal of Honor, and the admiration of his son, Douglas MacArthur.

The Union army attacked nearby Missionary Ridge the next day—again, with success. The Confederates were forced to leave Chattanooga for good. Chattanooga then became the supply point for Gen. William Sherman's infamous—at least in Georgia—march to the sea.

Following the Civil War Chattanooga became a manufacturing center, but in recent years tourism has become an increasingly important source of income. Lookout Mountain, with its historical, natural, and sometimes overblown attractions, has become the focal point of the city.

Chattanooga has made two lasting contributions to American culture. Adolph Ochs, the publisher of the *New York Times*, cut his journalistic teeth on the *Chattanooga Times*. And Coca-Cola, although invented in Atlanta, was first bottled commercially in Chattanooga.

HOW TO GET THERE

The Chattanooga Airport is served by Delta, Piedmont, and Republic airlines, as well as two commuter lines.

Most people arrive by one of the three interstate highways that form a large *X* at Chattanooga. I-75 comes southwest from Knoxville and northeast from Atlanta; I-24 comes southeast from Nashville; and I-59 approaches the city in a northeasterly direction from Birmingham.

If you are a blue highway fan, you might prefer U.S. 41 or 11. These highways cross the same way the interstates do, and on them you will pass by the diners and small towns that those on the interstates miss.

Drivers coming from the westernmost part of North Carolina should take U.S. 64, a Tennessee-designated scenic parkway that leads through some spectacular scenery including the TVA flume along the Ocoee River.

ONCE YOU'RE THERE

Despite the lures of the Chattanooga Choo Choo and a few other attractions, downtown Chattanooga is not the nicest place to lay your head. For the best lodgings head for the hills—to Lookout Mountain. Find a room with a view of the city. You'll be closer to the attractions on the mountain and above the steamy heat that sometimes fills the Chattanooga basin.

Take the Incline Railway up Lookout Mountain and inspect the battlefield at Point Park, which is also a good place to have a picnic. If the weather is hot, a trip to Ruby Falls is a good remedy. Don't miss the Tennessee Valley Railroad and Museum.

Lookout Mountain can sometimes get crowded, and when it does it's time to head for Raccoon Mountain. Follow U.S. 41 north out of the city to the TVA's Raccoon Mountain Pump Storage Project. On the way you might stop and watch the daredevils at the Raccoon Mountain Flight Park.

TOWNS AND ATTRACTIONS

CHATTANOOGA. Once noted as a manufacturing and transportation center, this is an attractive destination for travelers. Knoxville may have the main campus of the University of Tennessee and the accompanying cultural amenities, but Chattanooga is rich in historical sites and things to do. Railroad buffs would be hard pressed to find a city that offers more model railroads, incline railways, and museums devoted to the glories of the iron horse. Ironically, they cannot get there by train anymore.

History lovers, particularly Civil War enthusiasts, will find the site of the Battle Above the Clouds one of the more interesting battlefields in the country.

Historical Sites

Chickamauga-Chattanooga National Military Park. Comprising eight thousand acres, this park commemorates one of the bloodiest battles in American history, when thirty-four thousand men were wounded or killed. When the park was established in 1890 it comprised the Chickamauga Battlefield alone, but since then land on Lookout Mountain, Missionary Ridge, Signal Point, and Orchard Knob have been added to the grounds.

The headquarters of Chickamauga-Chattanooga National Military Park are located just off U.S. 27 south of Chattanooga. They include a visitors' center and a large collection of military shoulder arms. Demonstrations and lectures are held frequently. Admission is free, and the park is open year round from 8:00 A.M. until dusk. It is closed on Christmas and New Year's Day.

Confederate Cemetery. Whereas Chattanooga's National Cemetery was created by order of a Union general in 1863, the Confederate Cemetery came about through efforts by returning Confederate troops in 1865. It is located between East Third and East Fifth streets in downtown Chattanooga. No admission is charged, and the grounds are open from 8:00 until 4:30.

Cravens House. At the top of Lookout Mountain, this house was used, at different times, as the headquarters for Union and Confederate troops. National Park Service guides in period costumes show visitors the historic house and grounds. Trails lead from here to Park Point and archeological remains.

Cravens House is located off U.S. 41 and 11 via Tennessee 148. It is open Monday through Saturday from 9:00 to 5:00 and Sunday from 1:00 to 5:00. It is closed from December through February. A small admission is charged.

National Cemetery. Following the carnage of the battles of Chickamauga and Chattanooga, the Union commanding officer had the bodies collected and buried in one place. Union and Confederate troops were placed side by side, their graves marked by simple stones.

Civil War buffs often take notice of the graves of Andrews's Raiders, Union spies who sneaked into Georgia and stole the General, a Confederate locomotive. They made their way north with the Georgians in hot pursuit. Captured by the Southerners, they were all hanged. They were the first Americans to be awarded the Congressional Medal of Honor. A replica of the General is atop a special monument on their grave.

The National Cemetery is located in downtown Chattanooga just east of Central Avenue and off Bailey Avenue. No admission is charged, and it is open from 8:00 until 4:30 seven days a week.

Museums

Chattanooga Museum of Regional History. Located atop Missionary Ridge, this museum focuses on Chattanooga's history. Exhibits concern such subjects as the Civil War, early Americana, toys, and World War I. A large collection of old photographs rounds out the collection.

Located at 176 South Crest Road, the museum is open from April through November. Hours are Tuesday through Friday from 9:00 to 3:00 and Saturdays from 12:00 to 5:00. Admission is charged.

Confederama. Devotees of toy soldiers, this is your place. Over five thousand tiny soldiers are forever fighting the battles of Lookout Mountain and Chattanooga. The display covers 480 square feet, and a recorded narration booms forth while tiny lights flash and miniature cannons puff smoke.

Located at 3742 Tennessee Avenue, near the Incline Railway, Confederama is open daily 9:00 to 8:00 from June through Labor Day, and 9:00 to 5:00 the rest of the year. It is privately owned and admission is charged.

Houston Antique Museum. Situated across from the Hunter Museum of Art, this museum displays the life-long collections of Anna Safley Houston, who left them to the city when she died in 1951. The museum houses fifteen thousand pitchers, Toby jugs, Chinese export porcelain, quilts, early lamps, toys, and pewter. Not a good place for children.

The museum is in a house built in the 1890s and furnished with period pieces. It is open Tuesday through Saturday from 10:00 to 4:30 and on Sundays from 2:00 to 4:30. Admission is charged. The museum is located at 201 High Street.

Hunter Museum of Art. Overlooking the Tennessee River, this museum features a permanent collection of eighteenth-, nineteenth-, and twentieth-century American art, as well as special exhibitions throughout the year. Located at 10 Bluff View, the museum is open from 10:00 to 4:30 Tuesday through Saturday and 1:00 to 4:30 on Sunday. A small donation is requested.

Lookout Mountain Museum. Across from Point Park atop Lookout Mountain, this wax museum features scenes of noteworthy events, including some from Indian history. Objects on display include Civil War rifles and pistols, swords, and military equipment. Indian artifacts include ceremonial axes and tools, stone pendants, and early game balls.

The Lookout Mountain Museum is open all year from 9:00 to 5:00, and in the summer months from 9:00 to 8:00. A small admission is charged.

National Knife Museum. Operated by the National Knife Collectors Association, this museum houses over five thousand sharp and gleaming pieces. Located off I-75 at the Shallowford Road exit, the museum is open Monday through Saturday. No admission is charged.

Rabbi Harris Swift Museum of Religious Art. This museum contains religious artifacts from several cultures, including Chinese gods, Buddha figures, and rare Jewish scrolls. The museum is located in the Siskin Foundation building at 526 Vine Street, and is open Monday through Friday from 9:00 to 5:00. No admission is charged.

Tennessee Valley Railroad and Museum. Here steam and diesel locomotives pull passenger trains on a five-mile run that includes a 960-foot pre-Civil War tunnel under Missionary Ridge. Visitors can see Pullman cars, office cars, dining cars, and cabooses. The rare private cars are especially interesting. Children usually enjoy the excursion.

Located at 4119 Cromwell Road (Tennessee 153) at the Jersey Pike exit off I-75, the museum is open from 10:00 to 5:00 daily, May through October. Admission is charged for the train ride and entrance to the museum. Call (615) 622-5908.

Theaters and Films

Backstage Playhouse. Chattanooga's only dinner theater presents enthusiastic amateurs in popular musicals and drama. Located at 3264 Brainerd Road. Call (615) 629-1565.

Little Theater. This group of amateur thespians performs about six productions a year. Located at 400 River Street. Call (615) 267-8534 for information and tickets.
Tivoli Theatre. This old movie palace serves as a home for the Chattanooga Symphony, opera productions, and touring companies offering Broadway shows. Occasionally films made before 1950 are shown. Located at 709 Broad Street. Call (615) 757-5042.

Miscellaneous Amusements

Chattanooga Choo Choo. This complex began as the city's elegant Southern Railroad Terminal. Built in 1909, it at one time had 68 trains arriving a day on 14 tracks. Passengers disembarking in Chattanooga stepped into a building that is still impressive. The grand dome of the lobby is 85 feet high; it is said to be the largest free-standing dome in the world. The station was closed in 1970 and would have been destroyed had it not been for the efforts of some businessmen and preservationists.

Now the Choo Choo, as it is called, is the centerpiece of downtown Chattanooga. It is filled with shops, lounges, and restaurants with turn-of-the-century decor. For those who would like to spend more than a day, outside the station is a unique hotel. Twenty-four railroad cars located along the tracks have been converted into rooms with Victorian-style brass beds and Tiffany-style lamps. Other attractions include an 1880 Baldwin steam locomotive, a display of the world's largest HO-gauge model railroad layout, an ice-skating rink, and a 1920s trolley from New Orleans that offers rides for only twenty-five cents.

The Chattanooga Choo Choo is located at—where else?—1400 Choo Choo Boulevard in the downtown area. Call (615) 266-5000.
Raccoon Mountain Flight Park. If you've always hankered after hang gliding, this is the place to go. Chattanooga, with Lookout Mountain and nearby Raccoon Mountain, is ideally situated for the growing sport, and

this park claims to be the oldest commercial hang-gliding resort in the United States. The average student takes lessons for seven days before he or she is ready to go aloft. Those with less time may prefer to sample hang gliding on the flight simulator, a device that enables one to soar for seven hundred feet—a flight of about twenty-five seconds—over a height of as much as a hundred feet.

If you do complete the lessons and decide to fly for real, you are invited to take off from the top of Raccoon Mountain, 825 feet above the landing field. The flight park is located off U.S. 41 on Raccoon Mountain. Call (615) 825-1995.

Incline Railway. Getting there can be more than half of the fun if you take the Incline Railway up the side of Lookout Mountain. At one point this railroad bed reaches a grade of 72.7 percent, the steepest passenger incline in the world. From Memorial Day through Labor Day there is a shuttle bus at the top to take revelers to Rock City and Ruby Falls.

In operation since 1895, the Incline Railroad is a National Historic Site, and is clearly visible on the side of Lookout Mountain. Board at Saint Elmo Avenue. Admission is charged.

Raccoon Mountain Pump Storage Project. Built by the TVA, this complex employs one of the more unusual means of producing electricity in the country. During the night and other times when demand for electricity is low, water is pumped from the Tennessee River to the top of Raccoon Mountain to fill a lake. Whenever electricity demand reaches a peak, the water is released to spin turbines and produce the needed power.

Picnic areas and observation points are available for visitors. Tours of the power-generating facilities, which are nine hundred feet underground, can also be arranged. The Raccoon Mountain complex is located west of downtown Chattanooga off U.S. 41. It is open from 8:00 until dusk. Call (615) 751-3356.

Reflection Riding. One of the more beautiful attractions of Lookout Mountain lies at the foot of it. Reflection Riding is a three hundred-acre nature and wildflower preserve offering self-guided walks and an auto drive through the park. One portion of the Great Warpath is still visible. Reflection Riding is located at the foot of lookout Mountain off U.S. 41 and U.S. 11. It is open Monday through Saturday from 9:00 till dusk, and on Sunday from 1:00 till dusk. A small admission is charged.

Rock City. Perhaps more famous for its "See Rock City" signs than the attraction itself, this long-time tourist destination has been in business since 1932. To publicize it, the owner dispatched crews with an offer to paint a farmer's entire barn for free if he would let them paint a sign on the roof. In 1956 there were over eight hundred such signs, but the Highway Beautification Act and competing businesses have reduced the "See Rock City" barns to a handful. Some of these have been placed on the National Register of Historic Places.

Whatever influences people to come to Rock City, they find themselves on a ten-acre tract on top of Lookout Mountain. Designed primarily for children, Rock City consists of a series of trails through large rock formations that have been given imaginative names. A very narrow passage, for example, is called Fat Man's Squeeze. One overlook is dubbed Lover's Leap. In Fairyland Caverns small figurines represent characters from nursery rhymes, and flower gardens appeal to those with a green thumb.

Just as the ads promise, you can stand at one point and see seven states. At least one child was disappointed, though, that the state lines in reality weren't as distinct as those on maps. Perhaps one more state is necessary to truly appreciate Rock City—a childlike state. Rock City is located on Lookout Mountain—follow the signs—and is open every day of the year from 8:30 to sundown, and from 8:00 to sundown May 21 through Labor Day. Admission is charged. Call (404) 820-2531.

Ruby Falls. The perfect rainy-day attraction. Ruby Falls is inside Twin Caves, which once opened near the Tennessee River. The natural opening was sealed when a railroad was constructed, and in 1928 drilling was begun to create a new opening so tourists could see the caves. During this construction Ruby Falls was discovered.

The water falls 145 feet in a chamber that is 1,120 feet below the top of Lookout Mountain. The caves themselves are worth seeing, if only because every formation that remotely resembles anything has been given a name—like Steak and Potatoes, Leaning Tower, Beehives, or Elephant's Foot. Andrew Jackson signed his name on one of the cave walls in 1833. Ruby Falls is open daily from 8:00 A.M. to 9:00 P.M., and from April through Labor Day from 7:30 A.M. to 10:00 P.M. It is located on Tennessee 148 on Lookout Mountain, and is privately owned. Admission is charged. Call (615) 821-2544.

Events

Autumn Leaf Special Train Excursion. At the height of the autumn colors in October, a steam-powered train leaves Chattanooga for a tour of the local foliage. For more information write the Tennessee Valley Railroad and Museum, 4119 Cromwell Road, Chattanooga 37421. Call (615) 894-8028.

Chattanooga Downtown Arts Festival. Local arts and crafts, music, theater, and dance are displayed in early June. For more information write the Chattanooga Chamber of Commerce, 1001 Market Street, Chattanooga 37402; or call (615) 756-2121.

Chattanooga Riverbend Festival. Held in mid-June, this gathering features a triathlon, concerts by such celebrities as Dizzy Gillespie and Chrystal Gayle, cloggers, karate demonstrations, power-boat races, and kid's events such as puppet shows. For further information write Friends of the Festival, P.O. Box 886, Chattanooga 37401. Call (615) 756-2211.

Dining

Chattanooga Choo Choo. Five restaurants are included in this temple of trains, and together they offer seating for over a thousand. The most impressive among them is the Dome Room, located under the great dome of the renovated train station. Gourmets may flock to Le Grand Diner, where patrons are seated in a restored railroad car and offered French cuisine and an impressive wine list. The other restaurants are the Trolley Cafe, the Stationhouse, and the Palm Terrace. Located downtown at 1400 Choo Choo Avenue. Call (615) 266-5000 for reservations.

Edison Restaurant. Situated at 5308 Ringgold Road, this place specializes in home-style cooking and Southern staples such as fried chicken and country ham. Call (615) 867-1742.

Epicurean Restaurant. Located at 4301 Ringgold Road, this restaurant offers everything from steak to Greek pastries. Call (615) 622-4139 for reservations.

Fehn's Restaurant. This place offers a view of the Tennessee River, with its commercial and pleasure boat traffic. Southern food is served family-style. Located at 600 River Street. Call (615) 267-6430 for reservations.

Green Room. Located in the Read House, Chattanooga's grande dame of hotels, this restaurant offers continental cuisine in a formal atmosphere and live entertainment on the weekends. Located at 827 Broad Street downtown. Call (615) 266-4121 for reservations.

Hunan's. This place offers the best Chinese food in Chattanooga. Located at 5911 Brainerd Road. Call (615) 899-2225.

Loft Restaurant and Lounge. Steak and seafood are the offerings here. Located at 328 Cherokee Boulevard. Call (615) 266-3601 for reservations.

Narrow Bridge. Situated in a restored 1920s house, this restaurant offers food grilled over a mesquite fire. Located at the intersection of East Brainerd and Jenkins roads approximately one and a half miles from I-75. Call (615) 855-5000 for reservations.

Town and Country Restaurant. This place primarily offers steak, along with live entertainment. Located at 110 North Market Street. Call (615) 267-8544 for reservations.

Lodging

Chanticleer Lodge. Atop Lookout Mountain one block from the Rock City gardens, this lodge offers stone cottages with antique furnishings and lovely grounds. Located at 1300 Mockingbird Lane. Call (404) 820-2015.

Chattanooga Choo Choo. Besides visiting the trains, seeing the model railroad, and eating one of the finest meals in town, at the Choo Choo you can spend the night without stepping off the property. The 373 rooms include 48 railroad parlor sleeping cars. The railroad cars are often booked far in advance, so reservations are strongly recommended. Located at 1400 Choo Choo Boulevard. Call (615) 266-5000.

Johnson's Scenic Court. This motel on top of Lookout Mountain offers the famed view of seven states. Situated on seven acres, it features a swimming pool, 16 units with private wooden decks, and a cabin. The furnishings are modern, and rooms come with TV and private bath but no phone. The motel is closed from January through April. Located two miles past Rock City on Georgia 157. Call (404) 820-2000.

Read House. Chattanooga's grand old hotel for decades, the Read House offers luxurious accommodations with a health club, Jacuzzis, and an outdoor swimming pool. Located at 827 Broad Street. Call (615) 266-4121.

CHEROKEE NATIONAL FOREST. This national forest—the only one in Tennessee—runs the length of the border with North

Carolina, broken only by the Great Smoky Mountains National Park. Although larger than the national park, Cherokee National Forest is often overlooked by travelers who see the Great Smokies on the map and head straight for them. Unfortunately, thousands of others are always doing the same.

This area offers beautiful scenery, campgrounds, hiking trails, and picnic areas. The TVA lakes here are small, but the mountains come right down to the edge of the water. For those who wish to spend the night, camping is the way to go. Along U.S. 64 from Ocoee eastward there are five campgrounds and numerous picnic areas. This national forest offers no amenities like restaurants or inns, yet neither does it offer the crowds that accompany such attractions.

The Cherokee National Forest is divided into six ranger districts, three of which lie in the Chattanooga area (the other three are described in Chapter 1). Each is briefly described below. For further information and maps write the Forest Supervisor, 2800 North Ocoee Street, Northwest, Cleveland 37311; or call (615) 476-9700.

Ocoee Ranger District. The action here lies along the Ocoee River, with its TVA flume and white-water rafting. Five campsites are along the river, or very close to it, and two others lie further south. For additional information and maps write the Ocoee Ranger District, U.S. Forest Service, Route 1, Parksville, Benton 37301; or call (615) 338-5201.

Hiwassee Ranger District. Six campgrounds in this district lie along the Hiwassee River. Places of interest include the TVA's Appalachia Powerhouse and Maggie's Mill. For further information write Hiwassee Ranger District, U.S. Forest Service, 1401 South Tennessee Avenue, Etowah 37331; or call (615) 263-5486.

Tellico Ranger District. The Tellico area of the Cherokee National Forest is famous among hunters for the wild boar, bear, and other big game that are found here. Others may be interested in seeing the Bald River Falls and the Pheasant Fields Rearing Station. There are seven campgrounds along the Tellico River. For further information write Tellico Ranger District, U.S. Forest Service, Route 3, Tellico River Road, Tellico Plains 37385; or call (615) 253-2520.

CLEVELAND. Named for a Revolutionary War general who fought at King's Mountain, Cleveland is the jumping-off point for explorations of the southernmost Tennessee mountains. The Cleveland area is also the scene of one of the more shameful things ever done by the U.S. government: the forced removal of the Cherokees on the "Trail of Tears."

The Cherokees were the dominant Indian tribe in the southern Appalachians. Unlike the nomadic plains Indians, the Cherokees lived in stable villages and raised crops. As more and more settlers came West, however, the Cherokees were pushed further and further out of their ancestral lands. At first they agreed to treaties, but it seemed that each agreement increasingly favored the white people.

Andrew Jackson was a passionate Indian hater, and his arrival in the White House marked the beginning of the worst times for the tribes. By the time of his presidency the Cherokees were highly civilized, according to white standards; they had a written language, a newspaper, and a sophisticated governmental structure that included a supreme court. All of this carried no weight in Washington. Orders were given to the army, and approximately fifteen thousand Cherokees were rounded up, put in concentration camps in the Cleveland area, and marched off to a barren reservation in Oklahoma. A few managed to escape and hide out in the Great Smoky Mountains; their story is told under the town of CHEROKEE, North Carolina.

Red Clay State Historical Area. This was the last council ground of the Cherokee Nation in Tennessee. Here the Cherokees learned they would have to go to Oklahoma. They moved here in 1832 after the state of Georgia stripped them of all rights except the right to sell land,

and they stayed until forced out in 1838. A visitors' center contains a small museum and a theater where slides and films are shown. Near it is a reconstructed council house and a Cherokee farm. A path leads to the huge spring that attracted the Indians here. The spring is 17 feet deep and provides over four hundred thousand gallons of water a day. There are also picnic areas and a three-mile loop trail leading to a limestone overlook tower.

The Red Clay Historical Area is located on the Georgia border. From Cleveland take Tennessee 60 south for 13 miles; turn right onto Weatherly Switch and follow the signs approximately 2 miles to the park. The museum is open daily from 8:30 to 4:30. No admission is charged. Call (615) 472-2627.

Primitive Settlement. This museum of pioneer life is housed in a collection of authentic log cabins, some of them 150 years old. The structures have been restored to their original condition and filled with antique furniture, which is interesting to see even if it doesn't always fit the rustic lifestyle that typified cabin life. Privately owned, the Primitive Settlement is located one mile off U.S. 64 five miles east of Cleveland. Follow the signs. Open daily 10:00 to 6:00. Admission is charged.

COPPERHILL. Approached from the east or west along U.S. 64, the Copperhill area gives a shock even to those who know what to expect. After driving through verdant forests and lush farmland, the visitor comes upon land that resembles a moonscape. It is stripped of trees, bushes, and in some places even grass. There is no topsoil. If you leave the main highway and drive toward Copperhill, the devastation intensifies.

The Copperhill Basin, as it is called, is the result of one of the world's worst cases of industrial pollution. In 1850 the first copper mine was dug here, and by 1899 copper production was in high gear. Huge copper roasters ran day and night, and the surrounding countryside was stripped of timber to feed the flames. Sulfur dioxide, a byproduct of the smelting process, was released into the air and killed any vegetation remaining. Erosion did the rest. The damage covers 56 square miles, and is said to be visible from orbiting spacecraft.

All of this does not seem to appreciably concern the locals, some of whom refer to the red hills as "a beloved scar." The area does have a kind of beauty that is often compared to that of the Badlands or other desert lands in the American West. Copper is still mined here, but, oddly enough, the sulfur dioxide that caused all this havoc is now processed into sulfuric acid, which has surpassed the copper as the main product of the industry. A museum chronicles all of this. See the listing under DUCKTOWN.

DAYTON. In 1925 the Tennessee State Legislature passed a law forbidding the teaching of any theories of evolution in public school classrooms. The American Civil Liberties Union offered to defend anyone who would oppose the law in a test case. This was reported in a Chattanooga newspaper, and it attracted the attention of a group of Dayton boosters who were sitting around a small table in Robinson's Drug Store, the local watering hole.

John Thomas Scopes was a young biology teacher in the Rhea County High School, and when he approached the drugstore the men present asked him if he had ever taught evolutionary theory. He confessed that he had. The Dayton boosters decided that a test case would be just the item to stir things up and put Dayton on the map. They succeeded beyond their wildest dreams, but the publicity that emerged during the hot summer of 1925 was not exactly what they had in mind.

The American Civil Liberties Union was notified that Scopes had been arrested, and the circus began. Clarence Darrow, the eminent attorney, announced that he would defend Scopes, and William Jennings Bryan, three-time presidential aspirant and "silver tongued orator," came in to assist the prosecution. The trial lasted ten days, but every word of it was followed by newspapers, newsreels, and a Chicago radio station. Proceedings began in the Rhea County courthouse, but the heat and the huge number of spectators convinced the judge to reconvene outside under the trees. The climax of the trial came when Bryan took the stand to testify about the Biblical story of creation. Darrow pressed him relentlessly, asking the Great Commoner if a whale really swallowed Jonah, but Bryan's faith was not shaken.

The trial ended with the conviction of Scopes, although the verdict was later overturned on a technicality. Clarence Darrow returned to Chicago, and five days after the trial Bryan died in Dayton. The small town was now assuredly on the map, but through the writings of H. L. Mencken and others it was depicted as the home of ignorant backwoodsmen who would not tolerate scientific theory. Dayton was later pilloried in the play *Inherit The Wind*, which was subsequently filmed.

Rhea County Courthouse. The scene of the Bryan-Darrow confrontation is now listed on the Register of National Historic Places. The actual courtroom in which the trial began has been restored to its 1925 condition. Located on the town square, it is usually open from 9:00 to 5:00 on weekdays.

Robinson's Drug Store. The place where it all started, this drugstore still serves soft drinks at a small table where the discussion that led to the Scopes trial was supposedly held.

Scopes Museum. In the basement of the Rhea County Courthouse, the Scopes Museum displays artifacts and photographs of Dayton's famous trial. A small theater shows a documentary by the British Broadcasting Corporation on the Scopes Trial. The museum is open from 8:00 until 4:00 on Monday, Tuesday, Thursday, and Friday, and from 8:00 until 12:00 on Wednesday and Saturday. No admission is charged.

William Jennings Bryan College. This four-year Christian college was established in memory of the man who had testified under oath to the accuracy of the Bible. Approximately six hundred students attend the college, where they major in one of seventeen academic fields, including arts and sciences, Biblical history, business, and education. Presumably evolution is not on the list.

DUCKTOWN. This town was named for Chief Duck of the Cherokees, and was the center of the early copper mining industry in the area. It was a rough-and-tumble mining town in the Wild-West tradition, but the center of operations gradually shifted to Copperhill, further south.

   Ducktown Museum. This small and friendly place displays a collection of photographs and artifacts depicting the history of the area. Samples of copper ore and the finished product are displayed along with an explanation of how the refining process works. The Museum is located in Ducktown in the Burra Burra Mine Historical District, which is listed on the National Register of Historic Places. To get to the museum leave U.S. 64 and go north on Tennessee 68. Follow the signs. It is open Monday through Saturday from 10:00 to 4:30, and a small admission is charged.

FORT LOUDON STATE HISTORICAL AREA. This five-hundred-acre park contains a replica of Fort Loudon, constructed in 1756 by English colonists from South Carolina to resist French expansion from the southwest. Built to European standards, it did not look like the usual American frontier fort. Instead of being square or rectangular, Fort Loudon was diamond-shaped with a bastion at each corner.

   When the fort was built the colonists were on good terms with the Indians. Indeed, the Cherokees had requested the fort to protect their women and children while the men were off fighting the Indian allies of the French. But due to increasing French influence and British abuses of the Indians, things changed. The Cherokees lay siege to the fort. Five months later the English surrendered, but not before securing an agreement that they could leave in peace. The Indians let them out, but the next morning fell on the English, killing some and taking others prisoner. The fort was burned to the ground.

The replica of Fort Loudon is located off U.S. 441, south of a bridge over the Little Tennessee River near Vonore. It is open daily from 8:00 to 4:00. No admission is charged.

OCOEE. The Ocoee River has some of the wildest rapids to be found in the state of Tennessee. As travelers approach the North Carolina border on U.S. 64, the number of white-water outfitters and guide services increases; finally the river itself can be seen. More than one person has come to the Ocoee, however, only to be greeted by a trickle of water, barely enough to call a mountain stream. How can this be?

The answer lies overhead in a large wooden flume. When the TVA set up its hydroelectric system, the Ocoee was one of the smaller rivers tapped for power. The engineers found it necessary to construct a trough-like flume to transport the water from a dam downstream to a power plant. For three decades the water flowed through the flume, and no one considered rafting the Ocoee.

By the 1970s the flume needed repair. While it was being rebuilt, the waters were loosed in the riverbed once more, and white-water aficionados gloried in the Class I through Class V rapids. When the TVA completed the flume, considerable controversy arose; the rafters didn't want to give up their sport. A compromise was reached, and now electricity is generated only part time. When it isn't—generally on weekends—the Ocoee roars again. Visitors can choose from several companies that offer guided raft trips on the river. A few are listed here.

Cherokee Rafting
Route 1
Ocoee 37361
(615) 338-5124

High Country Ocoee
  Outpost
Route 1
Ocoee 37361
(615) 338-8634

Ocoee Outdoors
Box 172
Ocoee 37361
(615) 338-2438

Sunburst Adventures
Box 238
Ocoee 37361
(615) 338-8388

Smoky Mountain River
  Expeditions
Box 178
Ducktown 37326
(615) 496-7332

Wildwater, Ltd.
Ducktown 37326
(615) 496-4904

FOUR

Great Smoky Mountains National Park

WHAT IS THE LURE of the Great Smoky Mountains National Park? A lot of people like to express it in numbers. The park is the largest wilderness area in the eastern United States. It totals 517 thousand acres, and is within a day's drive of 65 percent of the nation's population. Portions of the park receive 80 inches of rainfall a year. There are over two miles of hiking trail for every mile of road—over eight hundred miles of trail in all.

The list goes on and on. But the lure of the Smokies cannot be reduced to columns of figures. How can you quantify a deep breath of air on the top of Clingmans Dome, air that is scented only with fragrant spruce? How can you put a numerical value on the way the sun looks as it rises over the top of a ridge? And who can calculate the joy experienced by a child playing for the first time in the waters of a mountain stream?

The value of a wilderness experience is intensely personal. Some people can get their fill by driving through an area with no billboards or fast food chains. Others focus on the delicate petals of a wildflower in a mountain

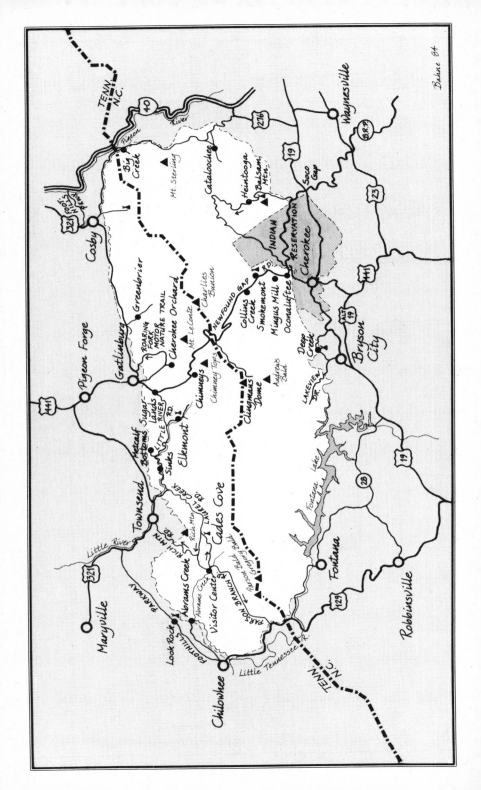

Bahre 84

meadow, and still others receive their due by carrying a tent on their backs for fifteen miles and sleeping at least five miles from the nearest road.

Whatever the lure, the Great Smoky Mountains National Park attracts more people than any other national park in the country—sometimes more than some of the other parks combined. No one knows the exact number of people who visit the park, but park authorities estimated that over eight million individual visits were made in 1983.

ABOUT THIS CHAPTER

People come to the park for many reasons. Some want pretty scenery; the more vistas they can see out the car window the happier they are. Others seek a more active experience; they want to get out and hike, bicycle, or jump from rock to rock in a stream. Quite a few see the park as a place for recreation, while others perceive it as a wilderness sanctuary, to be treated with care and respect. The rest of this chapter is broken down by activities. Since most people enter the park by car, we'll start off with driving.

MAIN ENTRY POINTS TO THE PARK

GATLINBURG. Over half of the park's visitors enter on U.S. 441, after making it past the temptations of Pigeon Forge and Gatlinburg. The Sugarlands Visitor Center and the park headquarters is on the right as you enter, and this is a good place to get oriented and to make plans. The center features natural history exhibits, a film, and books and pamphlets—some free—about the park.

Outside the Sugarlands Visitor Center drivers make a choice: head up the Newfound Gap Road over the mountain or turn right and head for the Cades Cove area along the Little River Road. Aside from the center, there isn't a great deal to do at Sugarlands. You have to drive five miles up 441 to the nearest picnic area, and most of the sights along the Little River Road lie on the other end.

CHEROKEE. This entrance leads straight onto the Newfound Gap Road, which heads over the mountain and on to Gatlinburg. Visitors can stop at the Oconaluftee Visitor Center and Pioneer Farmstead, the Mingus Mill, and the Smokemont area, but then there are no other roadside attractions until the Clingmans Dome Road, ten miles away.

TOWNSEND. Of the three main entrances to the park, this one is least used. It leads to an intersection of the Little River Road, which heads toward the Sugarlands Visitor Center and Gatlinburg, and Laurel Creek Road, which goes to Cades Cove.

SCENIC DRIVES

NEWFOUND GAP ROAD (U.S. 441). This is the only road that crosses the mountains from Gatlinburg to Cherokee. It is closed to commercial traffic, and virtually everyone who visits the park drives over it at least once.

As you leave the Sugarlands Visitor Center, you literally cannot see the forest for the trees. About five miles up, after leaving the Chimneys Picnic Area, the road makes a noticeable climb, and then you are right beside the Chimneys. Thereafter the road climbs quickly, so quickly that engineers were forced to install a unique feature called the Loopover to prevent the road from becoming too steep. Here the road goes in a giant circle and actually loops over itself.

Close observers will notice that the vegetation changes as the road ascends. The hardwood forests so prevalent in the lower elevations are gradually replaced by evergreen trees. Driving this road is like making a trip to Canada; the higher you get the more the trees are like those found in the northern United States. At the top of the mountain, the forest is like that of northern Canada.

If you are driving from Gatlinburg, most of the spectacular scenery will be behind you, and it's a good idea to pull off the road from time to time and drink it in. Finally the road reaches Newfound Gap, so named by early settlers because it replaced a passage in the mountains that had been used since Indian times. Here Pres. Franklin D. Roosevelt dedicated the park in 1940. Here, too, one can see the mountains in North Carolina stretching to the horizon.

The Clingmans Dome Road (described further on) heads off to the right here. If you continue on into North Carolina, it's all downhill from here. The trees slowly change from softwoods to hardwoods, and within seven miles you are back in a valley again. The Collins Creek Picnic area appears on the right, followed shortly by the Smokemont Campground and Mingus Mill. This is a good place to stop and get out. Then the road passes the Oconaluftee Pioneer Farmstead, which is more or less North Carolina's answer to Cades Cove. The road finally passes the Oconaluftee Visitor Center, and if you keep driving you will find yourself on the Cherokee Indian Reservation.

CLINGMANS DOME ROAD. This seven-mile road along the ridge of the mountains is closed to cars during the winter, when it becomes a cross-country skier's delight. While open, however, it offers spectacular views of the North Carolina side of the park. The road ends at a big parking lot and the beginning of a half-mile paved trail to the top of Clingmans Dome. Here a spiral ramp—accessible to those in wheelchairs—leads to an observation tower and the best view in the entire region, if not the entire eastern United States. Misty mountains extend in every direction, the air is cool and scented with the evergreens, and being there makes the drive and the walk all worth it.

The Newfound Gap and Clingmans Dome roads are the best places to see the mountains, but on certain summer and fall weekends they are jammed with traffic. At such times it is useful to consider driving on some of the roads that lie outside of the park for a look at the mountains.

FOOTHILLS PARKWAY. This road was once designed to go all the way around the northern boundary of the park, but was never finished. There are two segments, one near Cosby and the other on the western end of the park. The Cosby section connects I-40 and Tennessee 32 and is only six miles long.

The longer—17 miles—and much more scenic section runs from U.S. 321 between Townsend and Maryville to U.S. 129. The best way to see this road without having to drive it twice is to go to Cades Cove, take the Parson Branch Road to U.S. 129, turn right, and pick up the parkway to Chilhowee. It ascends to Look Rock, where there is a fire tower to climb, and then continues on back to U.S. 321, all the way providing a good view of the mountains.

Note: The Foothills Parkway may be closed in the winter.

BLUE RIDGE PARKWAY. As it draws near its southern terminus, this famous highway weaves through the Cherokee Indian Reservation climbing higher and higher. Sometimes visitors like to take the Parkway to Soco Gap and then go east on U.S. 19 to U.S. 276, where they go north to I-40, one of the more scenic interstate highways in the eastern United States. They follow I-40 north around the eastern end of the park.

CHEROKEE TO FONTANA. This route is entirely out of the Great Smoky Mountains National Park, but it affords many views of the underside of the park as it winds through the equally beautiful mountains of the Nantahala National Forest. From Cherokee take U.S. 19 to Bryson City. One good side trip leads six miles up Lakeview Drive, all that was built of a road planned to replace one that Fontana Lake covered up. This is a dead-end road, but it has some nice views of the lake and the mountains. Continue on U.S. 19 out of Bryson City until you come to North Carolina 28 on the right. Follow 28 all the way to Fontana, after which it joins U.S. 129. This route is extremely curvy, and might not be suitable for large recreational vehicles or passengers who are subject to carsickness.

NATURE ROADS

In a sense all of the roads in the Great Smoky Mountains National Park are nature roads, but the ones below do not command wide views of distant peaks. These quiet byways enable the visitor to see things close up, to experience nature a little more intimately, and to get out now and then to examine an old cabin, a waterfall, or a small mountain stream.

LITTLE RIVER ROAD. One of the two main roads in the park, this one leads from the Sugarlands Visitor Center over Sugarlands Mountain, descends to the Little River, and follows it toward the Cades Cove area. Some of this 18-mile road was constructed on the remains of the Little River Railroad, which was used to bring logs out of the mountains in the early part of this century.

A turnoff to the left leads to the Elkmont community, a group of cabins occupied by families who owned them when the Great Smoky Mountains National Park came into existence.

Back on the road, a turnoff to the right leads to Metcalf Bottoms, where a log school and several old cabins can be seen. These are indicative of the way people lived in the area in the early part of this century.

The Little River grows in volume the further it goes, and plunges over a small waterfall at the Sinks, a popular if bone-chilling swimming hole. Further downstream visitors may see people riding inflated automobile inner tubes on the river. The National Park Service takes a dim view of this sport, for it is hazardous, especially when the water is high, but so far they have done nothing to stop it. The Little River Road ends at an intersection with the Laurel Creek Road, which leads to Cades Cove, and the road out of the park to Townsend. The Laurel Creek Road is pleasant enough, but offers little to see besides trees along the way.

CADES COVE ROADS. The Cades Cove Historical Area is dealt with in another section of this chapter, but the roads leading from it are worth describing here. Many people think of Cades Cove as an end to itself, but it marks the start of two gravel roads that are little known and little traveled.

Rich Mountain Road. This route was taken by Cades Cove residents when they went to town in Maryville. The seven-mile road starts out one-way as it winds up out of the cove, offering several views of the farmlands, and crosses Rich Mountain at the park boundary. Now two-way, it descends to U.S. 321 near Townsend. Recreational vehicles are banned, and the road is closed in the wintertime.

Parson Branch Road. If you want to drive only one of the roads out of Cades Cove, this is the one to take. An eight-mile one-way road, it leaves the cove just beyond the Cable Mill parking area and wanders down to U.S. 129 between Fontana and Chilhowee. The road is surrounded by beautiful, lush growth of mountain laurel and ferns. It fords a creek several times. The Cades Cove area can often become crowded, and this is an excellent way to exit. The road is closed in the wintertime.

CHEROKEE ORCHARD ROAD. Lying just outside Gatlinburg, this is the road to take when you've had too much of gimcrack and souvenir T-shirts. Follow the Airport Road in Gatlinburg to Cherokee Orchard Road. It runs three and a half miles through an old orchard and past the site of several log cabins. The forest here is very new, so it is a good place to see wildflowers.

ROARING FORK MOTOR NATURE TRAIL. This delightful five-mile drive just outside of Gatlinburg leads visitors uphill to the Grotto Falls parking area and then downhill back to town along a rushing stream. The water cavorts over rocks, cooling the air and providing moisture for luxurious growth of ferns and mosses. This is one of the best places to take photographic portraits of your fellow vacationers. Recreational vehicles are banned, and the road is closed in the wintertime.

HISTORIC AREAS

As you drive or hike through the forests and along the streams, you may easily assume that the Great Smoky Mountains National Park was always as it is now. It wasn't. From the times of the Cherokee until the creation of the park, people lived here. When the park was put together there were over six thousand landowners, and over two-thirds of the land had been logged. Throughout most of the Smokies there are little traces of its earlier inhabitants—particularly the Indians—but in a few sections the visitor can gain a sense of what life here used to be like.

TENNESSEE SIDE

Cades Cove. This stretch of low land surrounded by mountains is believed to have been named for Kate, the wife of a Cherokee Indian chief. It is the best place in the park to see historic structures and an accurate depiction of how the mountain people lived.

The buildings and farms lie along an 11-mile one-way loop that is the best road in the park for bicycling. Visitors can rent bicycles at the campground store at the beginning of the loop, and on late Saturday afternoons in the summer and early fall automobile traffic on the road is banned so that bicyclists can have it all. There are shortcuts across the cove for a quick trip, and two roads—Rich Mountain and Parson Branch—lead from the cove out of the park. Several hiking trails lead up from the cove to the surrounding mountains. One popular day hike leads to 20-foot-high Abrams Falls, the waterfall with the largest volume in the park. The campground in Cades Cove is one of the more popular ones in the park, and the only one with a store. There is also a picnic area.

White settlers moved into Cades Cove in 1821, and 30 years later the cove reached a peak population of 685. This community farmed fifteen thousand acres and supported several churches and a couple of mills. Many of their necessities were grown or made, and everything else came over Rich Mountain on a wagon trail from Maryville. The land could not support 685 people, however, and families began to move on to other places. When the area became a part of Great Smoky Mountains National Park in 1936, most of the remaining families moved out, although they still made use of their churches and cemeteries.

Today the National Park Service allows farmers to graze cattle in the cove to prevent the forest from growing back and to keep the area looking as it did in old times. The barbed wire fences and modern farming implements are a necessary concession. Deer often mingle with the cattle as they graze, and an occasional wild turkey can be seen at a distance.

The farms along the loop, such as the Elijah Oliver Place and the Tipton Place, give a glimpse of the ingenuity of the early mountain farmers. The Tipton Place has a replica of a cantilevered barn, an example of an unusual style of architecture that permitted keeping some items within four walls while providing outdoor shelter for work or for animals.

The highlight of the cove is the Cable Mill area, which contains a working mill, a frame house, and several typical farm outbuildings. Cornmeal produced in the mill is for sale in the visitors' center during the summer months. Periodic craft and farming demonstrations are presented here, and sorghum molasses are made one weekend in October. Postcards and film are sold in the visitors' center, and restrooms are provided.

Cades Cove is extremely popular with park visitors. It's a good idea to arrive early in the morning or late in the afternoon.

Elkmont. Some visitors are shocked to discover a group of vacation homes in the middle of the national park. Back when the Smokies were still being logged, prosperous Knoxvillians came by railroad to build second homes and a private club here in the mountains. When the park was established, these people had the clout to set up an agreement whereby the families could keep the cabins as long as the children lived. The youngest of these "children" are now in their fifties. The one-time club became the Wonderland Hotel, one of only two lodging places in the park. It is slated to close in the 1990s. Elkmont is located off the Little River Road.

Metcalf Bottoms. Located off the Little River Road about nine miles from the Newfound Gap Road, this flat area includes the Little Greenbrier Schoolhouse and the Walker Sisters' cabin. These are probably not worth a special trip, although Metcalf Bottoms does contain more picnic sites than any other area on the Tennessee side of the park.

Noah "Bud" Ogle Place. The name Ogle is seen on several commercial establishments in Gatlinburg. This farmstead, located on the Cherokee Orchard Road, is an example of how an ancestor of the Gatlinburg Ogles lived. A short nature trail near the house and an accompanying brochure describe this section of land and its history.

NORTH CAROLINA SIDE

Cataloochee. Twelve hundred people once lived in this area, which lies on the eastern extreme of the park. Nowadays the visitor will find a school building, churches, and a few houses and barns. If you've seen Cades Cove, don't knock yourself out to see this place. To get there either take the Big Creek-Cataloochee Road off Tennessee 32 near Cosby and follow the edge of the park around, or take U.S. 19 near Cherokee, NC to U.S. 276, drive north and follow the signs. The road is unimproved and not recommended for recreational vehicles.

Mingus Mill. Most people think of a mill as having a large overshot or undershot wheel, like the one in Cades Cove. This "tub mill," as the mountain people called it, is of a more advanced turbine design. It operates from May through October, and is located off the New-found Gap Road north of the Oconaluftee Pioneer Farmstead.

Oconaluftee Pioneer-Farmstead. This is North Carolina's answer to Cades Cove. From May through October, the typical mountain farm is the scene of demonstrations of farming methods. Small farm animals are allowed the run of the place. It is on the Newfound Gap Road near the entrance to the park.

NATURAL WONDERS

Several distinct natural features in the park are worth special trips. Most of these are some distance from the roads. A little exertion, however, can put you away from the noise of traffic and bring the wilderness a little closer.

WATERFALLS ALONG THE ROADS. For an area with so much rainfall, the Smokies have few spectacular waterfalls. The high ones usually come from small streams, and the biggest one in volume drops only 20 feet. If you have toured the waterfalls in western North Carolina, you might not want to spend half a day getting to one of the falls in the park.

Along the Little River Road you will find the **Sinks** and **Meigs Falls.** The Sinks are about twelve miles from the Sugarlands Visitor Center; a small parking area is available. Meigs Falls are in a small valley about one mile further down the road. They are on the far side of the stream, and can easily be missed if you drive too quickly. Of the two, Meigs Falls are more impressive.

Closer to Gatlinburg, on the Roaring Fork Motor Nature Trail, lies the **Place of a Thousand Drips.** Here hundreds of little streams seep from a tall bank when the water table is high. During dry periods the number of drips may drop considerably, but after a rain this place can be very appealing.

WATERFALLS ON THE TRAILS

Abrams Falls. Named after a Cherokee Indian chief, this waterfall is on the wide stream that drains Cades Cove. Though large in volume, it falls only 20 feet. Visitors can reach the waterfall via a two-and-a-half-mile walk from Cades Cove, but a better hike approaches it from the Abrams Creek Ranger Station at the park's western boundary.

Grotto Falls. Since they are just a one-and-one-half mile walk off the Roaring Fork Motor Nature Trail near Gatlinburg, these falls are good to take children to see.

Laurel Falls. These falls are reached by a one-and-a-quarter-mile trail off the Little River Road.

Rainbow Falls. Although originating in a small stream, these falls drop 80 feet. In the wintertime hikers sometimes find a towering column of ice. The three-and-a-half-mile trail begins at the Cherokee Orchard Road near Gatlinburg.

Ramsay Cascades. The highest waterfall in the park— 100 feet—is a cascade instead of a straight drop. It is reached by a four-mile hike from the Greenbrier Cove area between Gatlinburg and Cosby.

There are five other falls in the Great Smoky Mountains National Park. Information on where they are and how to reach them is available in any of the visitors' centers.

GRASS BALDS. A unique and still unexplained phenomenon in the park are grass balds—treeless patches on the tops or ridges of mountains that are otherwise covered with trees. Theories as to the origin of balds involve lightning, plant disease, actions by early Indians, and fire.

The white settlers in the area used the balds as pasture for their sheep and cattle. Residents in the Cades Cove area, who had to laboriously remove trees from their fields by hand, were glad to have pasture they didn't have to clear. In the spring of each year the men and boys would drive the cattle up to the mountain heights, always keeping watch to make sure they weren't attacked by a bear or panther. All summer the animals would graze under the watchful eye of an old man or boys who were appointed to look after the herd. In the meantime, the fields below were filled with corn or other grains, safe from the hungry cattle who would knock down fences to get the grain. In the fall the animals, fattened by the mountain grass, were returned to the farms.

However they came about, the balds are a worthwhile destination for a hike. It is exhilarating to emerge from a forest into a mountain meadow filled with long grass or wildflowers. Often one can see for miles from a bald, and it is a good place for a picnic and nap.

Most of the grass balds are along the crest of the Smokies. Andrews Bald, near Clingmans Dome, is the closest to a road. Other balds include Little Bald, Gregory Bald, Spence Field, Silers Bald, and Parson Bald. Hikes to several of the balds are listed below under HIKING.

After the Cades Cove farmers left their homes and no one drove cattle to the mountaintops anymore, the forest began to slowly reclaim the grassy areas. This posed a problem for the National Park Service, which as custodian of the wilderness was supposed to let nature take its course. The National Park Service finally decided to maintain two balds, Gregory and Andrews, by cutting back new growth.

ANIMALS IN THE PARK

As a wilderness area, the park is home to creatures ranging from the black bear to the tiny salamander. The vast majority of these animals pose no threat to people, but visitors should be mindful of three in particular.

BEARS. The park is famous for its bears, and many people have gone home with tales of a marauding bear eating up the contents of an ice chest or coming up to a car for handouts. Unfortunately, some people have gone home with a face full of stitches. Though they look awkward, bears move very fast; over a short distance a bear can outrun a horse. Females with cubs are particularly dangerous. If someone gets between the mother and her cubs, even inadvertently, she may attack.

The authorities of the Great Smoky Mountains National Park have constant problem with people feeding the bears. This harms the animals in three ways. First, hamburger buns and the like are not good for a bear. Second, if they lose their fear of humans the bears are more likely to come close and get in trouble. Finally, poachers have been known to listen on citizens' band radios for reports of bears near a road. They park near where a bear has been spotted and leave a trail of bread far into the woods. If the bears follow it, the mother is often killed and her cubs kidnapped.

Backcountry hikers sometimes encounter bears near camping shelters or on highly traveled trails. Bears are intelligent animals, and they know that those packs contain more than dirty socks. It is not uncommon for a bear to rush at a hiker while making a "snuffling" sound. The hiker, utterly terrified, flings down the pack and sets an Olympic record in the 100-yard dash. The bear immediately stops the chase and settles down to dine. Unless cubs are involved, most encounters between bears and humans center on food. One wants it, and one wisely decides to let the other have it.

WILD HOGS. The European wild hog was imported to stock a hunting preserve in North Carolina in the early part of this century. The hogs escaped into the mountains and over the years worked their way into the Great Smoky Mountains National Park, where they have created ecological havoc. They have destroyed patches of wildflowers, fouled once pure springs, and competed with bears for naturally occurring foods.

The hogs can reach weights of four hundred pounds, and they have razor-sharp tusks that can easily kill dogs and seriously hurt people. Fortunately, the hogs are largely nocturnal and have keen senses of smell and hearing. Usually they will stay away from people. If cornered, however, they can be vicious.

SNAKES. There are several species of snakes in the park, but only two that are poisonous: the timber rattlesnake and the copperhead. The timber rattler may be encountered soaking up the sun on a rock. Its distinctive rattle usually alerts people to its presence.

The copperhead is more insidious. It prefers the lowlands, and is likely to be found in and among rotting timber and logs, and around rocks and outbuildings. Copperheads give no warning; they just bite. Be especially careful when picking up firewood.

It is easy to become paranoid about snakes. Many long-term visitors in the park have never encountered either a rattlesnake or a copperhead. It doesn't hurt, however, to stay on guard.

RECREATIONAL ACTIVITIES IN THE PARK

BICYCLING. Few people think of the Great Smoky Mountains National Park as a good place to ride bikes. The roads are crowded with cars and they climb high mountains. Cades Cove is considered the only decent place to take to the bicycle saddle.

With the right equipment, however, bicycling in the Smokies can be downright pleasurable. A multigeared bike can cut the hills down to size. For example, the climb up the Newfound Gap Road from Cherokee or Gatlinburg to Clingmans Dome is not as bad as it sounds. The rider starts at an elevation of about two thousand feet, and climbs 20 miles to forty-six hundred feet. That's not an impossible ride if you're in good shape and have a good bike. Best of all, if you do the work to get to the top, there is a blissfully easy ride down the other side or back down the way you came.

Off-the-road riding has come into vogue in the past few years, but vehicles—and this includes bicycles—are barred from National Park trails. For the rough-and-tumble set, however, gravel roads such as the Cataloochee Road or the Parson Branch Road out of Cades Cove are good ones to take.

The most dangerous thing about riding in the park, as elsewhere, is the automobile traffic. Not all drivers are accustomed to sharing the road, and even if they are they may be looking at the scenery instead of at you. The roads are too narrow for a recreational vehicle to pass a bike, so you may find yourself holding up traffic going uphill. Downhill is another matter; a bicyclist can easily keep up with everyone else.

Helmets should be worn on all roads, and tire repair equipment should be on board every bike. The park has no service stations or bike repair shops. Riding on any paved roads outside of Cades Cove is not a good idea for children.

CAMPING. Some people don't consider their trip to the Smokies complete unless they spend a night out under the stars, and camping is certainly the least expensive form of accommodations. It can also be educational. From mid-June through September 1 the park offers interpretive and entertaining programs at the developed campgrounds. There are hikes for children only, nighttime programs, and other activities that promote greater appreciation and understanding of the park.

The park offers seven developed campgrounds and three primitive campgrounds. For those who are up for a little hiking, there are shelters on the Appalachian Trail and backcountry camping sites.

Park personnel define a developed campground as one with water, flush toilets, tent sites, tables, fireplaces, and some space for recreational vehicles. Showers and RV hookups are not provided. There are dumping stations at

Cades Cove, Cosby, and Smokemont campgrounds, as well as one across from the Sugarlands Visitor Center. Developed sites cost six dollars a night, and visitors are limited to seven days at all campgrounds during the peak season. You can make reservations at three campgrounds—Cades Cove and Elkmont in Tennessee and Smokemont in North Carolina—by writing Ticketron, P.O. Box 2715, San Francisco, California 94126. You cannot make reservations by phone. Reservations are recommended; they are taken up to two months in advance.

　　Primitive campgrounds offer water, pit toilets, and fire rings, but no tables.

Tennessee-side Campgrounds

Developed

　　Cades Cove. 161 sites. This part of the Smokies is rich in things to do. Besides the historic homes and the Cable Mill, a number of trails lead to attractions such as the Rich Mountain Fire Tower, Spence Field and Gregory Bald, and Abrams Falls. This is the only campground with a store, and the loop road is the best place to bicycle in the entire park.

　　Cosby. 175 sites. This campground is away from the crowds that fill Cades Cove and some of the other campgrounds. It is a good base to explore the Greenbrier area and perhaps hike to Ramsay Cascade, the highest waterfall in the park. "Tubing" on Cosby Creek is the favorite activity here.

　　Elkmont. 320 sites. The biggest campground in the entire park, this one is close to the Metcalf Bottoms historical area and the delightful Little River. Laurel Falls is nearby, too, and this is the closest campground to Gatlinburg.

　　Look Rock. 92 sites. This campground often has space when the others don't, due no doubt to the fact that it is located on the western extreme of the park. It does offer access to the Abrams Creek area, which is described below.

Primitive

Abrams Creek. 16 sites. The smallest campground on the Tennessee side, this one is located in an area of exceptional beauty, where tall fir trees lend a cathedral effect to the forest. It is the trailhead for a walk to Abrams Falls.

North Carolina–side Campgrounds

Developed

Balsam Mountain. 46 sites. This is a good base for exploring the Cherokee Indian Reservation, perhaps visiting their museum and taking in an evening of "Unto These Hills," an outdoor drama. Mingo Falls on the reservation is worth a side trip. (See Chapter 7 for more about the reservation.) This campground is also close to the Blue Ridge Parkway, which is often less crowded than park roads.

Deep Creek. 119 sites. Located near Bryson City, this campground is within two miles' hike of three waterfalls: Juneywhank Falls, Indian Creek Falls, and Toms Branch Falls.

Smokemont. 140 sites. This is the biggest campground on the North Carolina side, and a good place to stay while taking in the Pioneer Farmstead at Oconaluftee and the Mingus Mill. It is also the closest park campground to Cherokee, North Carolina.

Primitive

Big Creek. 9 sites. The smallest campground in the park, Big Creek is located at the eastern edge of the park.

Cataloochee. 27 sites. Also on the eastern edge of the park, this one is at the end of a rough, unpaved road that will guarantee you freedom from crowds. The Cataloochee area contains several old buildings remaining from a community of twelve hundred settlers.

Trail Shelters

These shelters, most of them on the Appalachian Trail, offer accommodations for hikers who do not want to carry tents. Inside are from 8 to 14 beds made of wire mesh strung between logs in a bunk-bed fashion. Each shelter has three solid walls; the fourth side is made of chain link fencing to keep out the bears.

The shelters can be a godsend if you're an overnight hiker without a tent, but the total stranger who sleeps beside you may be the wildest thing you encounter on the trip. The shelters may pose hazards for the environment, too, by concentrating campers in a few spots. By the end of the fall, for example, it is impossible to find any firewood within a half-mile radius of some of the shelters. A shelter may also attract bears, which is fine for the people inside, but somewhat unnerving for the hiker who is chased for a pack full of food.

Good or bad, the shelters are available by reservation. There is no charge for their use, but you must have a permit from Park Headquarters or one of the ranger stations. Reservations may be made up to one month in advance.

Backcountry Camping

The best wilderness experience, some claim, is sleeping on the ground in the backcountry. The park encourages this experience by offering around a hundred backcountry camping sites. Garbage may not be buried or tossed down privies; users are asked to pack out everything they pack in. Tents should not be trenched, and hand-dug toilets should be well away from the campsite and any water source. Campers can build fires if fire rings exist, but park officials prefer the use of portable stoves to minimize the impact on the environment.

Backcountry sites are all over the park; locations are changed from time to time to minimize the damage to the land. The sites can accommodate from 8 to 20 people, and campers can stay up to three days in each site. Reservations are required. You can reserve a campsite at no cost up to a month before you plan to start out by writing Backcountry Permits, Great Smoky

Mountains National Park, Gatlinburg, Tennessee 37738, or by calling (615) 436-9564. Once you secure a reservation, you have to pick it up in person no earlier than 24 hours before your hike and no later than noon on the day you are hitting the trail.

Park rangers are very strict about camping in unauthorized places. This means you cannot spend the night in a picnic area or on the side of the road, even if all the campgrounds are full and it is ten o'clock on a Saturday night. The same holds true for the backcountry. Allow enough time to get to your destination.

Dozens of privately owned campgrounds surround the park. They range from simple affairs to full-blown "campground condominiums" complete with water slides. The best bet here is to use one of the annual campground guides such as *Woodalls*.

FISHING. Approximately 730 miles of streams in the park await the angler, and four lakes border the Smokies. Despite the fact that the park is federal territory, those over age 16 who fish must have either a Tennessee or a North Carolina fishing license. The Cherokee Indian Reservation has its own set of permits.

The park is one of the last refuges of the brook trout, the only trout native to these waters, and these cannot be kept. The more aggressive rainbow trout and brown trout tend to crowd the native fish into the upper reaches of the streams, and these newcomers are fair game. Rock bass are also found in some streams, and the lakes have smallmouth bass and blue gills. The daily limit for fish in any combination is five, and any trout in your possession must be seven inches long.

Miscellaneous rules: Natural bait cannot be used. Fishing is permitted year-round from dawn to dusk. You do not need a trout stamp to fish in the park. Anglers are limited to one hand-held rod and single-hook lures. Certain streams are closed to fishermen, and others—some of the less fished ones—can be reached only on foot. Complete information is available at any visitors' center or ranger station. Buy your Tennessee or North Carolina fishing license outside of the park.

HIKING. Whether it means a fifteen-minute stroll on a nature path or a week-long trek on the Appalachian Trail, hiking is one of the more popular activities in the Smokies. The trail descriptions that follow provide a general idea of what to expect. Before setting out, it's a good idea to have a topographical map and a more detailed trail guide. The very best is the *Hiker's Guide to the Smokies*, published by the Sierra Club and on sale at visitors' centers and local bookstores.

The Appalachian Trail

This nationally famous trail is the interstate highway of hiking in the Smokies. Running 70 miles along the mountain crest that divides Tennessee and North Carolina, it offers the best views in the park. Maine-to-Georgia hikers mingle with weekend hikers who walk along with day hikers who stroll along with tourists who just want to say they have been on the trail. The result, especially in the Newfound Gap area, is a crowded trail on which it is increasingly difficult to get away from it all.

No permit is required to hike on the trail, but you need one to camp either in a shelter or at a backcountry site. These are described more fully under CAMPING.

If you are interested in hiking a long section of the Appalachian Trail, you can write for detailed maps and trail guides to the Appalachian Trail Conference, P.O. Box 236, Harpers Ferry, Virginia 25425. Keep in mind that good sections of the trail lie above and below the park, and these are much less crowded.

Here are some sections of the Appalachian Trail that are good for day hikes.

Charlie's Bunion. Leave the Newfound Gap parking lot and head east for four miles to this sheer drop of one thousand feet. A spectacular view awaits. The trail climbs almost a thousand feet in the first three miles, so plan on doing some huffing and puffing.

Newfound Gap to Clingmans Dome. This section of the trail goes along the ridges of the highest peaks in the park. Start at Newfound Gap and follow the trail west for seven and a half miles to Clingmans Dome. The trail climbs sixteen hundred feet; if you want to do it the easy way you can start at Clingmans Dome. Either way, arrange for a driver to meet you at the other end if you don't think you'll feel up to the return trip.

Day Hikes

Most visitors to the Great Smoky Mountains National Park do not have the time or the equipment for a first-class wilderness backpacking expedition. Others prefer hiking unencumbered, and then following the outing with the creature comforts of a fine meal and a good bed. Here are some day hikes through various parts of the park. Most have some attraction either along the way or at the end.

Cades Cove Hikes

Abrams Falls. Five miles round trip. Begin at the Cades Cove Loop Road and walk two and a half miles downhill to the falls, or begin at the Abrams Creek Ranger Station at the park's western boundary and hike the same distance. The latter hike, which starts on the Cooper Road and follows Abrams Creek upstream, is the more interesting of the two.

Gregory Bald. Nine miles or eleven miles round trip. Two trails lead to this mountain meadow where old-timers used to graze their cattle. The **Gregory Ridge Trail** begins at the turnaround at the start of the Parson Branch Road and runs five and a half miles up Gregory

Ridge to the bald. You can expect to climb about twenty-six hundred feet. The **Gregory Bald Trail** begins further down the Parson Branch Road and runs for four and a half miles up to the bald. You will climb about twenty-one hundred feet. (Keep in mind that Parson Branch is a one-way road leading out of the park.)

Rich Mountain. Five miles round trip. Leave Cades Cove on the Rich Mountain Road, mindful that you cannot return on it, and stop at Rich Mountain Gap. This is the park boundary, and from here on the road is two-laned. Walk east along a fire road until the trail takes off to the left. Follow it to the top of the mountain and the intersection with the Indian Grave Gap Road. A good view of the mountains and Cades Cove awaits. This trail is less steep than those to the various balds.

Spence Field. Thirteen or nine mile round trip. Another mountain bald, this is reached by two trails. The first begins on the Laurel Creek Road, which leads to Cades Cove from the rest of the park. Begin at the **Bote Mountain Trail**, a jeep road that is clearly marked. Walk 13 miles to Spence Field for a total elevation gain of twenty-nine hundred feet. A shorter but steeper hike begins at the Cades Cove Picnic Area and follows the Anthony Creek Trail to intersect with the Bote Mountain Trail. It is nine miles round trip with a thirty-two-hundred-foot elevation gain.

Mount LeConte Hikes

Five trails lead to the summit of Mount LeConte, where hikers will find a trail shelter and Mount LeConte Lodge, as well as splendid views of the Tennessee side of the park. This is one of the more heavily climbed mountains in the park, and it's rarely lonely at the top. Many people take one trail up and another one down. One suggestion is to begin with the Boulevard Trail and come down the steep Alum Cave Bluffs Trail.

Alum Cave Bluffs Trail. Eleven miles round trip. This is the shortest and steepest way up Mount LeConte, but it offers a lot of attractions along the way. The first is a natural tunnel, and the second is the "cave," which is actually an eroded cliff under which one can escape the rain. The trail begins at the Alum Cave Bluffs parking lot off the Newfound Gap Road, and climbs twenty-five hundred feet to the top.

Boulevard Trail. Sixteen miles round trip. Why not start high and avoid some of the climbing? You can on this trail, which branches off the Appalachian Trail near Newfound Gap. It climbs only around fifteen hundred feet.

Bullhead Trail. Fourteen and a half miles round trip. So named because the mountain it crosses is said to look like the head of a bull, this trail begins in the Cherokee Orchard parking lot near Gatlinburg. The elevation climb is a healthy four thousand feet.

Rainbow Falls Trail. Thirteen and a half miles round trip. Another trail leading from the Cherokee Orchard parking lot, this one passes to see an eighty-foot-high waterfall. The bad news is that the elevation gain is four thousand feet.

Trilliam Gap. Thirteen miles round trip. Of the three trails approaching Mount LeConte from the Gatlinburg area, this one has the least elevation gain, since it begins further up the Roaring Fork Motor Nature Trail. The elevation gain is about thirty-three hundred feet.

Other Tennessee Trails

Chimney Tops. Four miles round trip. This is one of the more popular trails in the park. On paper it looks pretty easy. It isn't, especially for people who aren't dressed for hiking. The trail goes right up the Chimneys for an elevation gain of thirteen hundred feet in just two miles. You don't have to be Einstein to figure that this is a steep pull. At the end hikers are using hands and feet, but the view from the top is worth it.

Grotto Falls. Three miles round trip. This hike is cool on the hottest days. Leave the Roaring Fork Motor Nature Trail at the Grotto Falls Parking Area and follow the streams up to this waterfall. The climb totals about five hundred feet, and you can look for salamanders on the way. There are 23 kinds of salamanders in the park.

Henwallow Falls. Four miles round trip. Leaving from the lightly used Cosby Picnic Area, this trail climbs only six hundred feet through a forest with enormous poplars and hemlocks. At the end is a pleasant waterfall that spreads 20 feet across from a two-foot-wide creek.

Ramsay Cascades. Eight miles round trip. This is one of the few dead-end trails in the Smokies, but what a finale! The one-hundred-foot Ramsay Cascades, while not a straight drop, is the highest waterfall in the park. The trail begins in Greenbrier Cove, about six miles east of Gatlinburg on Tennessee 321. It gains sixteen hundred feet in elevation. Hikers should be careful at the falls; several people have slipped and been killed.

North Carolina Trails

Andrews Bald. Four miles round trip. Begin at the Clingmans Dome parking lot and hike south to the bald. The experience of walking onto the ridge as the forest melts away and the horizon opens up is worth fighting the traffic to get to the parking lot. In September you can pick blueberries.

Chasteen Creek. Ten miles round trip. Leave the Smokemont Campgrounds and hike up a jeep road until you reach the trail to Hughes Ridge. About one and a half miles from the campground lies a 15-foot waterfall. The climb is about twenty-four hundred feet.

Flat Creek Falls. Four miles or two miles round trip. Two trails lead to this moderate waterfall, and both start off downhill. The four-mile hike begins at the Heintooga Picnic Area, and the shorter stroll begins one mile south of Polls Gap on the Balsam Mountain Road. The first trail drops six hundred feet, and the two-miler goes down one hundred eighty feet.

Indian Creek. Two miles round trip. Leaving the Deep Creek Road one-half mile from the campground amphitheater, this trail more or less follows Deep Creek to a 60-foot waterfall. The elevation gain is one hundred feet.

Juneywhank Falls. One and one-half miles round trip. Go one-half mile from the campground amphitheater along the Deep Creek Road to begin this stroll to a lovely cascade. The elevation gain is one hundred fifty feet.

Mingus Creek. Four and one-half miles round trip. This trail leads from the Mingus Mill parking area off the Newfound Gap Road to the Mingus Cemetery, which is 748 feet higher than the beginning of the trail.

Mount Sterling. Twelve miles round trip. It is a tough climb—4,130 feet—to the top of this mountain from Big Creek Campground via the Baxter Creek Trail. A good view from an old fire tower awaits. Another trail up this mountain begins at the Cataloochee Schoolhouse, for a twelve-mile round-trip hike; the elevation gain is only 2,430 feet.

HORSEBACK RIDING. The hooves of horses are tough on trails; some estimate a horse does as much damage as ten hikers. Park officials have therefore cut down on the number of trails available to equestrians. Visitors can being their own horses, but no stables are available to keep private horses inside the park, and all food for horses must be packed in.

For this reason most people choose to rent a horse. Park officials require the stables to send a guide with each horse party to make sure the rules are followed. The stable in Cades Cove offers hayrides lasting one and a half to two hours on Thursday, Saturday, and Sunday evenings. Here are the addresses of some of the firms that provide horses. All have stables inside the park.

Cades Cove Riding Stables
RFD 1, P.O. Box 2885
Walland, Tennessee 37886
(615) 448-6286
In Cades Cove

McCarter's Riding Stables
Gatlinburg, Tennessee
   37738
(615) 436-5354
Operates near the park
headquarters on Newfound
   Gap Road

Smoky Mountains Riding
   Stables
P.O. Box 728
Gatlinburg, Tennessee
   37738
(615) 436-5634
Two miles east of
   Gatlinburg on U.S. 321

Cosby Stables
c/o E.G. Bryant
Route 2
Newport, Tennessee 37821
No telephone
Operates out of Cosby
   Campground

Smokemont Riding Stable
P.O. Box 72
Cherokee, North Carolina
   28719
(704) 497-2373
Near Smokemont
   Campground

HUNTING. Hunting is prohibited in the park.

LODGING. There are two inns in the park, and they are as different as night and day.

Wonderland Hotel. Located in the Elkmont community off the Little River Road, this hotel is open from Memorial Day through October and contains 27 rooms. Rates include breakfast and dinner. Write the Wonderland Hotel, Gatlinburg, Tennessee 37738; or call (615) 436-5490.

LeConte Lodge. This extremely popular lodge is open April through October. It offers ten cabins: eight with one bedroom, one with two bedrooms, and one with three bedrooms. Breakfast and dinner are included in the price.

   LeConte Lodge is special in that you have to hike a long way to get there. You can choose from five different trails, all at least five and one-half miles long—

one way. Located just below the summit of Mount LeConte, it provides literally one of the peak experiences of a trip to the Great Smoky Mountains National Park. For reservations, which should be made well in advance, write P.O. Box 350, Gatlinburg, Tennessee 37738; or call (615) 436-4473.

PICNICKING. This is a favorite activity in the park, and there are nine sites from which to choose. The Chimneys, with 89 places five miles from the Sugarlands Visitor Center, is open year-round. The others are open from April through November. Each picnic area contains tables, grills, and restrooms. On the Tennessee side there is Cades Cove with 81 places; Look Rock, 51 places; Metcalf Bottoms, 165 places; Cosby, 95 places; and Greenbrier, 12 places. On the North Carolina side there is Collins Creek, 182 places; Deep Creek, 47 places; and Heintooga, 41 places.

Note: You can picnic anywhere in the park except in a campground, but you can drink alcoholic beverages only in a *designated* picnic area, campground, or overnight lodge. Having an alcoholic beverage in an open bottle or can within reach in your automobile is against the law.

SKIING. There is no downhill skiing in the Smokies, but cross-country aficionados can take to the roads that are closed to cars in winter, such as the Clingmans Dome Road. It can get very cold along the tops of the ridges, so dress warmly.

WATER SPORTS. The streams in the Smokies are filled with water that is chilling even on the hottest days, and there are no beaches or swimming pools for public use in the park. This does not, however, keep people out of the water. The Sinks along the Little River Road is perhaps the best swimming hole in the park, and the pool at the bottom of Abrams Falls has seen a swimmer or two. The rocks—slippery or underwater—can make swimming hazardous.

Riding automobile inner tubes in the water is a popular

sport with local, although park officials take a dim view of it. The two best places for tubing, as it is called, are in the Little River below the Sinks in Tennessee and in the Deep Creek area near Bryson City in North Carolina.

It is virtually impossible to canoe in the Smokies, and kayaking is possible only when the spring rains swell the rivers. Even then it is dangerous. If white water is your preference, you'd do better to try some of the rivers outside of the park.

FIVE

Upper North Carolina

JOHN EHLE, A WRITER who has set several novels in northwest North Carolina, once compared the area to a fine wine-producing country. The stock of the people, the land in which they are rooted, and the conditions in which they live, he said, are just right for storytellers. This part of North Carolina has certainly produced its share of writers. Thomas Wolfe, who called the state Old Catawba in his fiction, is probably the best known. William Sidney Porter, writing under the pseudonym O. Henry, is noted for his short stories, although they are not about the region. More recently, Wilma Dykeman's fiction and nonfiction have given a true picture of life in the mountains.

Anyone writing a novel about the mountains today could choose as a setting a ski resort, a 150-year-old inn, or a multimillion dollar condominium development. Northwest North Carolina has a keen sense of the appeal of its mountains and villages, and is better equipped than any-where in southern Appalachia to accommodate visitors.

The area has a long history of out-of-towners. In 1670 a German physician, John Lederer, was sent by the English

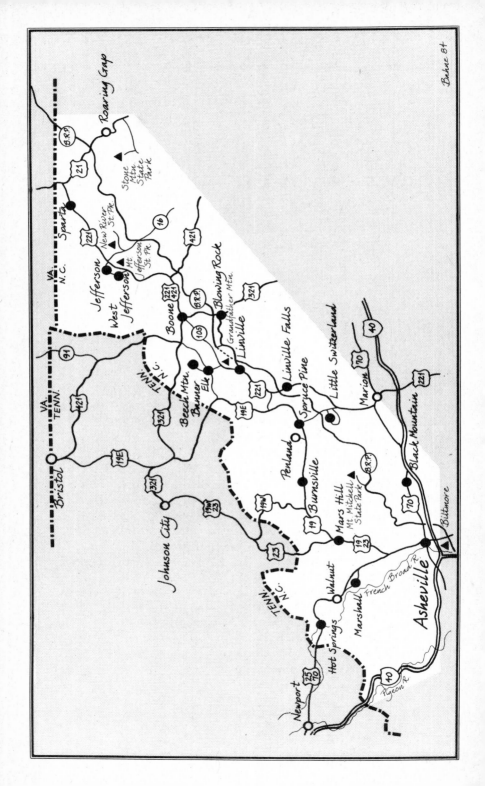

Balue 84

governor of the colony to explore the mysterious land to the west. Thomas Jefferson's father explored the northernmost part of the area, and Ben Franklin's brother settled near the future town of Linville Falls.

Other settlers cleared land and built farms, and the population rose steadily but slowly, for the opening of the Cumberland Gap and the promise of flatter, richer land beyond it lured the people away. Daniel Boone explored the area around the town that bears his name, but he too moved west. It is interesting to note that Asheville, now the largest city in this end of the state, was for years a mere stopping place on the Buncombe Turnpike between two larger towns—Greeneville, Tennessee, and Greeneville, South Carolina. The Civil War largely bypassed the area, although a considerable number of skirmishes between Northern and Southern sympathizers occurred here. The economy of the region, like that of the entire South, was ravaged by the war.

The railroad changed all this. Like the early settlers in their covered wagons, the railroad builders had for years avoided the mountains. With dynamite and gangs of laborers, however, the iron horse pushed its way into the mountain valleys and coves, providing a speedy and dependable outlet for local products and an opportunity to lure Northern capital. And although it wasn't immediately apparent, the railroad gave a big boost to what would become the region's largest moneymaker—tourism.

The first vacationers had come from the low country of South Carolina to escape the heat, and they had brought their slaves and their society ways with them. The railroads enabled people of more moderate means to visit the mountains. These newcomers branched out from the railroad stations to explore the region and to sample the cuisine in various inns.

The 1940s and 1950s saw the rise of tourism as we know it in the high country of northwest North Carolina. The Blue Ridge Parkway funneled travelers from the north into the area. Tweetsie Railroad, a narrow-gauge train that

served the mountain towns of Johnson City, Tennessee, and
Boone, North Carolina, was opened as an early theme park.
Grandfather Mountain, billed as the oldest mountain in
the world, began luring visitors to the summit.

The 1960s saw the coming of the ski resorts. Skeptics
snorted at the idea of snow skiing in the South, but the
resorts prospered, helped by people with money in their
pockets and the growing technology of artificially produced snow.

Today northwest North Carolina has the slickest tourist
business in the southern Appalachian region, complete with
toll-free telephone numbers, computerized operations, and
skillful marketing plans. Despite this, the majesty of the
highest mountains in the eastern United States, the seren-
ity of the Blue Ridge Parkway, and the individual charms
of the mountain towns combine to keep visitors returning
year after year.

HOW TO GET THERE

BY AIR. The Asheville Regional Airport is served by Piedmont and Atlantic Southeast airlines.

The Tri-Cities Airport near Johnson City, Tennessee, is
served by Piedmont, USAir, and Eastern airlines.

The airport in Charlotte, North Carolina, is served by
Delta, Eastern, Piedmont, USAir, Ozark, and United airlines.

FROM TENNESSEE. There are three main routes from Tennessee into North Carolina. From south to north, they are
as follows.

The first and easiest is I-40 into Asheville. This highway
takes the driver through some of the most rugged and remote territory crossed by any interstate in the East. With
high mountains on one side and the Pigeon River on the
other, it is one of the more twisting interstate highways
anywhere.

Indeed, corkscrew roads characterize all of the approaches into North Carolina from Tennessee. History buffs may decide to take U.S. 25/70 from Newport to Asheville. This route follows the French Broad River, and was used by drovers and wagon drivers of the 1700s and the 1800s on their way to the markets of Charleston, South Carolina. The road is mostly two-laned, with occasional sections where you can pass a slow truck or bus.

U.S. 23 leaves Erwin and heads straight up the side of a mountain toward Asheville. Before I-40 was constructed, this was one of the primary routes between the states. Route 19E and U.S. 321, both from Elizabethton, Tennessee, offer good views of the mountains and the hillside farms. U.S. 321 and U.S. 421, one of Tennessee's Scenic Parkways, lead to the northernmost section of North Carolina.

FROM VIRGINIA. The most obvious route from Virginia is the Blue Ridge Parkway. If you're in a hurry, however, you might want to come down I-77 until it intersects with I-40. Or take I-81, get off on Virginia 91, and head south.

ONCE YOU'RE THERE

A great many visitors to the upper part of the North Carolina mountains fall prey to the Blue Ridge Parkway Syndrome—they get on the famous highway and never get off. This is fine if they wish to see the scenery from a chaste distance, but they are cheating themselves if they do not stop and visit some of the mountain villages, drop in on a festival or two, and spend the night in an inn.

A far better mountain experience is provided by variety—by driving a stretch on the parkway and then getting off and exploring a town, perhaps even on foot. Blasphemous though this might sound, you can even skip some of the Parkway without ruining your trip.

Note: For a full description of the Blue Ridge Parkway, see Chapter 6.

TOWNS AND ATTRACTIONS

ASHEVILLE. The economic and cultural center of western North Carolina, Asheville was never a fort or an outpost in the sense that Knoxville, its East Tennessee counterpart, was in its early days. Indeed, for a long time Asheville was just a stop on the road from Greeneville, Tennessee, to Greeneville, South Carolina—a place where drovers and their herds of cattle, hogs, or turkeys spent the night before moving on. The Civil War largely passed the town by.

Asheville is the seat of Buncombe County, one of the few counties in America whose names have passed into the language. When pressed to state his point after a rambling, inconclusive speech, an early congressman from the area replied, "I was just talking for Buncombe." The contracted version of this word—*bunk*—is used to this day.

The coming of the railroad in 1880 marked the period of Asheville's biggest growth, and within twenty years came two men who put the town on the map. In 1889 George Vanderbilt, a New York capitalist, rolled into town. He bought up 130 thousand acres of mountain land and proceeded to build the largest privately owned house in the world, which he called Biltmore. About the same time E. W. Grove, who had made his money in the patent medicine business, moved in from St. Louis; in 1913 he completed construction on the Grove Park Inn, which was and is the finest hotel in the area.

Prominent doctors in the East began recommending Asheville to patients with tuberculosis or any ailment that required rest and fresh air. The railroad made it easy to get to Asheville, and the health seekers poured in. Many recovered and decided to stay on, and the city responded with the construction of hotels, sanitariums, and over one hundred boardinghouses. One of the latter establishments was run by a Julia Wolfe, whose son Thomas was to scandalize the town he thinly disguised in his novel, *Look Homeward, Angel.*

When the crash came in the 1920s many of the people

who had speculated on North Carolina real estate lost all they had. Advances in medical science eliminated the need for people to come to the mountains to cure tuberculosis, and most of the vacationers were broke. Asheville was hard hit.

Since that low point the city has been coming back. Tourism is today at an all-time high. George Vanderbilt is gone, but his house pulls in thousands of people a year, and the Blue Ridge Parkway funnels nature lovers of all kinds into the city. Having the Great Smoky Mountains National Park just 40 miles away doesn't hurt either. Today's visitor finds a city with mountains to be seen in all directions, with young people who are revitalizing the downtown area, and with lots of the amenities (and few of the problems) of a much larger city.

Asheville is well equipped to guide visitors to the city and the region. The Chamber of Commerce Convention and Visitors' Bureau is full of brochures, maps, and courteous people. Several signs direct motorists to the bureau, which is located off I-240 at 151 Haywood Street. It is open from 8:30 to 5:30 on weekdays and 9:00 to 5:00 on weekends. During the late spring, the summer, and the early fall the bureau stays open on weekdays until 7:00 P.M. Call (704) 258-3916 for further information.

Historic Places

Biltmore House and Gardens. This monument to unbridled spending often affects visitors in one of two ways. Either they lust after the money and power that could build such an edifice, or they decry a system in which one person can accumulate fantastic sums.

However they may react, visitors should not leave Asheville without seeing Biltmore House and Gardens. Completed in 1895, the house took five years and the efforts of a thousand workers to build. It has over 255 rooms. The original estate totaled 130 thousand acres, though it is now down to a mere eight thousand. The grounds were laid out by Frederick Law Olmstead, who also designed New York's Central Park.

Biltmore takes at least a half day to see. On the grounds of the estate are a winery, a restaurant located in a former calf barn, and one of the largest collections of azaleas in the world. The tour of the house is broken into two sections, Upstairs and Downstairs. Upstairs covers the main portion of the house, the opulent bedrooms, the ten thousand leather-bound books, and the imposing great rooms. The Downstairs tour displays the hidden works of the house—the laundry and servants' quarters (Biltmore required the services of 80 people)—and the recreation rooms, consisting of an indoor swimming pool and a bowling alley. Try to take both tours.

Biltmore House and Gardens is open daily from 9:00 to 5:00. It is in western Asheville in Biltmore Village, on U.S. 25E. The admission is steep.

Biltmore Village Historic District. Beyond the gates of the Biltmore estate a village was constructed in 1898 to serve the needs of the Vanderbilts, their servants, and their guests. Twenty-four of the original buildings remain, including three designed by Richard Morris Hunt: **All Souls Church, Biltmore Railway Station**, and **Biltmore Estate Office**. This is a charming place to eat lunch, walk around, and visit the many small shops that surround the historic buildings. The village is located off U.S. 25E west of the downtown area.

Chestnut Hill Historic District. Located along Charlotte and Chestnut streets, this area includes more than two hundred late nineteenth- and early twentieth-century houses reflecting the boom times in Asheville.

Downtown Asheville Historic District. Approximately 170 buildings, some built as early as 1840, make up the largest collection of historic architecture in Asheville. Centering on Pack Square, they include the art deco **S & W Cafeteria** at 56 Patton Avenue, the Spanish baroque **Church of St. Lawrence** at 97 Haywood Street,

and the neo-Georgian **Battery Park Hotel** at Battle
Square.

Vance Birthplace. Zebulon Vance was North Carolina's
political man for all seasons. Among other things, he
was a governor and U.S. senator. He was born north
of Asheville in a log house that has been restored to its
1830 condition. Located on Rheem Creek Road in
Weaverville. Open Tuesday through Saturday from 9:00
to 5:00 and on Sunday from 1:00 to 5:00. No admission
is charged.

Western North Carolina Heritage Center. This museum
of local history is located in the Smith-McDowell house,
a restored 1840 home. It is constructed of brick—an
unusual building material for the time and place—and
features a double porch supported by short white columns. This house originally faced the old Buncombe
Turnpike. From June through October it is open Tuesday through Saturday from 10:00 to 4:00 and on Sunday from 1:00 to 5:00. A small admission is charged.
Located at 283 Victory Road. Call (704) 253-9231.

Cultural Sites

Asheville Art Museum. The permanent collection here
is twentieth century American art, including paintings,
sculpture, prints, and various crafts. Touring exhibits
are presented as well. Located in the Asheville Civic
Center Complex downtown, the museum is open Tuesday through Friday from 10:00 to 5:00, and on weekends from 1:00 to 5:00. No admission is charged.

Colburn Mineral Museum. North Carolina is noted for
its extensive and varied mineral deposits, and this museum features gemstones, fossils, and reproductions of
world-famous diamonds. Located in the Civic Center,
the museum is open from Tuesday through Friday from
10:00 to 5:00, and on weekends from 1:00 to 5:00. No
admission is charged.

Riverside Cemetery. Buried here are two of Asheville's
famous writers, Thomas Wolfe and O. Henry, whose

real name was William Sidney Porter. Some visitors waste their time hunting for Thomas Wolfe's famous stone angel. Don't bother; it's in a cemetery in Hendersonville. Riverside Cemetery is on Birch Street.

Thomas Wolfe Memorial. For anyone who has read the tortured story in *Look Homeward, Angel*, this house is a required stop. The setting for the 1934 novel is a boardinghouse called Dixieland. This was the real boardinghouse, and it contains furniture that was there when Wolfe was, as well as some of the items from his final New York apartment. The memorial is located at 48 Spruce Street in downtown Asheville. It is open Tuesday through Saturday from 9:00 to 5:00, and from 1:00 to 5:00 on Sunday. A small admission is charged.

Theaters and Films

Asheville Civic Center and Thomas Wolfe Auditorium. These city-owned facilities are often visited by touring theater, dance, and musical groups. They are located downtown at Hiawassee and Flint streets. Call (704) 255-5771 for ticket information.

Asheville Community Theater. This amateur company performs musicals and plays all year. Located at 35 East Walnut Street. Call (704) 254-1320 for ticket information.

Miscellaneous Amusements

Health Adventure. This facility enables children and older folks alike to learn about their bodies, how they work, and how to keep them in good health. "Hands-on" exhibits employ electronic displays, computers, and various mixed media. Visitors can watch puppet shows, put together a skeleton, and participate in a mock operation compete with masks, gowns, and instruments.

Health Adventure is heavily used by the local school systems, and cannot always accommodate people who drop in; visitors are advised to call ahead. Located between Memorial Mission and Saint Joseph's Hospitals at 501 Biltmore Avenue, Health Adventure is open from 8:30 to 5:00 Monday through Friday. A general tour is offered at 3:00. A small admission is charged. Call (704) 254-6373.

National Climatic Center and National Weather Records Center. Records on the weather all over the country are collected and stored here in the largest such archive in the world. In guided tours visitors can see meteorological data being entered into computers, paper and computer-tape archives, and the agency's large printing facilities.

Architecture enthusiasts will appreciate the Gothic building, which contains other federal offices and occupies an entire city block. Originally called the Grove Arcade, it was built in the 1920s by E. W. Grove, who also designed the Grove Park Inn. The building is sometimes called America's first indoor mall, and is replete with brass railings, spiral staircases, and gargoyles. It is listed on that National Register and is located in the city block bounded by Battery Park, Page and O. Henry avenues, and Otis Street. The center is open Monday through Friday from 8:00 to 5:00, and no admission is charged. Call (704) 259-0682.

University Botanical Gardens. Occupying ten acres of the campus of the University of North Carolina at Asheville, these gardens contain twenty-six thousand native plants, a sculpture garden for the blind, and a log cabin. Located off U.S. 25N near Merrimon Avenue. No admission is charged, and the gardens are open all year during daylight hours.

Western North Carolina Farmer's Market. This state-owned facility covers 37 acres outside of Asheville. In modern buildings farmers display their wares, which include local fruits and vegetables, jams and jellies, handcrafted goods, and ornamental plants. The market is located at 570 Brevard Road, and is clearly marked from both I-40 and I-26. Open April through December. No admission is charged.

Western North Carolina Nature Center. Western North Carolina used to be the scene of various roadside "See the Bear" exhibits, in which unfortunate bruins were kept in filthy cages. Legislation now forbids such abuse of the state's largest animal, but here people can still see bears—in an environment more like their natural one. Occupying seven acres, the Nature Center is home to a selection of wild and domestic animals. In the wildlife line are a bear, a cougar, and a golden eagle, as well as deer and some descented skunks. Snakes, wild turkeys, and foxes round out the list. The bear and deer can be viewed from a boardwalk that takes the visitor above the animals' enclosures.

Children like the barnyard petting zoo, which offers lambs, calves, and goats. Exhibits such as the "World of Night" and the "World of the Sea" round out the experience. Located on Gashes Creek Road, the center is open Tuesday through Saturday from 10:00 to 5:00 and on Sunday from 1:00 to 5:00. A small admission is charged. Call (704) 298-5600.

Crafts

Allanstand Mountain Craft Shop. Located on the Blue Ridge Parkway, this shop belongs to the Southern Highland Handicraft Guild, which guarantees the quality and authenticity of the handcrafted items sold there. Located at Milepost 382. Call (704) 298-7928.

Biltmore Homespun Shops and Antique Automobile Museum. The Homespun shops were opened by Mrs. George Vanderbilt in 1901 to preserve the mountain crafts of spinning and dying wool. Here visitors can watch craftspeople at work and buy their finished products, which are as good as any woolens available in the British Isles. The Antique Car Museum offers a look at five or six elegantly restored old cars. These two establishments are open daily from 9:00 to 4:00. They are on the grounds of the Grove Park Inn on Macon Avenue. No admission is charged.

Guild Crafts. Another member of the Southern Highlands Handicraft Guild, this shop is located at 930 Tunnel Road. Call (704) 298-7903.

High Country Crafters. This cooperative presents the work of close to two hundred artists and craftspeople. Here visitors can find quilts, dulcimers, pottery, wooden toys, and art works in various media. Located at 34 Haywood Street. Call (704) 255-9355.

New Morning Gallery. Probably the fanciest shop of its kind in the entire area, this gallery features the work of local artists and craftspeople. Located in Biltmore Village at 7 Boston Way. Phone (704) 274-2831.

Stuart Nye Silver Shop. Copper and silver creations from this shop are sold at Guild Crafts next door. Located at 940 Tunnel Road. Hours are Monday through Friday from 8:30 to 11:30 and from 12:30 to 4:00. Call (704) 298-7988.

Dining

The Annex Restaurant. This restaurant in the eclectic Wall Street neighborhood features sandwiches, salads, and other inexpensive dishes. Located at 22 Battery Park Avenue. Call (704) 253-2158.

Bill Stanley's Barbecue and Bluegrass. Hickory-smoked meats, bluegrass music, and the fancy footwork of cloggers are the attractions of this lively eatery. A live band is featured every night. Lunch and dinner include ribs, chopped barbecue, and cold beer. The restaurant is at 20 South Spruce Street in downtown Asheville. Call (704) 253-4871.

The Biltmore Village Inne. Offering brunch, lunch, high tea, and dinner, this charming place is found in the historic Biltmore Village west of town. Features a good wine cellar and "strolling minstrels." Located at 5 Boston Way. Call (704) 274-4100.

Edgewood Restaurant. Greek food is the specialty here. Dine on gyros, shish kabob, and baklava. Located at 1435 Merrimon Avenue. Call (704) 252-2623.

Grove Park Inn. Overlooking Asheville and the mountains, this old inn is perhaps the most romantic place to dine in town. In the summer you can eat outdoors on a terrace. Three meals a day are served in six separate dining rooms. Located at 290 Macon Avenue. Call (800) 438-5800.

The Marketplace. This is one of the more expensive restaurants in Asheville. Main dishes include rack of lamb, roast duckling, and fresh mountain trout. The dessert specialty is a seven-layer Marjolaine cake. The dining room is formal, and reservations are a very good idea. This place has one of the best wine cellars in the region. The **Grill and Lounge** downstairs is less formal and less expensive, but the food is cooked to the same standards as in the main dining room. Located at 10 Market Street. Call (704) 252-4162.

Steven's. A restaurant and pub, Steven's is in a structure made from portions of several turn-of-the-century buildings, and the furnishings date from the same period. The lunch menu includes sandwiches, pizza, and Mexican food. The dinner menu includes veal and scallops.

Stone Soup. This place is worth a visit if just to see the building. Stone Soup is in the Manor House, the oldest operating hotel in Asheville. Unusual in that it is owned and run by the workers, the restaurant serves lunch and Sunday brunch in the main dining room of the Manor House. Soups are the specialty, and these are complemented by a salad bar and homemade breads. Located on Charlotte Street near the Grove Park Inn. Call (704) 258-3993.

The Windmill. Meals here are a far cry from the usual overcooked Southern food, which can get tiresome after a while. Eastern European dishes are featured here. Lunch and dinner is served at 76 Haywood Street. Call (704) 253-5285.

Lodging

Bed and Breakfast. For a complete list of bed-and-breakfast places in the Asheville area write the Asheville Chamber of Commerce, P.O. Box 1011, Asheville 28802. Call (704) 258-3858.

Flint Street Inn. This bed-and-breakfast inn offers four guest rooms. Built in 1915, the house is within walking distance of downtown. Located at 116 Flint Street, Asheville 28801. Call (704) 253-6723.

Grove Park Inn. Biltmore House is the place to see, and this longtime Asheville landmark is the place to stay. It was built in 1913 by E. W. Grove, who served as his own architect and contractor. The original portion of the inn is built out of massive boulders; the fireplaces inside can easily burn ten-foot logs. This was a favorite place for F. Scott Fitzgerald to stay when his wife Zelda was being treated at a local mental hospital.

The old inn was open only seasonally for some years, and got a little shabby, but it has been renovated and is now open all year. A new wing in the front yard somewhat spoils the symmetry of the grounds, but the inn still holds its charm. The rooms are relatively high-priced. Located at 290 Macon Avenue, Asheville 28804. Call (800) 438-5800 or (704) 252-2711.

Events

For further information on any of the events described here write the Asheville Chamber of Commerce, P.O. Box 1011, Asheville 28802; or call (704) 258-3858.

Bel Chere. This mixed-bag event includes road races, mountain music and dancing, cooking, craft demonstrations, games, and all manner of foolery. Held in the streets of downtown Asheville in late July.

Guild Fair. The Southern Highland Handicraft Guild sponsors this annual event, which is held in July and October at the Asheville Civic Center downtown. One of the better crafts shows in the region, it provides an opportunity to buy genuine handcrafted goods from the mountains.

High Country Christmas. Here is a chance to buy locally handcrafted goods for Christmas presents. Held in December at the Asheville Civic Center.

Mountain Dance and Folk Festival. This event features competitions and demonstrations of clogging and mountain music. Held indoors at the civic center, it occurs over several evenings in early August.

Shindig on the Green. This weekly hoedown is held outdoors on the City Hall Plaza every Saturday night during the summer at 7:30. Local bands play and local dancers dance.

BANNER ELK. This town was named for early settlers and the river they settled near. They were the Banner family, and the river was the Elk. A sleepy resort town for many years, Banner Elk became the center of North Carolina's skiing boom in the 1960s.

Edge of the World Outfitters. Locals might not agree with its name, but this place may be your only stop before a hiking, canoeing, or cross-country skiing outing. Edge of the World sells and rents equipment for all of these activities, and organizes group trips as well. Write the Edge of the World at Route 3, Box 510-A, Banner Elk 28604; or call (704) 898-9550.

Lees-McRae College. This two-year college is housed in an attractive collection of buildings made of native stone. It often sponsors concerts, lectures, and other events. For information call (704) 898-5241.

BEECH MOUNTAIN. At an elevation of 5,505 feet, this town is the highest in North Carolina. It began as a ski resort in the 1960s, and has survived warm winters and high interest rates to become the biggest development of its kind in the state (the skiing is described later in this chapter). For casual visitors, there is an array of shops and eateries.

Lodging

The Pinnacle Inn. Not an inn in the usual sense, this place offers one- and two-bedroom detached "villas." Each comes with an outdoor covered hot tub, and a heated indoor pool, Jacuzzi, and steam room and sauna are shared by all. Write the inn at P.O. Box 1136, Banner Elk 28604. Call (704) 387-4276.

BLACK MOUNTAIN. This quiet mountain town has been a home to religious retreats and one of the more famous progressive colleges. Black Mountain College was founded in 1933 by Professor John Rice, who had three goals: to keep the college small so that no one would have to do administrative work full time, to integrate academic work with community life, and to develop in the students "resourcefulness and general intellectual and emotional fitness." Some of the people associated with Black Mountain College were Buckminster Fuller, Merce Cunningham, John Cage, and Franz Kline. It shut down in 1956. The religious organizations, however, are still going strong.

Downtown Black Mountain has a good collection of crafts shops and quiet restaurants. It has little in way of night life, at least in the heathen sense.

Black Mountain College Site. A lot of innovative thinking went on at this place, which now makes up Camp Rockmont, a summer camp. To get there take the old U.S. 70 west of town to the Lake Eden Road. Follow the signs to Camp Rockmont.

Blue Ridge Assembly. The Young Men's Christian Association, better known as the YMCA, has been running a conference and training center here since 1906 for their local organizations in the Southern states. On U.S. 70 in Black Mountain.

Christmont Christian Assembly. This property was owned by a Spanish architect who worked on Asheville's Biltmore estate and who designed the dome on St. Lawrence Church in Asheville. Now it is owned and operated by the Christian Church. Located nine miles from Black Mountain on North Carolina 9.

In the Oaks Episcopal Conference Center. One of the smaller retreats, this is owned by the Episcopal Diocese of Western North Carolina. It is located on Vance Avenue in Black Mountain.

Montreat. This is a combination retreat, junior college campus, and residential community. The retreat is owned by the Presbyterian Church; the college is Montreat-Anderson; and the community's most famous resident is Billy Graham. The college often presents events that are open to the public. Call (704) 669-8011 for information. Located two miles north of Black Mountain on North Carolina 9. The dining room of the retreat is open to the public.

Ridgecrest. This conference center, owned by the Southern Baptist Convention, is the largest of Black Mountain's religious retreats. Over fifty thousand people come here each year. It is located on U.S. 70 east of Black Mountain. Visitors are welcome to drive around, and a Baptist bookstore is on the premises.

Lodging and Dining

Monte Vista Hotel. Sixty-seven rooms make up this hotel, which is a good place to stay if you are not connected with one of the religious groups that run retreats in the area. The dining room is open to the public. Write the hotel at Black Mountain 28711; or call (704) 699-2119.

BLOWING ROCK. This is the name of a rock and a town. The town is one of the oldest resorts in the mountains; it was incorporated in 1889 and has been heavily dependent on tourism since then. Information on any of its attractions can be obtained by calling (800) 438-7500 from the eastern United States or (800) 222-7515 in North Carolina, or by writing High Country Host, 600 Highway 105 Extension, Boone 28607.

Blowing Rock. This large rock sticks out over a cliff at the head of a valley. When the wind blows up the valley it meets the cliff and is forced upwards. Any light object tossed over the cliff will rise with the wind, or at least not fall as quickly as it would elsewhere. The rock is privately owned; admission is charged. The view is pleasant, but similar ones are available for free on the Blue Ridge Parkway and other places in the region. Blowing Rock is located on U.S. 321/221.

Blowing Rock Crafts. The home of **Goodwin Guild Weavers**, this is a fascinating place. Cotton and wool are woven at antique looms into beautiful placemats, napkins, tablecloths, and coverlets. The looms are of the same types that were powered by water in New England mills a hundred years ago. Their power is now supplied by electricity, but the clicking and clacking is just the same as always.

Admission to the weaving room is free, and you can buy finished products in the gift shop. Both are open Monday through Saturday all year, and located on Main Street in Blowing Rock. Call (704) 295-3577.

Expressions Crafts Guild and Gallery. Cooperatively owned, this shop and gallery features pottery, photographs, woodwork, basketry, leather work, and jewelry, among other things. It is located on U.S. 321 at the turnoff to Appalachian Ski Mountain. Call (704) 295-9042.

Moses H. Cone Memorial Park. The Cone estate, which is now a part of the Blue Ridge Parkway, stretches down to U.S. 221 on the outskirts of Blowing Rock. From here you can take a short uphill hike to the Cone mansion. For a more complete account of the Cone park, see Chapter 6.

Mystery Hill. This wonderfully corny attraction is a delight for children and a test of anyone's equilibrium. The house has tilted floors, to which the furniture is bolted. In such a setting water appears to flow uphill, and making one's way is sometimes difficult. Located on U.S. 321, the house is open daily from 8:00 A.M. to 8 P.M. in the summer and 9:00 to 5:00 the rest of the year. Admission is charged.

Tweetsie Railroad. This is one of the older tourist attractions in the area, and one of the better ones. "Tweetsie" was the name mountaineers gave a narrow-gauge railroad engine that used to go from Boone, North Carolina, to Johnson City, Tennessee. The train is the centerpiece of the park, and it takes visitors on a three-mile loop that includes simulated Indian attacks and at least one train robbery. All this is quite exciting for the younger set.

The park also features carnival rides, a chairlift, and a display of antique steam engines. One price covers everything but food in the park, which is open from Memorial Day weekend through October. The full park is open every day from the second Monday in June through mid-August, but the rest of the time some activities are closed on weekdays. Located on U.S. 321/221 between Blowing Rock and Boone.

Events

Blowing Rock Horse Show. This long-running annual display of horses is held every August in Blowing Rock's Broyhill Park. For details write the Chamber of Commerce, P.O. Box 406, Blowing Rock 28605; or call (704) 295-7951.

Lodging and Dining

Gideon Ridge Inn. This small inn—it has just seven rooms—is located on U.S. 321 close to the rock that gives the town its name, and offers the same view. The inn was constructed of native stone; the walls are 14 inches thick. A garden surrounds the house. Open all year, Gideon Ridge Inn offers a complete breakfast with all rooms, and most guests take advantage of the fine dinners as well. As a result, the dining room is closed

to the public. Write the inn at P.O. Box 1929, Blowing
Rock 28605; or call (704) 295-3644.

Green Park Inn. Built in 1882, this inn sits at an elevation of forty-three hundred feet atop the Eastern Continental Divide. All 85 rooms have modern furniture.
Adjacent to the hotel is a golf course, and a swimming
pool and tennis courts are also available. The dining
room, which is open to the public, offers three meals a
day, primarily American style. The inn is open May
through February. Write P.O. Box 7, Blowing Rock
28605; or call (704) 295-3141.

Maple Lodge. This downtown establishment is in a white
two-story building with two large maple trees out front.
Inside are two parlors, one with a stone fireplace and
the other with a pump organ and piano. Visitors find
a bowl of fruit and a bottle of sherry waiting in each
of the eight guest rooms, all of which come with private
baths. Open April through October, the lodge offers
babysitting, golf, and tennis privileges. Write P.O. Box
66, Blowing Rock 28605; or call (704) 295-3331.

Ragged Garden Inn. Located on Sunset Drive near
downtown Blowing Rock, this inn was built in 1900 as
a summer residence. It is constructed of chestnut wood
with chestnut bark siding, and furnished with antiques.
All five guest rooms have private baths. The restaurant is open to the public, and features European
cuisine with an emphasis on the foods of northern
Italy. The inn is open April through January. Write
Box 1927, Sunset Drive, Blowing Rock 28605; or call
(704) 295-9703.

Sunshine Inn. In operation for sixty years, this bed-and-
breakfast inn offers nine units and a public dining room.
Located on Sunset Drive in downtown Blowing Rock,
the building resembles an old farmhouse; it is complete
with big porch, rocking chairs, and an old-fashioned
swing. The inn caters to people of all ages, and serves
family-style dinners with fresh vegetables in the dining
room. Open mid-May through mid-October. Write the

inn at Box 528, Sunset Drive, Blowing Rock 28605; or call (704) 295-3487.

BOONE. This town is named for Daniel Boone, who roamed here from 1760 through 1769. The area contains the headwaters of four great river systems: the Ohio (New River), the Tennessee (Watauga River), the Pee Dee (Yadkin River), and the Santee (Johns and Catawba rivers). It is the largest town in northwestern North Carolina, and with Appalachian State University (ASU) it is the intellectual center of the region. It is refreshing to find here a bookstore that does not regard Barbara Cartland as the greatest female author of all time.

Information on Boone and its vicinity is readily available from the High Country Host. From the eastern United States call (800) 438-7500; in North Carolina call (800) 222-7515. Or write or drop by 600 Highway 105 Extension, Boone 29607.

Appalachian State University. Ten thousand students are enrolled at this center of learning. The main campus in downtown Boone occupies 75 acres, and a 180-acre campus is located west of town. The latter is home for the Center for Appalachian Studies, which sponsors the new **Appalachian Culture Center** in University Hall. Cultural activities at ASU are open to the public. Call (704) 262-2090 for information.

Blue Ridge Hearthside Crafts. Three hundred fifty craftspeople contribute to this cooperative, which is located on North Carolina 105 one mile south of the Boone city limits. Travelers can choose from quilts, pottery, weavings, and carvings. Call (704) 963-5252.

Daniel Boone Native Gardens. Daniel Boone was never noted as a gardener, but his name adorns this six-acre collection of native plants. The property also includes the Squire Boone Cabin, where Daniel Boone is supposed to have lived, and a wishing well. Adjacent to Horn in the West, it is open daily except Monday from 9:00 to 5:00, and from 9:00 to 7:00 in July and August. A small admission is charged.

Hands Crafts Gallery. This cooperative offers pottery; woven goods; etched and stained glass; drawings and paintings; sculptures in cloth, clay, copper, and brass; and art work in various media. It is located on North Carolina 105 near the High Country Inn, one mile from the intersection of U.S. 321 and North Carolina 105. Call (704) 264-9743.

Horn in the West. This outdoor drama works in Daniel Boone and the Indians, then climaxes with a re-enactment of the Battle of Kings Mountain, a major turning point in the Revolutionary War. The professional company has been in operation since 1951. The Horn in The West complex includes the Daniel Boone Native Gardens, a Museum of Scouting, a farmers' market, and a nature trail. A second, smaller theater, the Powderhorn, offers various productions on the weekends. Curtain time for the main show is 8:30 every night except Monday. It's a good idea to dress warmly. Write P.O. Box 295, Boone 28607; or call (704) 264-2120. Admission is charged.

Events

Blue Ridge Hearthside Annual Crafts Festival. One hundred craftspeople from the Blue Ridge area set up booths to display their techniques and finished products. Held in mid-August and mid-October at the Holiday Inn Convention Center on U.S. 321 south of Boone. Write P.O. Box 269, Banner Elk 28604 for details. Call (704) 963-5252.

Octoberfest. Held in downtown Boone, this festival takes place in early October. The main street of town is lined with craftspeople who sell and demonstrate their work. Mountain music and dance are performed, and local delicacies are sold. For further information write the Boone Chamber of Commerce at 600 Highway 105 Extension, Boone 28607; or call (704) 264-2225.

Watauga County Spring Festival. Occurring sometime between mid-April and mid-May, this festival is much like the Octoberfest, except it takes place inside two gymnasiums at ASU. Write the Chamber of Commerce for details.

Winter Week of the Arts in Watauga County. Centering on the visual and performing arts, this festival is held in December. Write the Chamber of Commerce for details.

Lodging and Dining

The Center for Continuing Education. Situated atop a thirty-seven-hundred-foot mountain, this place offers 83 well-appointed rooms. Although they are often occupied by groups who are participating in seminars or courses, rooms are also available to individuals. Breakfast, lunch, and dinner are served at the Commons, a restaurant on the grounds. Write the center at Appalachian State University, Boone 28607; or call (704) 264-5050.

The Dan'l Boone Inn. Located at the edge of the ASU campus in Boone, this restaurant serves up Southern-style food three times a day. Try the country ham and biscuits or the fried chicken, or pick up one of the box lunches for an outing. In the summer and fall the restaurant serves lunch and dinner from 11:00 to 9:00. In the winter and spring dinner only is served, from 5:00 to 9:00. Breakfast is served on the weekends only. Located at the intersection of U.S. 421, 321, and 221. Call (704) 264-8657.

BURNSVILLE. This town always looks familiar to New Englanders, for it is built around a green common. Burnsville was established in 1834 as the seat of Yancey County, which has the highest average elevation of any county in the state. The town is named for a Captain Otway Burns, a War of 1812 hero who endeared himself to the locals by casting the winning vote in a legislative battle to establish the county.

Burnsville was the home of Jack Dempsey's grandfather, a blacksmith of prodigious strength who weighed

250 pounds and stood six feet, six inches tall. The story is told that eight mountain men jumped on him in a "free for all," an early form of entertainment. When the merriment was over all eight assailants lay unconscious on the ground. The next day the Town Council passed an ordinance declaring Dempsey's fists as deadly weapons, and forbade him to strike anyone with them.

Parkway Playhouse. In business since 1946, this summer stock playhouse is operated by the Theatre Division of the University of North Carolina at Greensboro. The playhouse offers musicals and drama. For further information write Parkway Playhouse, Burnsville 28714. Call (704) 682-6151.

Events

Lumberjack Day. Held in mid-October, this festival features relaxing events such as log rolling, cross-cut sawing, axe throwing, pole felling, and tobacco spitting contests. For further information write the Yancey County Chamber of Commerce, Burnsville 28714. Call (704) 682-7413.

Mount Mitchell Crafts Fair. Held on the first Friday and Saturday in August, this event features over two hundred craftspeople demonstrating and selling their work. Live music and mountain dancing are performed, and there is a chicken barbecue. For further information write the Yancey County Chamber of Commerce, Burnsville 28714. Call (704) 682-7413.

Music in the Mountains. This highbrow event offers five weeks of Sunday afternoon chamber music concerts beginning the first Sunday after Independence Day. For more information call the Toe River Arts Council, Town Square, Burnsville 28714. Call (704) 682-7215.

Lodging and Dining

The Nu-Wray Inn. Don't miss this place. Built in 1833, it is one of the oldest inns in the region and is noted for its "Southernboard" family-style dinners. Guests are seated at long tables and served heaping platters of food. During the meal they are entertained by an antique Steinway player piano and an elegant music box.

Located on the town square, the inn is filled with antiques, and the front porch is lined with rocking chairs. If there is a quintessential inn in western North Carolina, this is it. The Nu-Wray Inn is open from April 29 through December 1. It serves breakfast daily, dinner on weekdays, and lunch on Sundays. Write the inn at Box 156, Burnsville 28714; or call (704) 682-2329.

Yancey County Country Store. Located across the town square from the Nu-Wray Inn, this one-time country store is now a restaurant and art gallery. The restaurant features barbecue and home-baked goods for lunch and more sophisticated fare in the evenings. Call (704) 682-3106.

HOT SPRINGS. This small town on the French Broad River has seen better days. Once known as Warm Springs, it was an important stop on the road from Cumberland Gap to the markets of Charleston. In those days huge droves of cattle, hogs, and even turkeys would come down the road. In one year between one hundred fifty and one hundred sixty thousand hogs alone came through.

With the coming of the railroad the livestock drives halted, and health seekers in greater numbers began to come to the town, whose name was changed to Hot Springs. The local hotel lured them with descriptions such as the following: "These waters . . . bring the bloom back to the cheek, the lustre to the eye, tone to the languid pulse, strength to the jaded nerves, and vigor to the wasted frame."

The town had three successive hotels, all of which were eventually destroyed by fire. Hot Springs reached its zenith in the 1920s, although it probably had the most residents during World War I, when the U.S. government interned 517 German officers and 2,300 sailors in and about the Mountain Park Hotel.

There is now nothing to see of the old hotels that drew so many people to Hot Springs. Nor can one see the springs themselves, which are on private property. Nowadays the French Broad River attracts most of the travelers who come through town. The French Broad District of the Pisgah National Forest is headquartered in Hot Springs (see PISGAH NATIONAL FOREST).

Paint Rock. This is a one hundred–foot cliff overlooking the French Broad River. The rock is stained dark red from the iron oxide in it. A more lurid explanation of the rock's coloring is given in a legend that involves two Indian lovers from rival tribes who jumped off the rock and stained it with their blood. Located off U.S. 70 three miles from the Tennessee state line. Follow the signs.

Smoky Mountain River Expeditions. From April through October this outfit runs guided raft trips on the French Broad River from North Carolina into Tennessee, as well as trips on the Ocoee and the Nolichucky rivers. Write them at Box 398, Hot Springs 28743; or call (704) 622-7260.

JEFFERSON. The first town to be named for Thomas Jefferson and the seat of Ashe County, Jefferson for a time rivaled Asheville as the largest city in western North Carolina. It is known for having pure water; two resorts used to offer bismuth water and radium water. All of the streams in Ashe County flow into the New River, which is the only large river in this country to flow due north.

Jefferson sits in the middle of an intensive farming district. The mountains here are small compared with those to the south, and dairy cattle can be seen grazing high on the slopes. The Kraft Food Company located a cheese plant here because of the good water and ample supplies of milk.

Mount Jefferson State Park. Mount Jefferson rises abruptly from the surrounding land to a height of forty-nine hundred feet. Identified on old maps as Nigger Mountain, it was said to be a frequent refuge of run-

away slaves. The park consists of 541 acres at the summit, from which one can see into Tennessee, Virginia, and North Carolina. There is also picnicking, hiking, and nature study. The park is closed during the winter. Write P.O. Box 48, Jefferson 28640. Call (919) 246-9653.
New River State Park. Reached by following North Carolina 88 and State Road 1588, this park consists of four separate sites totaling five hundred acres along the New River. The park has facilities for primitive and canoe camping, fishing, and hiking. Write P.O. Box 48, Jefferson 28640. Call (919) 982-2587.
New River Outfitters. The New River is a gentle stream well suited to family expeditions. This firm supplies the canoes and necessary equipment. Guided trips of one and two days are available. New River Outfitters are open mid-April through mid-October. Write P.O. Box 433, Jefferson 28640. Call (919) 246-7711.

Events

Blue Grass and Old Time Fiddlers Convention. Early in August this musical aggregation kicks off with contests for bluegrass bands, old-time bands, and flat-foot dancers. Visitors can also hear guitar, mandolin, banjo (clawhammer and bluegrass) and fiddle solos; electrical instruments are banned. The convention is held early in August at the Ashe County Park in Jefferson. Free camping is offered. For further information write Jack D. Miller, Jefferson 28640. Call (919) 246-9945 or 246-9579.

Lodging and Dining

Groves Guest House. Offering bed-and-breakfast accommodations for two families, this guest house is located on North Street, Jefferson 28640. Call (919) 246-3157.
Shatley Springs Inn. This inn still dispenses radium water, which devotees claim has healing properties. Ten cabins are available for rental, and a public dining room serves three meals a day. The inn is open from

May through October. Write to P.O. Box 64, Crumpler 28617; or call (919) 982-2236.

LINVILLE. With its classy second homes and out-of-state Cadillacs, Linville is reminiscent of Highlands, a town further south. And no wonder—they were laid out by the same man. But unlike Highlands, Linville is an odd mixture of tourism and taste. Grandfather Mountain is one of the more highly promoted attractions in the region, yet just a few miles away the Eseeola Lodge reigns in rustic splendor, far from the screaming youngsters and their parents in stretch pants.

Brown Mountain Lights. Brown Mountain is famous for the mysterious lights that rise above it and twinkle away to nothing. Various theories have been offered to explain their purpose, but the most reasonable one seems to be the propensity of couples who view the lights in the dark to wind up in each other's arms. The lights can be best seen from the Blue Ridge Parkway at Milepost 305.2 or from Wiseman's View on the Linville Mountain Road, formerly North Carolina 105.

Grandfather Mountain. The Indians named this mountain, which from a distance resembles a skyward staring face. It features a "mile-high swinging bridge." The bridge is a mile high, true enough—but this measurement refers to the elevation, not the depth of the chasm beneath the bridge. From the bridge and the two peaks it connects, stunning views can be seen. If it is at all foggy, however—as it often is in these mountains—you won't see a thing.

The privately owned park on Grandfather Mountain incudes fifteen to twenty miles of hiking trails in a forty-one-hundred-acre tract of wilderness. There is also a visitors' center with mineral and wildflower displays, a gift shop, a short-order grill, a U.S. Weather Station, a small zoo, and hang-gliding demonstrations. Children particularly like the zoo, which is maintained as close to the animals' natural habitats as possible.

The hang-gliding demonstrations are held daily, weather permitting, from May through October. The park is open daily from April through mid-November, and on sunny weekends during the winter. Summer hours are from 8:00 until dusk; off-season hours are from 9:00 to 5:00. Grandfather Mountain is on U.S. 221 near Linville. Admission is charged. Call (704) 733-4337.

Events

Grandfather Mountain is the site of a wide variety of special events, including those described as follows. Information on all of them can be obtained by writing Grandfather Mountain, Linville 28646.

Highland Games and Gathering of Scottish Clans. This is one of the better Scottish displays of color, athletic prowess, and music and dance in the eastern United States. Held every year on the second weekend in July.

Masters of Hang Gliding Championships. Late August brings top hang gliders to the mountain and the hearts to the mouths of those who watch them.

Singing on the Mountain. This gathering of gospel singers and their fans is held on the fourth Sunday in June. Usually a speaker of national fame is present.

Lodging and Dining

Eseeola Lodge. This is perhaps the best inn in the mountains. Its exterior is covered with bark from the almost extinct chestnut trees, and inside the rooms have simple yet elegant furnishings. A trout stream gurgles under the building, and the cuisine in the formal dining room is the best to be found in this area. A golf course, tennis courts, and a swimming pool are all open to guests. There are 28 units in all, in the lodge and the adjacent cabins. Open May 27 through September 6. Write the lodge at Box 98, Linville 28646; or call (704) 733-4311.

LINVILLE FALLS. This is the name of both a town and a set of waterfalls.

Linville Falls. In volume, this is the biggest waterfall in the southern Appalachians. The Linville River shoots through a double set of falls and into Linville Gorge. Located just off the Blue Ridge Parkway and U.S. 221. Follow the signs. No admission is charged.

Linville Caverns. The North Carolina mountains get a lot of rainfall, so it's useful to have one attraction at which the weather doesn't matter. Linville Caverns can be a welcome respite from the rain or the heat. Guided tours take the visitor through collections of imaginatively named stalagmites and stalagtites and to an underground stream where blind cave fish swim. Open April through October from 9:00 till 6:00 and November through March from 9:00 till 4:30, the caverns are located about three miles south of Linville Falls on U.S. 221. Admission is charged.

LITTLE SWITZERLAND. This town was supposedly named because of the area's resemblance to Switzerland. It is more likely, however, that the name was picked to entice prospective customers to a summer colony founded in 1910.

Alpine Lookout. One mile south of Little Switzerland on North Carolina 226A, this place offers a lookout with a fine view of the southern lands below the mountains.

Toe River Craftsmen. This cooperative in Little Switzerland is open daily except on Mondays during the summer. Call (704) 675-4555.

MARSHALL. Located on a narrow strip of land between the French Broad River and a high cliff, this town is said to be "one mile long, one street wide, and sky high." The local school occupies Blennerhasset Island in the middle of the river.

French Broad Rafting Company. This company guides raft trips over seven and a half miles of the French

Broad River. Located in the town of Walnut, between Marshall and Hot Springs, it offers trips daily in the spring, summer, and fall. Write the French Broad Rafting Company at Route 5, Box 372, Marshall 28753; or call (704) 649-3574.

Southern Whitewater Expeditions. The firm offers one- and two-day rafting trips on the French Broad River. It is located on the river near the town of Walnut. Write Southern Whitewater Expeditions at P.O. Box 29, Walnut Rural Station, Marshall 28753; or call (704) 649-3679.

MARS HILL. Named for a hill in Athens, Greece, this town is the home of Mars Hill College, a Baptist liberal arts college that has the honor of being the nation's oldest institution of higher learning on its original site, west of the Catawba River.

The earliest construction of the college was financed in a curious manner. When the first building was completed twelve hundred dollars was owed to the contractor, but the fledgling college had no more funds. A slave named Joe was sent to Asheville to guarantee payment of the loan, and when the debt was paid this human collateral came back home. He is commemorated by a marker on the college grounds, and for a long time his descendants worked for the institution.

The campus totals 150 acres, and is a cultural center for the surrounding area. Some activities at the college are open to the public. Call (704) 689-1217 for information.

The Country Boutique. Operated by the Madison County Crafts Association, this shop features quilts, toys, musical instruments, and carvings. The shop is housed in the restored Old Frog Level Schoolhouse on the campus of the college. Call (704) 649-3231.

Rural Life Museum. This museum provides a look at the life of a pioneer family one hundred to one hundred fifty years ago. It includes tools, artifacts, and furniture. Open Tuesday through Friday. Call (704) 689-1244.

Southern Appalachian Repertory Theater. From June through August this company presents six musicals and dramas. Write P.O. Box 53, Mars Hill 28754; or call (704) 689-1203.

Events

Bascom Lamar Lunsford Mountain Music and Dance Festival. This festival offers mountain music, dancing, and crafts. It is held on campus in October. Write the college at Mars Hill 28754; or call (704) 689-1332.

Lodging and Dining

Baird House Inn. This small inn features six guest rooms with poster beds and working fireplaces. It is open year-round. Write the inn at 121 South Main Street, Mars Hill 28754; or call (704) 689-5722.

Deacon's Bench Restaurant. Located in a former church built in 1917, this restaurant features plain old American food made with fresh ingredients—worth noting in a region where canned green beans are all too well known. Located on U.S. 23, the restaurant is open all year. Reservations may be necessary during the fall foliage season. Call (704) 689-3898.

Wolf Laurel Inn. The inn comprises 78 rooms, plus log cabins and cottages. During the wintertime this is a ski resort, but during the off-season, as the innkeepers term it, facilities for golf, swimming, tennis, horseback riding, and hiking are available to guests. The number-12 hole on the golf course is the highest hole on any green east of the Rockies. Write the inn at Route 3, Mars Hill 28754. Call (704) 689-4111.

PISGAH NATIONAL FOREST. "Get thee up to the top of Pisgah, and lift up thine eyes westward, and northward, and southward, and eastward, and behold it with thine eyes." These words were directed at Moses in the Old Testament, but they constitute worthy advice for those who want to see mountain scenery. The Pisgah National Forest (PNF) covers 478 thousand acres in two separate tracts that include some of the highest peaks in the eastern United States.

Various natural attractions within the national forest are better known than the forest itself, and for this reason they are listed separately. Although not as large as the neighboring Great Smoky Mountains National Park, the PNF has higher peaks, many more waterfalls, and wildflower areas that surpass anything in the Smokies (for more on the waterfalls see Chapter 7). There are hiking trails, campgrounds, picnic areas, and wilderness areas. All of these, however, are scattered between towns, and a scenic wonder may be just down the road from a fast food joint. This can be a blessing or a curse, depending on how you look at it. For a big chunk of wilderness, head for the Smokies. For a wider variety of things to see and do, stay in the PNF.

Like the southerly Nantahala, the PNF is divided into four administrative areas. The Toecane, Grandfather, and French Broad ranger districts lie north of Asheville, while the Pisgah Ranger District sits beside the Nantahala National Forest further south. Each will be briefly described here. For further information about the forest generally, and the precise location of campsites and picnic areas, write to the Supervisor, National Forests in North Carolina, P.O. Box 2750, Asheville 28802, or to one of the district offices. Call (704) 258-2850.

Pisgah Ranger District. This is the smaller of the two sections of the forest, and is located southwest of Asheville. It is a part of the immense landholdings accumulated by George Vanderbilt in his Biltmore Estate. The district includes several waterfalls as well as the Cradle of Forestry museum north of Brevard. Also notable is the Shining Rock Wilderness Area, a 13,400-acre preserve that is a delight for hiking. A free permit is required to camp in the wilderness; one can be obtained from the District Ranger, whose office is two miles north of Brevard on U.S. 276. Write the District Ranger, U.S.

Forest Service, P.O. Box 8, Pisgah Forest 28768. Call (704) 877-3265.

Toecane Ranger District. This district is located to the north and east of Asheville, and extends to the Tennessee state line. It includes Mount Mitchell, the highest peak in the eastern United States, and two areas of intense growths of rhododendrons, which flower profusely in the spring. Craggy Mountain Scenic Area is located near Craggy Gardens, a stop on the Blue Ridge Parkway. Roan Mountain is on the Tennessee state line. The district office is located in Burnsville on the U.S. 19E bypass. Write District Ranger, U.S. Forest Service, P.O. Box 128, Burnsville 28741. Call (704) 682-6146.

Grandfather Ranger District. This is the northernmost part of the Pisgah National Forest, and includes the Linville Gorge Wilderness Area and four campgrounds. The District Office is located in the public library building in Marion. Write to District Ranger, U.S. Forest Service, P.O. Box 519, Marion 28752. Call (704) 652-4841.

French Broad Ranger District. Located on the French Broad River northwest of Asheville, this district office is located on the main street in downtown Hot Springs. Write the District Ranger, U.S. Forest Service, P.O. Box 128, Hot Springs 28743. Call (704) 622-3202.

SPARTA. Allegheny County produces a lot of tobacco; it also produces pipes in which to smoke it. The Dr. Grabow Pipe factory, located southwest of Sparta on U.S. 21, is the largest manufacturer of smoking pipes in the country.

Stone Mountain State Park. This park centers on a six-hundred-foot-high granite face whose base is three miles in circumference. It is a favorite of wild goats and mountain climbers, who tackle climbs with names such as the Great Brown Way, Electric Boobs, and Rice Krispies. Less athletic visitors may camp, picnic, view waterfalls, and fish for trout. The park is located near

Roaring Gap. Write the park at Route 1, Box 17, Roaring Gap 28668. Call (919) 957-8185.

Events

Blue Ridge Mountain Fair. This event features a crafts show, a ten-kilometer road race, live music, a wagon train, a horse show, a puppet show, and many other events. Held in late June and early July. Write the Allegheny County Chamber of Commerce, P.O. Box 337, Sparta 28675; or call (919) 372-5473.

SPRUCE PINE. Western North Carolina is rich in minerals, and much of the underground wealth is around this small town. Kaolin, a fine white clay used in ceramics, is mined in open pits here. Mica, asbestos, iron ore, and feldspar are some of the other minerals mined in Spruce Pine. Not surprisingly, this is a center for rockhounds. There are several mines in the area where one can prospect for gemstones.

Hensley's Forge. Unadvertised but worth a stop is this father-and-son blacksmith shop. Ben and Mike Hensley hammer out gates, railings, andirons, and delicate items such as chandeliers. They can make virtually anything of iron a customer requests. Their shop is five miles south of Spruce Pine on U.S. 226.

Museum of North Carolina Minerals. Some seven hundred of the finest examples of North Carolina minerals are housed in this museum. Located at milepost 331 of the Blue Ridge Parkway, it is open from May through November from 9:00 to 5:00. In April it is open on weekends only.

Penland School of Crafts. This school was open in 1929 to prevent the disappearance of traditional mountain crafts. Now the oldest and largest school for art and crafts in North America, it annually draws students from all over the world. Instruction is offered in fibers, ceramics, glass, metals, wood, and photography, to name a few. Most students come for intensive two- or three-week sessions. At peak times the school has 160 people teaching and learning among 47 buildings spread over 460 acres.

This is a school, not a tourist attraction. Tours are available, but it's a good idea to call ahead. The school has a shop where the students' works are sold. The school is located northwest of Spruce Pine and can be reached by U.S. 19E or North Carolina 226. Whichever you take, turn off at Penland Road and follow the signs for five miles. Write the Penland School at Penland 28765; or call (704) 765-2359.

Events

Mineral and Gem Festival. The first week of August marks this gathering of rockhounds. Local mineral mines are open to the public, lectures are given, and innumerable sessions of specimen trading are held. Write the Mitchell County Chamber of Commerce, Pinebridge Center, Spruce Pine 28777. Call (704) 765-9483.

WEST JEFFERSON. Jefferson was once the main town in this county, but, as happened to so many other once prosperous communities, the railroad bypassed it. West Jefferson became the larger town.

Ashe County Cheese Factory. A lot of the milk produced in the area is channeled into this factory, which has been in operation since 1930 and was once owned by the Kraft Company. The usual unit of production is a 24-pound wheel, but visitors can purchase smaller amounts of cheddar, colby, and Monterey Jack cheese at a shop at the plant. It is located at 106 East Main Street in West Jefferson. Call (919) 246-2501.

Blue Ridge Mountain Frescoes. In 1973 an Episcopal priest was approached by Ben Long, a North Carolina artist who wanted to try his hand at fresco, a technique in which paint is applied to wet plaster. It was a medium often used by Leonardo da Vinci and other great masters, but one that had never been used much in modern times, and certainly not in rural churches in North Carolina.

The priest gave his consent, and in 1974 Long painted *Mary Great with Child,* a depiction of the pregnant Virgin in Saint Mary's Church in West Jefferson. He painted two more frescoes in the church, and while he did so his work began to attract international acclaim.

In 1980 Long came back to the area with a group of students in tow and painted another fresco in the Holy Trinity Church in nearby Glendale Springs. Entitled the *Last Supper,* it measures 17 by 17½ feet. A final fresco was painted in the undercroft of the Holy Trinity Church.

These two churches and their unusual art attract thousands of visitors a year. Saint Mary's is located off U.S. 221 on the old North Carolina 194 at Beaver Creek, on the outskirts of West Jefferson. Holy Trinity is in the center of Glendale Springs, which is about seven miles from West Jefferson on North Carolina 16. The churches are open every day.

Greenfield. This privately owned outdoor recreation center offers camping, fishing, horseback riding, and a restaurant. It is located in the shadow of Mount Jefferson State Park. Follow North Carolina 163 out of West Jefferson to State Road 1149. Turn left. Write the park at Route 2, West Jefferson 28694. Call (919) 246-9106.

SKIING

Appalachian Ski Mountain. Located near Blowing Rock and Boone, this firm offers eight slopes with two chairlifts and three surface lifts. The vertical drop from the top of the mountain is 365 feet. Write P.O. Box 106, Blowing Rock 28605. Call (704) 295-7828.

Ski Beech. This resort, which is incorporated as the highest town in North Carolina, offers fourteen slopes, including the highest one in the eastern United States. The maximum vertical drop is 830 feet, and there are six chairlifts and two surface lifts. Ski Beech also offers a nursery and ice skating. Off-season activities range from golf to swimming to an Oktoberfest. The resort is located on North Carolina 194 near Banner Elk. Write Ski Beech, P.O. Box 1118, Banner Elk 28604. Call (704) 387-2011.

Cataloochee. Located near Maggie Valley and Waynesville, this resort offers two slopes, each of which has a surface lift. The vertical drop is 740 feet. Write Route 1, Box 500, Maggie Valley 28751. Call (704) 926-0285.

High Meadows. Roaring Gap is the town closest to this mountain, which has a vertical drop of 80 feet, two slopes, and two surface lifts. Write P.O. Box 222, Roaring Gap 28668.

Hound Ears. This resort has two slopes with a vertical drop of 107 feet. One chairlift and one surface lift are provided. Skiing is permitted Friday through Monday only. Write P.O. Box 188, Blowing Rock 28605. Call (704) 963-4321.

Mill Ridge. Located near Banner Elk, Blowing Rock, and Boone, this resort has three slopes with a vertical drop of 225 feet. One chairlift and one surface lift are provided. Write Route 1, Banner Elk 28604. Call (704) 963-4500.

Sapphire Valley. This ski area is near Cashiers. Its four slopes have a vertical drop of 425 feet, and one chairlift and two surface lifts are provided. The resort features a nursery and ice rink. Write Route 70, Box 80, Sapphire Valley 28774. Call (704) 743-3441.

Scaly Mountain. The southernmost ski area in the state, this one offers three slopes with a 225-foot vertical drop, one chairlift, and one surface lift. Write Box 80, Scaly Mountain 28775. Call (704) 526-3737.

Ski Hawksnest. Two chairlifts and two surface lifts bring skiers to this resort's six slopes. Two of the slopes are for advanced skiers and two are for beginners. The maximum drop is 618 feet. Night skiing, equipment rentals, and a ski school are offered, as are group rates, food, a lounge, and entertainment. Located on North Carolina 105 near Banner Elk. Write Rt. 1, Box 256, Banner Elk 28604. Call (704) 963-6563.

Sugar Mountain. A mile-long chairlift carries skiers to the top of Sugar Mountain, where they can choose from 16 trails, the longest of which is 1.3 miles and has a vertical drop of twelve hundred feet. The most challenging run is forty-one hundred feet, and for those who are not quite up to it there are eight intermediate and six beginner slopes. Sugar Mountain offers a nursery, a cafeteria, and lodging. For information write P.O. Box 369, Banner Elk 28604.

Wolf Laurel. Located near Mars Hill, this resort features nine slopes with a vertical drop of seven hundred feet. One chairlift and three surface lifts are provided. Write Route 3, Mars Hill 28754. Call (704) 689-2222.

SIX

The Blue Ridge Parkway

MOST PEOPLE WHO CONSIDER VACATIONING in western North
Carolina think first of the Blue Ridge Parkway. This 469-
mile road is the longest scenic drive in the world, and it
attracts millions of motorists and bicyclists who come to
see the panorama of the highest mountains in the eastern
United States. The road is a driver's dream: there are no
billboards, no big trucks, and no potholes.

But nor are there farmers' markets, artists' studios, or
old inns—the sorts of things that make a trip to an area
like North Carolina so enjoyable. For these and other delights the traveler must descend from the heights to the
nearby villages and towns. Many guidebooks list these
towns as if they were accessory to the Blue Ridge Parkway—mere appendages to the two-laned road. This is not
the best way to approach them. There are many ways to
see the southern Appalachians, and the Blue Ridge Parkway is only one. Consequently the various villages, towns,
and attractions in the area, though they may lie right beside the parkway, are listed alphabetically in this book,
either in Chapter 5 (Upper North Carolina), Chapter 7

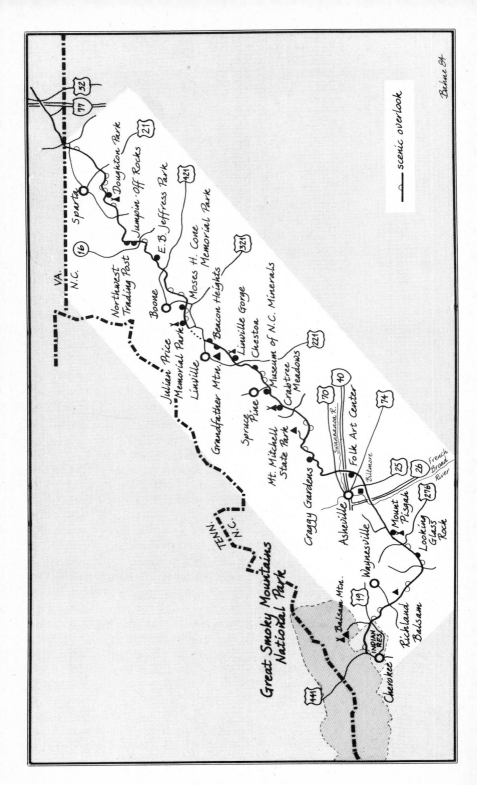

Behme St

→ scenic overlook

(Lower North Carolina), or Chapter 9 (Southwest Virginia). Ideally you should proceed along the parkway with this book and a map. If you want to investigate a town that is nearby, you can look it up.

HISTORY

Like social security and the TVA, the Blue Ridge Parkway is one of the few good things that came out of the Great Depression. A similar scenic road had been proposed early in this century, and in 1911 one was even surveyed from Tallulah Falls, Georgia, to Marion, Virginia. Known as the "Crest of the Blue Ridge Highway," a portion of it was constructed between Linville and Altapass in 1912. This was at a time when many of the commercial roads were still dirt, and support for a tourist-oriented highway was difficult to muster. World War I brought a halt to construction, and the project was quietly abandoned.

In the depths of the Depression the federal government came up with an idea for a road to connect the Shenandoah National Park to the Great Smoky Mountains National Park. This proposal was greeted with great enthusiasm by people in North Carolina and Tennessee, and each group set out to make sure that the road came through their state. The secretary of the interior decided to place the road in Virginia and North Carolina, and with this decision came the terms of the agreement: the federal government would build the road, but the states had to provide the land.

As with many projects designed for the public good, the regrettable part was the action taken against landowners. All the people who owned land along the route were paid for their property, but quite a few did not want to sell, and court proceedings were eventually necessary to secure the right of way. The acquired property averaged one thousand feet in width to insure that no commercial development could spring up alongside the road.

Construction began in 1935. One important reason for building the road was to provide jobs for the unemployed, who were happy to work for 30 cents an hour. Private contractors did the road construction, but their efforts were augmented by the Civilian Conservation Corps, whose members worked at building fences, controlling erosion caused by the excavation, and planting trees and grass. Many of the men who hired on the work gangs had never before seen jackhammers or modern construction equipment.

The work was difficult. Twenty-seven tunnels were blasted out, and often a tunnel would open onto a section where a bridge was needed. The mountains did not easily yield to the efforts of the contractors, nor was the weather always cooperative. On many mornings the men would come to work in a fog so thick they couldn't see thirty feet in front of them.

Because the governor of North Carolina placed a priority on getting access to the most scenic areas and to providing employment where the Depression had hit hardest, the parkway was built in unconnected sections. Only later were these sections linked. When the longest stretch of the road was finally opened, it was an immediate success, and began luring out-of-state tourists as well as local people who had never seen some of the wonders of their own mountains. Traffic on the parkway has increased every year, slowed only by gasoline shortages, and in 1983 an estimated 19 million people traveled some portion of the Blue Ridge Parkway.

GETTING THE MOST OUT OF THE PARKWAY

Perhaps the biggest mistake that travelers on the Blue Ridge Parkway make is to assume that it is some sort of two-laned interstate highway, a quick way of getting from point to point. Nothing could be further from the truth; most motorists average only 30 mph.

The Blue Ridge Parkway is an experience in and of itself. The old saw "Getting there is half the fun" really holds true here. The road is designed to be traveled slowly;

the maximum speed permitted is 45 miles per hour. The people who laid out the road took into consideration where the best views and overlooks are to be found, and routed the road accordingly. Often it will swing to the west of one ridge and then to the east of the next one.

The opposite of the person who tries to barrel down the parkway is the one who never gets off it. You can certainly see the sights this way, but you'll have little interaction with the people of the region. This is akin to the behavior of the traveling Americans who, intent on mingling with the people in Scotland, picked out a rustic inn, only to find to their dismay that everyone there was from the United States. Besides, after three or four hours of staring at stunning mountain vistas, even the most ardent scenery lover gets satiated. Dropping into a village or town for a while can make the excursion through North Carolina much more interesting and fun.

While you're following the parkway, try to get off the pavement now and then. The scenic overlooks are beautiful, but not many of them have hiking or nature trails on which to stretch the legs and get the cardiovascular system cranked up a notch or two. At places such as Craggy Gardens, Moses Cone Memorial Park, and Mount Pisgah, you can escape the confines of your car and experience nature up close. Children particularly enjoy a chance to get out and release some energy. An hour or two in the woods— or even a few minutes—can make the rest of the driving much more pleasant.

The smooth asphalt and superbly engineered curves, so relaxing and easy to drive, can conceal the danger present on the parkway. This region is infamous for pea soup fogs that rival any in Victorian London. Such fogs are common in the early morning, and at night. At these times drivers cannot see thirty feet ahead, and are much more likely to plow into the rear of other cars. During fogs it is hazardous even to park on the side of the road. Another driver coming from behind may assume that a parked car is still moving and run right into it.

Visitors should keep in mind that wintertime brings ice and snow to the mountains. The higher portions of the parkway close from the first sign of the ice until April 15th.

BICYCLING ON THE PARKWAY

In many ways the parkway is perfect for bicycling. There are no trucks, no driveways or sidestreets for motorists to pull out from, and no dogs. The shoulders are usually free of glass, and the air is as pure as you'll ever find.

There's one big catch: the hills. This road follows the mountaintops, and the inclines can be incredibly hard to pull on the way up and thrillingly dangerous on the way down. In the first 25 miles north of Asheville, for example, the elevation increases 3,460 feet. That's a lot of pedaling! If you have the proper gears and plenty of stamina, it can be done.

Bikers should carry air pumps and everything necessary to change a flat tire. There are service stations along the parkway, but they are few and far between. A final note: Many of the tourists on the parkway are unaccustomed to sharing the road, and lots of them are busy looking at the scenery. A loud horn or a good set of lungs is helpful. As with any cycling, so is a helmet. A bicycle light is required by law for safe passage through the tunnels.

CAMPING ON THE PARKWAY

Just as in the Great Smoky Mountains National Park, the campgrounds on the Blue Ridge Parkway are simple affairs. Water and central toilet facilities are provided, but there are no showers. You can stay for only 14 consecutive days during the summer, and camping is allowed only in designated areas. Each campground offers lectures or other interpretive activities during the summer season.

None of the campgrounds accept reservations; their

policy is strictly first come, first served. This is important to remember if you are counting on staying at a particular one. Furthermore, few spaces are designated for recreational vehicles, and even these lack hookups. There are plenty of private campgrounds close to nearly every exit of the parkway. One of the annual guides to campgrounds is a good thing to carry with you.

Here, from north to south, are the five North Carolina campgrounds on the Blue Ridge Parkway:

Doughton Park. Located at milepost 241.1, this park is open May through October. It has 81 tent sites and 26 RV sites.

Julian Price Memorial Park. Located at milepost 297.1, this campground is open year-round. It has 129 tent sites and 68 RV sites. With its lake and proximity to Moses H. Cone Memorial Park and the town of Blowing Rock, it is very popular. Arrive early in the day to get a site.

Linville Falls. Located at milepost 316.4, this park is open year-round. It has 55 tent sites and 20 RV sites, but no dumping station. It also fills up quickly because of the attraction of Linville Falls and Gorge.

Crabtree Meadows. Located at milepost 339.5, this campground is open May through October. It has 71 tent sites and 22 RV sites, but no dumping station. This is one of the last campgrounds to fill up.

Mount Pisgah. Located at milepost 408.6, this one is open from May through October and has 70 tent sites and 70 RV sites. Since it is close to the Smokies, the campground is very popular.

In addition to the campgrounds, the Blue Ridge Parkway offers several backcountry camping sites. These are accessible only by hiking, and users must have permits from the rangers. For further information about camping on the parkway write the Superintendent, Blue Ridge Parkway, 700 Northwestern Bank Building, Asheville 28801; or call (704) 259-0779.

LODGING ON THE PARKWAY

As a service to visitors, two commercial lodges are allowed to operate along the parkway in North Carolina. Both are modern structures offering rooms at reasonable rates. They are open May through October, and both stay close to full during the season. It is particularly difficult to get reservations during weekends in October, when the leaves are at their height of color.

Bluffs Lodge. Located at milepost 241, this lodge sits in Doughton Park and offers 24 units and a restaurant. Write to National Park Concessions, Inc., Laurel Springs 28644. Call (919) 372-4499.

Pisgah Inn. Located at milepost 408.6, this inn sits on land once a part of the Biltmore Estate. It has 51 units and a spectacular view of the mountains. The dining room is open to the public. Write the inn at P.O. Drawer 749, Waynesville 28786. Call (704) 235-8228.

SIGHTS ALONG THE PARKWAY: NORTH TO SOUTH

DOUGHTON PARK. Mile marker 238. This six thousand–acre park is not as mountainous as areas farther south. Its most outstanding natural feature is the sheer cliffs of Bluff Mountain; the entire area was once known as the Bluffs. Aficionados of handcrafted goods will want to stop in at the Brinegar Cabin, the home of a one-time mountain weaver, for a demonstration of weaving and a chance to buy some of the products. The park also contains Bluffs Lodge and camping facilities.

NORTHWEST TRADING POST. Mile marker 258.6. Downhill from Doughton Park, this is another stop for those interested in crafts. The Trading Post, which is open mid-April through October, sells items made by local people, including quilts, carvings, and paintings.

JUMPINOFF ROCK. Mile marker 260.6. Fallinoff Rock might be a better name for this attraction, which consists of a sheer drop at the end of a half-mile trail. Don't let the children run ahead.

E.B. JEFFRESS PARK. Mile marker 272. Here a trail leads to one of the northernmost waterfalls in the state. There is an old cabin as well as picnic facilities within the park.

MOSES H. CONE MEMORIAL PARK. Mile marker 293. If you are short on time, skip all of the forementioned and head for this delightful place, which was once the home of Moses H. Cone, the "Denim King" of North Carolina. This particular Moses led his family into the wilderness, but he did so with elegant taste. The materials for Flat Top Manor, his 20-room house, were hauled by oxen up the mountain. Inside the mansion is a crafts shop.

Cone engaged in a hobby that few people could afford—road building. He had his workers build over 25 miles of carriage roads throughout the thirty-six hundred-acre estate, and these are terrific for easy hiking.

The mansion looks toward the town of Blowing Rock, which borders the lower end of the Cone grounds. One good hike descends from the mansion to the Trout Pond and Bass Lake; another goes to Flat Top Mountain. Both hikes are on carriage paths, which in the winter are excellent cross-country ski trails.

JULIAN PRICE MEMORIAL PARK. Mile marker 297.1. This 4,344-acre park is one of the better places to camp on the entire parkway. Trout fishing is featured at the lake; those who are just passing through may settle for a stroll.

UNFINISHED SECTION. Mile marker 300. This is the final section of the Blue Ridge Parkway to be completed, and the Linn Cove Viaduct is already an attraction in itself. This complex bridge is a quarter mile long and consists of 153 50-ton concrete sections, only one of which is straight. The bridge is said to be the only one of its type in America. Price: eight million dollars.

GRANDFATHER MOUNTAIN OVERLOOK. Mile marker 306.6. Grandfather Mountain was so named because it supposedly resembles an elderly man lying on his back and looking at the sky. Here's your chance to see if that description still applies.

LOST COVE OVERLOOK. Mile marker 310. This is one place where the mysterious Brown Mountain Lights can sometimes be seen at night. Daytime visitors can take a short trail to a bare quartzite outcropping.

LINVILLE GORGE WILDERNESS. Mile marker 316.3. John D. Rockefeller donated this 7,650-acre preserve of virgin timberland to the Blue Ridge Parkway. The Linville River roars—literally—through Linville Falls and into Linville Gorge, which has some of the toughest hiking trails in the region. There is an easy one-and-a-half-mile walk to the falls, which in volume are the biggest in the state. There are two levels of falls; the first is a cascade, and the second is more of a drop.

Hiking in the gorge, which was once used for training Green Berets, requires a permit. The trails leading into the gorge are very steep, and once you are down by the Linville River the scenery is reminiscent of the film *Deliverance*. You can get a permit up to 30 days in advance of your trip by contacting the District Ranger, U.S. Forest Service, P.O. Box 519, Marion 28752. You can also stop by the office on East Court Street in Marion or call (704) 652-4841.

CHESTOA VIEW. Mile marker 320.7. A short hike across Humpback Mountain leads to a cliff from which the flat Table Rock can be seen.

MUSEUM OF NORTH CAROLINA MINERALS. Mile marker 331. This modest museum contains samples of some of the gemstones and commercial minerals that are mined in the surrounding areas. It is open daily from 9:00 to 5:00 from Easter through Thanksgiving. No admission is charged.

CRABTREE MEADOWS. Mile marker 340. This 250-acre park is a good place for a pit stop. It has a campground, a service station, and a coffee shop. A pleasant 1.6-mile trail leads to Crabtree Falls, which drop 80 feet.

MOUNT MITCHELL STATE PARK. Mile marker 355.4. This park features the highest mountain in the eastern United States. For those who have seen New England's rocky Mount Washington, it may come as a surprise that this peak is wooded all the way to the top. Somewhat disconcerting, too, is the easy drive almost to the summit. At the top is an observation tower that provides a 360-degree view of rolling mountains.

The mountain is named for Dr. Elisha Mitchell, a professor at the University of North Carolina who first proved, in 1835, that this is the highest mountain in the East. His figures were challenged by Thomas Clingman, a North Carolina politician and amateur mountain measurer, who published an article in 1855 claiming that Mitchell had measured the wrong mountain, and had not been on the highest peak at all. Mitchell wrote an article defending his research, but the controversy continued, fueled by local newspapers and Clingman's arrogance.

Not to be outdone, Mitchell decided in 1857 to measure the mountain once more. He left his party in a rustic inn and set out for the home of Big Tom Wilson, a mountain man who had guided Mitchell on an 1844 expedition. He never got there. A search was organized, and Big Tom tracked Mitchell to the edge of a 40-foot waterfall. His body was in the pool below, his watch stopped at 8:10. The searchers theorized that he had tumbled over the falls in the dark. The next summer a Princeton professor measured the mountain and vindicated Mitchell's claim. The two professors' measurements differed by only one foot. Modern methods have placed the elevation of the peak at 6,684 feet above sea level.

Elisha Mitchell is buried at the summit of the mountain. The falls where he died are about one mile below the summit on the western slope. Mount Mitchell State Park can be reached by driving five miles from the parkway on North Carolina 128. No admission is charged.

CRAGGY GARDENS. Mile post 363. This area is a prime example of phenomenon known in the southern Appalachians as a heath bald. Such an area, which looks like certain hilltops in Scotland, has no trees, but is covered with dense and scrubby bushes of the heath family. The Catawba Rhododendron is the dominant one here, and when it blooms in mid-June the mountaintops are flush with the crimson and purple flowers. A visitors' center has exhibits on heath plants, and there are several nature trails. This area is very popular when the plants bloom; it's a good idea to visit early in the morning.

Bicyclists heading north are to be congratulated at this point. Those heading south should make sure everything—including the helmet—is on tight. From here to Asheville it's all downhill.

FOLK ART CENTER. Mile marker 382. This crafts shop, visitors' center, and auditorium is a good place to stop. The crafts shop is run by the Southern Highland Handicraft Guild, your guide to handcrafted gifts that did not first see the light of day in an East Asian factory. Open all year from 9:00 to 5:00. No admission is charged.

ASHEVILLE. Mile marker 390. The parkway swoops down over the Swannanoa River, its lowest point since entering the state. Asheville is a good place to spend some time, but those who wish a free look at the Biltmore House should gaze off to the right shortly after crossing U.S. 25. The parkway crosses part of the grounds of this Vanderbilt estate.

PISGAH INN. Mile marker 408.6. Once a halfway stop between the Biltmore House and George Vanderbilt's hunting lodge, this inn is one of two on the parkway in North

Carolina. Visitors can hike from the inn to the top of Mount Pisgah. There is also a campground, a service station, a crafts shop, and a restaurant.

LOOKING GLASS ROCK. Mile marker 417. The "looking glass" here is a four-hundred-foot-high granite cliff on a mountain across the valley from the parkway. When the cliff is covered with water or snow it is said to resemble a mirror.

RICHLAND BALSAM. Mile marker 431.4. A trail here leads to the highest point on the parkway—6,410 feet (technically speaking, Mount Mitchell is not on the parkway).

WOODFIN CASCADES. Mile marker 446.7. The water in these small falls flows down from Mount Lyn Lowry.

The Blue Ridge Parkway ends at the boundary of the Great Smoky Mountains National Park and the Qualla Reservation of the Cherokee Indians.

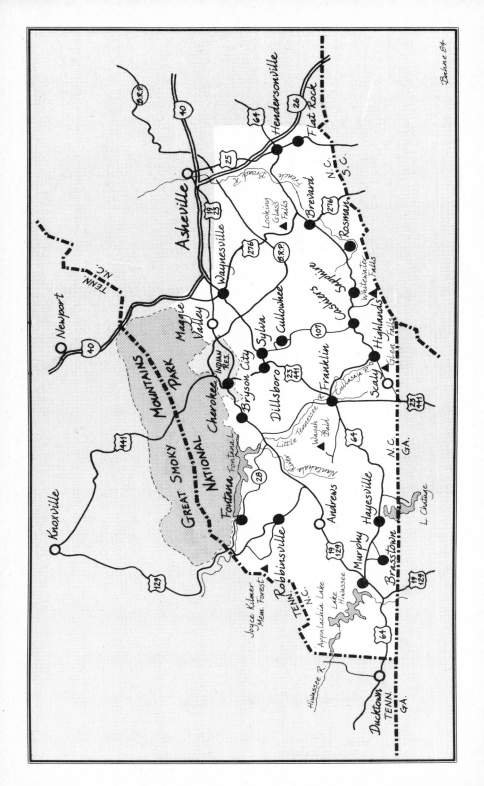

SEVEN

Lower North Carolina

SOUTHWESTERN NORTH CAROLINA has always been the most
remote part of the state. Murphy, for example, the seat of
Cherokee County, is closer to the state capitals of Tennessee, Georgia, Alabama, and Kentucky than it is to Raleigh,
North Carolina. Despite its relative isolation, however, the
beauty of the area and the riches within it have drawn a
steady stream of outsiders for almost four and a half centuries.

The Cherokee Indians, the dominant tribe in the region,
lived in a richly forested land. Towering chestnut trees
stood on mountains that reached above rushing rivers. The
valleys, some of which were cultivated by the Indians, were
also home to bison, bear, and deer. With a language that
would outlive their presence, the Cherokees gave names to
the mountains and rivers that reflected the beauty they
saw.

Then the first outsiders came. Searching for a city of
gold that the Indians kept telling him was farther away,
Hernando De Soto and over six hundred soldiers filed
through this area in 1540, plundering Cherokee crops and

forcing Indians to carry the Spaniards' gear as they pushed onward. This early exploitation of the native people set a trend that reached a low point in the 1830s when another armed force, this time from the United States, entered the area, rounded up as many Cherokees as could be found, and forced them to walk all the way to Oklahoma. The Indians still call it the "Trail of Tears."

About the same time that the Indians were rounded up and marched off, a different type of people began to arrive further east in southwestern North Carolina. The men wore high boots, the women wore silk dresses, and each family brought slaves. These were the planters from places like Charleston, South Carolina, and Savannah, Georgia, and they had come to the mountains to escape the summertime heat of the low country. They bought large tracts of land and built second homes—most of them larger than the homes the local people used all year. Their churches and their society ways came with these people, who set standards of taste in architecture that still hold sway in towns such as Flat Rock. During this time certain villages began to experience a seasonal variance in population—a common circumstance nowadays, but a novel one then.

The Civil War brought an end to these mountain pilgrimages, at least on such a grand scale, but the subsequent coming of the railroad brought another wave of outsiders who were determined to make money from the natural resources they found in the region. As the timber and minerals rode the rails out, money flowed in, enabling the mountain people to prosper. Naturalists and tourists began to come in greater numbers, and for their comfort a growing number of inns and mountain hotels were constructed.

In our own century Americans recognized the need to preserve the natural beauty of areas as remote as southwestern North Carolina, and steps were taken to insure that the mountains and forests would remain places of enjoyment and activity for a growing number of visitors. In the 1930s and 1940s the TVA constructed a series of dams on the rivers, providing electrical power as well as beautiful lakes. The Great Smoky Mountains National Park set aside the highest of the mountains, and the creation of the Nantahala and Pisgah National Forests insured that the resources of the area would be managed in a careful manner. Up to 70 percent of the land in some counties was put into the hands of the federal government, creating difficulties for the counties' tax assessors, but manifold delights for visitors.

For all the attention from the federal government and vacationers, southwestern North Carolina remains the most unspoiled section of the southern Appalachians. The millions of visitors to the Great Smoky Mountains National Park do not clog the roads here. There are very few tourist traps. The inns in the mountains are quiet, and in some places one can view landscapes that have not changed since the time of the Cherokees. The Cherokees themselves—descendants of those who refused to leave their homeland—keep their culture alive on a reservation. One of the most inspirational tracts of virgin timber in the East, the Joyce Kilmer Memorial Forest, is found here. The waterfalls in the area are the most striking in the region, and nowhere else in the country can visitors try their luck at finding so many kinds of precious stones. For those seeking natural beauty, outdoor activities such as white-water rafting and hiking, or simply some relief from the pressures of modern life, southwestern North Carolina is hard to beat.

HOW TO GET THERE

BY AIR. The closest airports to southwestern North Carolina are in Asheville, Chattanooga, and Knoxville.

FROM TENNESSEE. There are four main roads from Tennessee into southwestern North Carolina. From north to south, the first is I-40, which leads from Knoxville into Asheville, where it intersects with I-26. I-26 leads to the South Carolina line.

U.S. 441 goes through the Great Smoky Mountains National Park and takes travelers to Cherokee. This road is often crowded with visitors to the park, and the traffic may slow the through traveler. Another road from the Knoxville area is U.S. 129, which skirts the bottom of the park and leads to Fontana. This road is two-laned and very twisty.

Visitors from the Chattanooga area usually enter the state on U.S. 64, which is one of the more scenic highways in the area. It crosses the lower portion of southwestern North Carolina, passing through towns such as Franklin, Highlands, and Hendersonville.

FROM GEORGIA. A series of small roads connect the two states. The primary route is U.S. 23/441 up from Tallulah Falls.

FROM UPPER NORTH CAROLINA. The obvious way to come from northeastern North Carolina is by the Blue Ridge Parkway. Another road, and one that is always open in the wintertime, is U.S. 19, which runs down the middle of this area.

ONCE YOU'RE THERE

The further east you go in southwestern North Carolina, the more restaurants and lodging places you will have to choose from. You might stay somewhere in the triangle formed by Franklin, Asheville, and Hendersonville, and venture into the rest of the area on day trips.

The area has a number of good campgrounds, private and public. The private ones are listed in any good campground guide, such as *Woodalls,* and lists of the public ones can be obtained by writing the Nantahala and Pisgah National Forests.

TOWNS AND ATTRACTIONS

BRASSTOWN. Because it is located somewhere close to Tennessee's Copperhill, many people assume that this town lies above further copper deposits. It doesn't. The name

Brasstown is a corruption of a Cherokee word for "place of fresh green."

John C. Campbell Folk School. Billing itself as "the nation's only folk school," this institution endeavors to improve the lives of rural people by educating them in cultural, economic, and handicraft areas. Situated on 366 acres, the school offers courses in folk dancing, dulcimer playing, and homesteading, as well as such crafts as batik, enameling, lapidary, lap quilting, photography, rug braiding, and weaving. The courses range from 3 to 12 weeks, and offer an interesting sort of vacation for those who want something out of the ordinary. Lodging is provided for 75 students.

An offshoot of the school is the Brasstown Carvers, a cottage industry involving about forty people who create folk art from native walnut, cherry, and other woods. Their work can be purchased in a shop at the school.

The John C. Campbell Folk School is located off U.S. 64. Write it at Brasstown 28902; or call (704) 837-2775.

Events

Fall Festival. Held during the first weekend in October, this celebration offers demonstrations of mountain skills, folk dancing, live music, arts and crafts, and barbecue. For details contact the John C. Campbell Folk School.

BREVARD. This small town was incorporated in 1867 with seven residents, all of whom held public office. Now there are considerably more people, and Brevard consistently shows up on various lists of "Best Places to Live in the U.S." It is a popular retirement community.

Cradle of Forestry. When George Vanderbilt bought the land that made up Biltmore, he wanted his estate run right. A German forester, Dr. Carl A. Schenck, became manager of the Biltmore lands. In 1895 Schenck opened a school devoted to the new science of forestry.

The school closed in 1913, but visitors can now view
the reconstructed campus, which consists of a class-
room, a ranger's dwelling, and a lodge in the style of
the Black Forest. Located about three miles south of
the Blue Ridge Parkway on U.S. 276, it is open daily
from 9:00 to 5:00. No admission is charged.

Pisgah Forest National Fish Hatchery. This is one of the
largest trout hatcheries in the East. It is open daily
from 8:00 to 5:00 and is located on the Davidson River
Road off U.S. 276. No admission is charged.

Sliding Rock. Manufactured "waterslides" have become a staple in tourist-oriented sections of this region.
Here is a natural one. Sliding Rock is a 60-foot-long
smooth rock over which pours a cascade of bone-chilling water. Located on Looking Glass Falls Creek north
of Looking Glass Falls on U.S. 276. A bath house is
available. The slide is open from Memorial Day to Labor Day, and no admission is charged.

Waterfalls. Brevard is along North Carolina's waterfall
line, which follows U.S. 64 across the western part of
the state. Head south on U.S. 276 for one mile and look
for a parking lot for 100-foot-high **Maiden Hair Falls.**
They are privately owned. Five miles farther down the
road are the twin **Connestee Falls,** which are 110 feet
high. These are privately owned, and a fee is charged.

Eight miles north of Brevard on U.S. 276 is **Looking
Glass Falls,** which are 85 feet high. You can see these
for free.

Events

Brevard Music Center. Every summer two to three
hundred young people come to Brevard for the Transylvania Music Camp. They make up an orchestra that
performs at the Brevard Music Center, a lovely site with
a redwood and stone auditorium. Big-name performers
and conductors join these young musicians, and the
combination attracts music lovers for daily concerts
over a two-month period.

1984 saw appearances by such luminaries as Eugenia Zukerman, flutist, and William Brown, tenor, and the music ranged from opera to pops. Write for details to the Music Center, P.O. Box 592, Brevard 28712. Call (704) 884-2019 for ticket information.

Lodging and Dining

Colonial Inn. Bed-and-breakfast accommodations are featured at this turn-of-the-century inn that once hosted a reunion of Stonewall Jackson's troops. The building is listed on the National Register of Historic Places. Write to the inn at 410 East Main Street, Brevard 28712; or call (704) 884-2105.

Mountain Key Lodge. Located east of Brevard on old U.S. 64, this bed-and-breakfast lodge is in the Charles Patton House, which was constructed between 1860 and 1867 out of materials from the mountain behind it. The lodge offers six guest rooms, a tennis court, a pond, and a croquet court. Write 15 Seven Springs Road, Pisgah Forest 28768. Call (704) 884-7400.

The Womble Inn. Situated at 301 West Main Street, two blocks from downtown Brevard and one-half mile from the Music Center, the Womble Inn offers seven guest rooms furnished in eighteenth- and nineteenth-century antiques. Write to the Inn at Box 1441, Brevard 28712; or call (704) 884-4770.

BRYSON CITY. Of the various towns forming the doughnut of commerce around the Great Smoky Mountains National Park, Bryson City is the least visited. This fact is a source of consternation to the Chamber of Commerce, but a source of delight for visitors. The traffic jams of Cherokee and Gatlinburg are absent here.

High Country Outfitters. Specializing in raft rides on the Nantahala and Ocoee Rivers, this group also rents canoes and kayaks. Write them at P.O. Drawer J, Bryson City 28713. Call (704) 488-3153.

Nantahala Outdoor Center. This is one of the larger out-fitters in the area, offering rafting trips on the Nantahala, French Broad, Nolichucky, Ocoee, and Chattooga Rivers. They also rent rafts, canoes, and kayaks to those who want to go it alone. Write the center at U.S. 19W, Box 41, Bryson City 28713; or call (704) 488-9221.

Nantahala Rafts. This outfit leads raft rides on the Nantahala and Ocoee Rivers, wild hog and bear hunts, fishing expeditions, wilderness photo seminars, and ruby mining trips. Write U.S. 19W, Box 45, Bryson City 28713. Call (704) 488-2325.

Rolling Thunder River Company. Rafting trips on the Nantahala, Chattooga, Ocoee, French Broad, and Nolichucky rivers are offered by this firm. Write P.O. Box 88, Almond 28702. Call (704) 488-2030.

Lodging and Dining

Fryemont Inn. This inn was built under the direction of Amos Frye, a nineteenth-century timber baron, and the construction utilized local materials and craftsmen. The inn is made of chestnut, oak, and maple, the furniture of local cherry and black walnut. The chimneys could "draw a cat right out of the room." The inn, which has 37 rooms with private baths, is located above Bryson City. The dining room serves breakfast and dinner and is open to the public. Write P.O. Box 459, Bryson City 28713. Call (704) 488-2159.

Randolph House. Located in the middle of Bryson City, this is a two-story white house with 15 gables. The six guest rooms are furnished with antiques, and the dining room, open to the public by reservation, serves breakfast and dinner. Write the inn at Bryson City 28713. Call (704) 488-3472.

Hemlock Inn. Located on a 65-acre tract, this inn is open May through November and features 25 rooms furnished with country antiques. Breakfast and dinner are served family-style on tables with built-in Lazy Susans. The dining room is open to the public as space allows. Write the inn at Bryson City 28713. Call (704) 488-2885.

CASHIERS. Locals say the name of this town as if it were spelled *cashers*—a particularly apt pronunciation, for the chief activity at the crossroad is cashing in on high-rolling tourists who pass through.

Lodging and Dining

Cornucopia. The building once held the Cashiers Post Office, but now features lunch and dinner. Located on North Carolina 107 south of Cashiers.

High Hampton Inn. This is perhaps the only place in the southern Appalachians where a vacationer could easily fill a couple of weeks without stepping off the property. It was once the summer home of Confederate general Wade Hampton, who moved here after the war and stayed until his death in 1902.

The grounds total twenty-three hundred acres, and on them one can enjoy golf, tennis, horseback riding, fishing, sailing, canoeing, swimming, trap and skeet shooting, and hiking. The inn offers special programs for children. Guests stay either in the general's former house or in rustic cabins. The house is covered with chestnut bark, and has a commanding view of a lake backed by eastern America's highest sheer precipice— Whiteside Mountain.

The inn is not for everyone, as its own literature points out. For some people things are a bit too rustic here; however, several families return year after year. The inn is open from April 1 through November 1. Write to High Hampton, 22 Hampton Road, Cashiers 28717; or call (704) 743-2411.

Yesterday's Ltd. This restaurant is located in a renovated house that also contains a flower shop. It is on North Carolina 107 near the Cashiers crossroad. Call (704) 743-3101.

CHEROKEE. The largest Indian reservation east of Wisconsin focuses on Cherokee, which is the center of both government and tourism for the Eastern Band of the Cherokees. This group is all that is left of the thousands of Cherokees who populated North Carolina before the coming of the whites. Most of them were rounded up by the army in 1838 and forced to march to a reservation in Oklahoma, an event they still call the "Trail of Tears."

During the roundup about a thousand Indians escaped the efforts of Gen. Winfield Scott and his troops, and they hid out in the Smoky Mountains. Accounts of what happened next differ. In the Indian version of events, one brutal soldier was killed by Tsali and his kinsmen. The Army's account had Tsali and his kin attacking and killing two soldiers and wounding another. However it happened, this was the only act of bloodshed in the entire removal. General Scott was eager to get his distasteful business over with, so he agreed that the escapees could stay in North Carolina if Tsali, his brother, and three sons would come forward for punishment. They did, and were executed; their last request was that it be done by their own tribesmen.

The army departed, and this eastern band of Cherokees were left. They were penniless and did not own one acre of the land that had once belonged to them. Through the efforts of William Thomas, a trader and self-educated attorney who spoke the Cherokee language, the Indians received their portion of the money paid to the entire tribe for their land. With this they bought some fifty-seven thousand acres and began to rebuild their communities on it. They call this land the Qualla Reservation. Legally the Cherokees were put into an unusual situation; they were neither U.S. citizens nor citizens of North Carolina, and they could not own land individually. This seeming burden was to become a modern-day advantage.

Today Cherokee is a curious place. It is the center of Cherokee culture, a place where the old ways are perpetuated in classes and demonstrations, and yet it is a place of unbridled tourism. The town of Cherokee sits astride the entrance to the Great Smoky Mountains National Park, and all manner of rubber tomahawks, feathered headdresses, and other East Asian frippery is sold by the carload. Men wearing long headdresses—which their ancestors never wore—stand beside brightly painted teepees—which their ancestors never used—and invite tourists to pose with them for photographs. For a fee. Whether the causes of this center on the Indians or the tourists is a question for anthropologists.

If one can ignore the more blatantly tourist aspects of Cherokee, there are several places where the genuine culture of the Indians is displayed, and displayed well. Here is a sample of Cherokee's cultural, and sometimes capitalistic, offerings:

Cherokee Bingo. The peculiar legal status of Indians permits this high-stakes bingo game, which features five-figure cash jackpots. Located two miles north of Cherokee on U.S. 19, it is open year-round, and has room for twenty-five hundred players. Games are held twice a month. Call (800) 368-2464.

Cherokee Botanical Gardens. This quiet garden features properly identified wildflowers, bushes, and trees. Located next to the Oconoluftee Indian Village, it is open mid-May through mid-October. No admission is charged.

Cyclorama Wax Museum. One brochure said it best: "See the vast empire of the Cherokee Nation fade away on large scaled electronic maps." Over 75 life-sized wax figures make history stand still. Located on U.S. 19 north of Cherokee, the museum is open daily from April through October, and in the evenings from June through Labor Day. Admission is charged.

Magic Waters Park. A display of waterskiing prowess is the center of this park, and visitors can also watch high-divers and trained lions. For those who wish to get in on the act, there are two waterslides, an inner-tube ride, paddle boats, bumper boats, and several carnival rides. Magic Waters Park is open daily from June through Labor Day.

Medicine Man Craft Shop. Located on U.S. 441 across from the Cherokee Ceremonial Grounds, this is one of the better sources of authentic Cherokee crafted goods.

Mingo Falls. So far unadorned with wax figures, water slides, or plastic spears, this waterfall is on the Big Cove Road on the Qualla Reservation. There is a 15-minute walk from the parking lot to the falls. Open all year. No admission is charged.

Museum of the Cherokee Indian. This first-class museum is a must. Many small towns have displays of Indian artifacts, but this museum assembles them especially well and does an excellent job of explaining how they were used. A worthwhile feature of the place is an opportunity to hear the Cherokee language on special "hear phones." The museum is located on U.S. 441 at Drama Road. From mid-June through August it is open Monday through Saturday from 9:00 to 8:00 and on Sunday from 9:00 to 5:30. The rest of the year it is open daily from 9:00 to 5:30. Admission is charged. Call (704) 497-3481.

Museum of the American Indian. Exhibits on various Indian tribes make up this museum. Located on Main Street in downtown Cherokee, it is open from June through October. No admission is charged. Call (704) 497-2330.

Oconoluftee Indian Village. The Cherokee way of life in the eighteenth century is displayed in this re-creation of an Indian village. More than a museum, the village contains guides and craftspeople who demonstrate their work and answer questions. Visitors are encouraged to wander around and examine the buildings as well as the displays. This is a very good place for children who have seen too many rubber tomahawks. The village is open from mid-May through mid-October daily from 9:00 to 5:30. Admission is charged. Call (704) 497-2315.

Qualla Arts and Crafts Mutual. This organization is responsible for maintaining the old-time crafts of the Cherokee Indians. It is the best place on the reservation to buy baskets, beadwork, weavings, and pottery. Located beside the Museum of the Cherokee Indian, it is open all year. From mid-June through August hours are Monday through Saturday from 9:00 to 8:00 and on Sunday from 9:00 to 5:30. The rest of the year the shop is open daily from 9:00 to 5:30. Call (704) 497-3103.

Santa's Land. This theme park centers on Christmas, and includes carnival rides, a 125-year-old cabin, a grist mill, a moonshine still, a broom maker's shop, and the obligatory train on the circular track. Located on U.S. 19 on the Qualla Reservation, it is open daily May through October. Admission is charged.

Unto These Hills. The story of the "Trail of Tears" and the Indian version of events leading up to Tsali's death are vividly depicted in this outdoor drama. It was written by Kermit Hunter, who also wrote "Horn In The West," the outdoor drama in Boone. With a cast of 130, the show has been playing since 1950. It is presented in the evening from mid-June through August. It gets quite cool, and a jacket or sweater is advised. For reserved seats write P.O. Box 398, Cherokee 28719; or call (704) 497-2111. General admission tickets are also sold.

Events

Cherokee Indian Fall Festival. Held in early October at the Cherokee Ceremonial Grounds, this festival includes ceremonial dancing, blowgun demonstrations, archery, and beauty contests. The grounds are beside the tribal office on U.S. 441. For details write to Cherokee Tribal Travel and Promotion, P.O. Box 465, Cherokee 28719. Call (800) 438-1601.

Indian Stickball Games. Lacrosse is the gentle derivative of this rough-and-tumble sport, which in old times was used to settle disputes between villages. "When you see the game you'll know why," commented one observer of the event. Held in late October at the Cherokee Ceremonial Grounds.

Intertribal Traditional Dances. Various Indian tribes from all over the United States come for these dance competitions and demonstrations. Held in mid-August at the Cherokee Ceremonial Grounds.

CULLOWHEE. Perhaps anticipating nouvelle cuisine, this town takes its name from the Cherokee word for "place of the spring salad." It is most famous for Western Carolina University, an institution that began as a teachers' college in 1889. The university houses the largest library in southwestern North Carolina.

Jataculla Rock. This big boulder is covered with Indian carvings for which there is no agreed-upon interpretation. It is located in a field near East LaPorte, which is south of Cullowhee on North Carolina 107. Follow the signs on State Road 1737. No admission is charged.

Mountain Heritage Center. This small museum and library is dedicated to the preservation of mountain culture. It offers changing exhibits, programs, and slide shows. Located on the campus of Western Carolina University, it is open Monday through Friday from 8:00 to 4:00. No admission is charged.

Western Carolina University. This is the cultural center of the area. Here visitors can attend concerts, plays, and lectures throughout the year. Call (704) 227-7211 for information.

DILLSBORO. This town came about when a railroad tunnel was dug nearby. While workers bored and blasted out the tunnel, W.A. Dills set up Dillsboro. He also built and operated the Jarrett House hotel.

Riverwood Craft Shop. Across the Tuckasegee River from the Jarrett House is a collection of crafts shops and gift shops known collectively as Riverwood Shops. At least two are members of the Southern Highland Handicraft

Guild, which means the things travelers buy there have not been put together by hillbillies in Hong Kong.

The Old School. Just as its name suggests, this is an old schoolhouse. It contains antique, curio, and handicrafts shops. It is located on U.S. 441 four miles south of Dillsboro.

Lodging and Dining

Jarrett House. Whether you come to eat or to stay, the Jarrett House offers simple, down-home hospitality. The inn is famous for its Southern cooking; it features country ham and mountain trout. Guests can stagger out after a heavy dinner to sit in rocking chairs on one of the inn's three porches. The 22-room inn is closed for three months in the winter. It is located in downtown Dillsboro. Write the Jarrett House at Box 219, Dillsboro 28725; or call (704) 586-9964.

Squire Watkins Inn. This relatively new bed-and-breakfast inn is located in a restored Victorian house. Cottages are also available. Write the inn at Dillsboro 28725; or call (704) 586-5244.

FLAT ROCK. This is one of the more attractive towns in North Carolina, and has been so since 1827. Beginning in that year wealthy planters from Charleston and the surrounding area, seeking relief from the heat and the humidity of the South Carolina summer, made a two-week trip by carriage to Flat Rock. They brought their slaves, money, and sense of style with them, and all three worked to shape this town.

The summer season in old Flat Rock lasted from mid-May through October, and was characterized by balls, picnics, and carriage rides through the mountains. Most of these activities were halted by the Civil War, when many of the families who owned property in Flat Rock were impoverished.

Flat Rock still had appeal, however, and the pilgrimages continued, though on a less lavish scale. Today the town remains a quiet center of taste in a region that has often been too quick to demonstrate a lack of it. Students of architecture will appreciate the Flat Rock Historic District, which is listed on the National Register of Historic Places. Prime examples of Second Empire, Greek revival, and Gothic revival architecture can be seen.

Carl Sandburg Home National Historic Site. This stately white house was once the home of Christopher Gustavus Memminger, who was the secretary of the treasury for the Confederacy. The house is more famous, however, as the home of Carl Sandburg, poet and biographer of Abraham Lincoln.

Sandburg moved here in 1945 with his wife Paula Steichen, who was the sister of the American photographer Edward Steichen. Their arrangement was simple: he did the writing and she ran the farm. During their 22 years there he produced *Remembrance Rock*, his only novel, while she produced prize-winning goats.

The house is one of the best preserved writers' homes in America. Sandburg's study looks as if he just stepped out, and visitors can see his bedroom and the rest of the house much as the Sandburgs left it. It is located near the Flat Rock Playhouse off U.S. 25. Follow the signs. No admission is charged.

Flat Rock Playhouse. Sitting on the original flat rock, this playhouse has been designated the State Theater of North Carolina. With professional actors and actresses, it produces drama and musicals that are well worth a long drive to see. The season runs from July to September. Located on U.S. 25 in Flat Rock. For a schedule write the playhouse at Flat Rock 28731; or call (704) 692-2281.

Saint John in the Wilderness Church. This was the first Episcopal church in Western North Carolina. It was built in 1834 as the private chapel of a wealthy Charleston family. Later it was opened to the community, but it is said that the lady of the family who built it would not allow anyone to enter the church on Sunday mornings before her carriage arrived. She was preceded into the church by a maid carrying her prayer book and a large turkey fan on a velvet cushion. Only after she was seated could the rest of the parishioners enter. The church is located near the Flat Rock Playhouse, and is open most of the time.

Events

Historic Flat Rock Tours of Homes. The first Friday in August lends an opportunity to see the inside of some of the historic homes in Flat Rock. Write Historic Flat Rock, Box 295, Flat Rock 28731.

Lodging and Dining

Woodfields Inn. This charming inn is the place to stay in Flat Rock. Built in 1850, it is the oldest continually operated inn in North Carolina. It was a center of the antebellum society; when Yankee raiders threatened the community during the Civil War, the local people brought their valuables here. After the war the inn continued to offer hospitality to travelers.

The inn has 22 guest rooms, plus a secret room that the proprietors can sometimes be talked into showing. It is located off U.S. 25 and open all year. Write to the Woodfields Inn, Flat Rock 28731; or call (704) 693-6016.

FONTANA. At 480 feet, Fontana Dam is the highest dam in the eastern United States. It backs up the Little Tennessee River to form a lake covering ten thousand acres when full. It was built by the TVA during World War II to provide electricity for a Tennessee aluminum plant, and its construction led to the creation of Fontana Village, a group of small cabins for the workers on the project. Unlike Norris, Tennessee, a village built under similar circumstances and eventually sold cabin by cabin to individuals, Fontana Village was leased in one piece from the government and made a resort when the construction workers left.

Lodging and Dining

Fontana Village. Located in one of the more remote areas in the southern Appalachians, this resort consists of 250 cabins and a modern hotel. Outdoor activities, including tennis, horseback riding, golf, hiking, fishing, and boating, are stressed at the village. Twice a year the resort is taken over by Western square dancers. Write Fontana Village at Fontana Dam 28733; or call (704) 498-2211.

FRANKLIN. This seat of Macon County rests on an old Cherokee settlement. It also sits over some of the more unusual geological deposits in the United States. Tiffany's once owned an emerald mine in the area, and now rockhounds from novice to expert flock here to see if they can find emeralds, garnets, rubies, sapphires, and amethyst specimens. Almost all of the mines are located in the Cowee Valley off North Carolina 28 north of Franklin.

The proprietors of the mines usually provide the prospector with a bucket of mud alleged to contain wondrous stones. Gemstones are quite often found, and occasionally someone finds one that is indeed valuable. Seekers of fortune, however, should remember the example of Hernando De Soto, a tourist who passed through the area in 1540. He was also looking for riches from the earth, but went away empty-handed. Washing your bucketful of mud can be exciting—particularly for children—but if you really want to take home a gemstone, probably the best bet is to visit one of the many rock shops in the area.

Gem and Mineral Museum. This museum is in a 150-year-old jail on Phillips Street downtown. No admission is charged, and the museum is open from Monday through Saturday from 10:00 to 4:00.

Bulgin Forge. Blacksmiths at this small shop in downtown Franklin make pokers, shovels, and other fireplace accessories. The forge has been run by the same family for over seventy-five years. Located at 319 West Main Street.

Wayah Bald. Although not in Franklin, this place is worth a side trip. It is a 5,335-foot-high bald—a mountaintop devoid of trees—that is famous for its wildflowers and azaleas. There is a stone observation tower from which to view the flora. The best time to go is in May or June, when the flowers are in bloom. Take U.S. 64 west from Franklin; turn right on North Carolina 1310; then go right on Forest Service Road 69.

Lodging and Dining

Poor Richard's Summit Inn. On the highest hill in Franklin sits this 14-bedroom inn, which contains one of the finer restaurants in Franklin. The rooms are furnished in antiques, and there are no televisions. Dinners are served family-style on tables lit by kerosene lamps. Main dishes include lobster, steak, trout, and baked chicken. The soup and bread are homemade. The inn is open year-round, although in the winter months the dining room is open only on weekends. Write the inn at P.O. Box 511, Franklin 28734; or call (704) 524-2006.

Events

Festival of Festivals. This is a sampler of the various festivals held throughout the western North Carolina area. At this event visitors will find bagpiping, gospel singing, German Bavarian music, bluegrass music, folk dancing (including clogging), a pig barbecue, and displays of mountain crafts. Held in late June. For details write the Franklin Area Chamber of Commerce, 180 Porter Street, Franklin 28734; or call (704) 524-3161.

Macon County Fair. This display of agricultural products, ranging from cattle to jars of homemade jelly, is held in mid-September.

Macon County Gemboree. Rockhounds unite! You have nothing to lose but your stones at this annual gathering. It is held in late July.

HAYESVILLE. This is the seat of Clay County, the least populated of all the North Carolina mountain counties. The Nantahala National Forest occupies 85 percent of the county, and 80 miles of the Appalachian Trail runs through it. This is a particularly good section of trail to hike; there are nowhere near as many other hikers as you will find further north in the national park.

Hayesville was one of the places where the Cherokee Indians were rounded up and put in concentration camps prior to their removal to Oklahoma on the infamous "Trail of Tears."

Clay County Historical and Arts Center. This locally run museum is housed in the former county jail in the middle of Hayesville. The museum is open Monday through Friday from 9:00 to 5:00 and on Saturday from 9:00 to 3:00. It is closed from Labor Day through Memorial Day. Call (704) 389-6814. No admission is charged.

Jackrabbit Mountain. This campground on the shores of Lake Chatuge offers swimming, hiking, boating, and fishing. Take U.S. 64 east out of Hayesville; turn right on North Carolina 175; and turn right again on North Carolina 1155.

Lake Chatuge. The "Crown Jewel of the TVA lakes," as it has been called, is located in Clay County. The dam is 144 feet high. Unlike other lakes in the mountains, this one has flat ground around it. Here you'll find boat-launching ramps, campgrounds, and picnic areas. Maps of this or any TVA lake are available by writing the TVA Map Sales Office, Hanley Building, Chattanooga, Tennessee 37401.

HENDERSONVILLE. The seat of Henderson County, Hendersonville is the principal town along the oldest route for tourists entering the mountains of North Carolina. Beginning in the 1830s, plantation owners and others who could afford to escape the heat of the lowlands came by carriage through this area. Today travelers still pass through on U.S. 25 or I-26. The approach from South Carolina is most spectacular, as the mountains appear to rise up all at once at the state line. The climate of Hendersonville is exceedingly pleasant, and the town is a popular place to retire. The downtown area has been transformed into a pedestrian-oriented plaza with a gazebo where occasional concerts are held.

Henderson County Farmer Curb Market. For over fifty years local farmers have brought their fresh vegetables, dairy products, baked and canned goods, and handcrafted goods to this colorful market. Located behind the courthouse at 221 North Church Street, it is open January through April on Tuesday and Saturday from 8:00 till 1:00. From May through December it is open Tuesday, Thursday, and Saturday from 7:00 until 1:00.

Heritage Square Mall. *Mall* is a bad word in this book, but this mall is worth visiting. It is housed in a renovated warehouse and contains a cheese and wine shop, a crafts shop, and a small cafe. Located on Church Street.

Holmes State Forest. Ten miles west of Hendersonville is a small state park whose purpose is to explain forestry. The park includes three types of land—bottomland, hillsides, and a mountaintop. The proper use of a forest is explained through a visitors' center with exhibits and two trails: the half-mile **Forest Walk** provides recorded talks at intervals along the trail, and the two-mile **Forest Demonstration Trail** takes the hiker through different types of forest to the top of a mountain. Here the visitors can see an Eastern deciduous forest as well as one dominated by conifers.

To get to the park take Route 1127 from Hendersonville. No camping is allowed, but picnicking facilities are provided. Write Holmes State Forest, Route 4, Box 308, Hendersonville 28739. Call (704) 692-0100.

Jump Off Rock. This promontory overlooking Hendersonville is the subject of another of those Indian legends that involve lost love and someone jumping off a high place. Thirty-five hundred feet in elevation, the rock can be reached by following Fifth Avenue from town to the Laurel Park Highway. Follow the signs. Admission is charged.

The Mother Earth News Eco-Village. *Mother Earth News*, a journal of self-sufficiency, natural foods, and other delights of the alternative lifestyle, is headquartered in Hendersonville. The Eco-Village is where the staff practices what it preaches. Described as an educational vacation spot, it is worth a trip or an extended stay.

The visitor to the 622-acre village will find demonstrations of low-cost, do-it-yourself projects in such areas as food preservation, hydroelectric systems, and beekeeping, to name a few. Visitors can camp on the grounds. Those who are just passing through may observe various demonstrations, visit the Environmental Hall of Fame, and peruse books at the Eco-Village bookstore. A relatively steep admission is charged. For further information write the village at P.O. Box 70, Hendersonville 28791. Call (704) 693-0211.

Thomas Wolfe's Angel. Early in this century the grave of a minister's wife was marked by a carved stone angel from the Asheville shop of W. O. Wolfe. It has been identified as the angel in the title of his son Thomas's first book—*Look Homeward, Angel*.

For a long time the same cemetery contained a bizarre grave. Mrs. Charles B. Hansell, a tubercular patient, died and left a request that she be buried where the sun could always shine on her. A system of lenses was set up, and they did indeed cause the sun to shine on her remains. Unfortunately, they also drew the morbid and the curious, who peered down on her skeleton. In 1939 cemetery officials decided they had had enough of this, and covered the lenses. Oakdale Cemetery is located on Sixth Avenue in Hendersonville.

Events

Apple Festival. This takes place every year two weeks before Labor Day. It includes a parade, various forms of entertainment, and sporting events. You can taste virtually every possible food that can be made from apples. For details on the Apple Festival and other Hendersonville events write the Hendersonville Chamber of Commerce, 330 North King Street, Hendersonville 28793. Call (404) 692-1413.

Street Dancing. Live country music is provided and a street is roped off every other Monday from July through Labor Day.

Miscellaneous Festivals. Hendersonville likes having a good time. The town holds several festivals during the year, including a Fourth of July celebration, an antique fair in July, and, in August, the Western North Carolina Fair and the Arts and Crafts Fair. September brings the Carolina Mountain Folk Dance Jamboree.

Lodging and Dining

Echo Mountain Inn. This seasonal inn offers modern furniture and old-fashioned hospitality. It is situated at a three-thousand-foot elevation with nice views of the surrounding mountains. It has a swimming pool. Write to the inn at 2849 Laurel Park Hwy, Hendersonville 28793; or call (704) 693-9626.

Fo-Fo-Th-Bo, Ltd. An unusual name for an unusual place. This vegetarian restaurant offers a sometimes welcome change from the heavy Southern fare served at most places. No fried chicken here! The cuisine runs to Middle East and southern European tastes. Located at 330 North Main Street in Hendersonville. Offers lunch and dinner from Tuesday through Saturday, and brunch on Sunday. Closed in January and February.

Rubin's Osceola Lake Inn. This resort offers a touch of the Catskills in North Carolina. Its dining room, which is open to the public, is one of the few places in the region serving cheese blintzes, gefilte fish, and chicken soup, which is superb. Guests can enjoy tennis courts, a swimming pool, a golf driving cage, a putting green, rowboats, an indoor hot tub, and the all-important activities director. Open from May 1 to November 1.

Write to the inn at Hendersonville 28739; or call (704) 692-2544. In the wintertime write to 250 Palm Avenue, Palm Island, Miami Beach, Florida 33139; or call (305) 534-8356.

HIGHLANDS. At 3,835 feet, Highlands is North Carolina's second highest town. It was originally planned by two Kansas natives as a resort community. The tale goes that a line was drawn on a map from Baltimore to New Orleans, and another from Chicago to Savannah. Highlands was the point of intersection.

The Highlands area is the wettest in the eastern United States—it gets 80 inches of precipitation in an average year—and the plant life, from trees to lichens, is splendid. When the French botanist André Michaux came through in 1788 he located the shortia, a plant whose only other known habitat is Japan. Asa Gray rediscovered the plant a hundred years later, and botanists are still coming to do research in Highlands.

Most people, however, come to relax. Highlands has a fine collection of houses belonging to summer people and retirees. Tastes here are refined; the small grocery store carries caviar as well as bacon and eggs. Travelers delight in the lake at the west end of town and the waterfalls along U.S. 64 from Highlands to Franklin. For a more complete description of the waterfalls, see NANTAHALA NATIONAL FOREST.

Highlands Biological Station. Founded in 1927, this 16-acre research center is now overseen by the University of North Carolina. Its grounds are well kept, and inside is the **Highlands Nature Center**, a small museum of native flora and fauna. Included are North Carolina minerals, Cherokee Indian artifacts, and the cross section of a 425-year-old hemlock tree. The Biological Station is located on Horse Cove Street in Highlands and is open from late May through Labor Day, Monday through Friday from 10:00 to 5:00 and on Sunday from 1:00 to 5:00. No admission is charged.

Highlands Playhouse. This theater has been in operation since 1932. Every summer professional thespians perform dramas and musicals. Phone (704) 526-2695 for information and tickets.

Highlands Studio for the Arts. For theater with a lighter touch, this is the place to go. Improvisational acting and one-act plays are the specialties, and are offered from July through September. Performances are given Tuesday, Thursday, and Friday nights. For information call (704) 526-9482.

Sunset Rock. A road from downtown Highlands leads up to Ravenal Park, on a mountaintop from which one can see a panorama of peaks as well as some of the summer houses that grace Highlands. Open from daylight until dusk. No admission is charged.

The Stone Lantern. Highlands has several fine shops, but this is the most unusual. A small North Carolina town is not where you would expect to find a shop devoted to Oriental art, but The Stone Lantern is just that. Out back is an authentic Japanese garden. Located on U.S. 64 in Highlands. Call (704) 526-2769.

Events

Chamber Music Festival. This one-month festival, held in July, offers chamber music concerts in the Episcopal Church on Tuesday nights and Sunday afternoons. Details are available from the Highlands Chamber of Commerce, Highlands 28741. Call (704) 525-2112.

Helen's Barn. On Friday and Saturday nights in the summer the locals gather at this 50-year-old barn for a hoedown. Cloggers and square dancers raise the dust to live music, and food and drinks are available. Helen's Barn is on West Main Street. For information call (704) 526-2790.

High Country Arts and Crafts Fair. Eighty or more craftspeople gather in early June at Mountain Hillbilly Crafts, which is seven miles south of Highlands on North

Carolina 106. Write or call the Chamber of Commerce for details.

Japanese Flower and Art Festival. This week-long festival in July includes seminars on Japanese flower arranging and displays of art and rugs. Details are available from the Stone Lantern; call (704) 526-2769.

Lodging and Dining

Highlands Inn. Built in 1881, this is the prime place to eat and stay in Highlands. It has 46 guest rooms and five places to eat. The Dining Room is the most formal, with traditional Southern dishes served with crystal and fine china. Shan's Tea room offers a proper British tea, while the Porch overlooking Main Street is the place to see and to be seen. The Roof Garden offers lunches, and the Showroom features live entertainment along with seafood and steaks. The inn is open from May through October, and all the dining rooms are open to the public. Write to the Highlands Inn, P.O. Box 1030, Highlands 28741; or call (704) 526-9380.

On the Veranda. Sequoyah Lake is on the west end of Highlands, and overlooking the lake is this restaurant, which features American food "with a French touch." It is open all year and contains an art gallery. Call (704) 526-2338.

Skyline Lodge and Restaurant. Frank Lloyd Wright and Associates designed a casino for this site in the 1920s, and in the 1930s construction was begun. The Depression intervened, and the building, with some modifications, was completed in the sixties as a lodge. Located four miles east of Highlands, it sits on 55 acres. The grounds include a lake and a 30-foot waterfall as well as tennis courts and a swimming pool.

The rooms are modern, with televisions, telephones, and, in some cases, king-sized beds. The lodge serves breakfast only, to the public as well as overnight guests. The lodge is open from May through

October. Write P.O. Box 630, Highlands 28741. Call (704) 526-2121.

MURPHY. This is the westernmost town in North Carolina. General Winfield Scott had his headquarters at nearby Fort Butler as he supervised the roundup of the Cherokee Indians prior to their march west. Murphy was also the site of the last battle of the Civil War east of the Mississippi. It seems that a group of men had deserted the Confederate army and had formed a company of Federal troops. Most of them had legal cases pending against them, and all the papers were in the Cherokee County courthouse in Murphy. So they burned down the courthouse. The last battle, which took place on May 6, 1865, consisted of about a hundred Confederate troops routing this band of arsonists.

Indeed, Cherokee County has had a hard time keeping courthouses. Five have been built since 1844. The present one, built in 1927, was constructed to be as fireproof as possible. So far it is still standing.

Appalachia Lake and Dam. This is one of the smallest lakes in the TVA system, and it is unusual in that electricity is not produced at the dam itself. Instead the water is transported via an eight-mile long tunnel to a powerhouse downstream. The powerhouse is on the Hiwassee River, and to get to it you have to go into Tennessee along Tennessee 68. Maps of this or any TVA lake are available by writing the TVA Map Sales Office, Hanley Building, Chattanooga, Tennessee 37401.

Carolina Mountain Arts and Crafts Cooperative. Located eight miles west of Murphy on U.S. 64, this cooperative conducts workshops and demonstrations and sells the products of local craftspeople. Here you can find pottery, quilts, carvings, and various works of art. Call (704) 389-6661.

Cherokee County Museum. This museum contains a collection of Indian pottery, baskets, beadwork, and artifacts from various mounds and tombs in the area, as well as artifacts of the 1540 De Soto expedition. The collection also includes early pioneer paraphernalia and locally mined gemstones. It is open Monday through Friday from 9:00 to 5:00 and Saturday from 9:00 to 1:00. No admission is charged.

Episcopal Church of the Messiah. The stained glass windows in this 1896 church were built by Tiffany's of New York. The wood inside has an unusual herringbone pattern. The church is located across from the courthouse in Murphy, and is generally open from 9:00 to 5:00.

Hiwassee Dam and Lake. This 307-foot-high TVA dam and 22-mile-long lake are on the Hiwassee River. This is the highest overspill dam in the United States. Fishing and boating are permitted.

Fields of the Wood. This is one of those things that future civilizations will ponder over. Sponsored by the Church of Prophecy Marker Association, it consists of the world's largest cross (150 feet tall and 115 feet wide), the world's largest representation of the Ten Commandments on their tablets (300 feet square, with letters five feet high), a replica of the tomb in which Jesus was laid, and a likeness of the New Testament (34 feet wide and 24 feet tall). Visitors are invited to stand on top of the New Testament to take pictures. In addition there are a baptismal pool, an electric star of Bethlehem, and a lounge and gift shop.

This unusual collection of religious monuments is located in a remote section of Cherokee County. To get there take North Carolina 294 north from U.S. 64 and drive for about 15 miles. Fields of the Wood is open every day from sunup to sundown, and no admission is charged. It is billed as one of the Biblical Wonders of the Twentieth Century, which it undoubtedly is.

Walker Inn. This structure was built in 1840 and added onto in 1864. Now in private hands, the inn no longer takes in guests, but travelers can see it on Junaluska Road in the town of Andrews. Take U.S. 19/129 northeast from Murphy to Andrews. Walker Inn is shown by appointment April through October from 10:00 to 5:00.

Call (704) 321-4439. No admission is charged, although donations are encouraged.

Events

Streets Crafts Show. This is held every year on the Murphy Town Common the second weekend in May. Seventy-five craftspeople participate. Write the Cherokee County Chamber of Commerce at 104 Valley River Avenue, Murphy 28906; or call (704) 837-2242.

NANTAHALA NATIONAL FOREST. Visitors often confuse the purposes of a national park and a national forest, and are horrified when they see activities such as logging, hunting, and private building going on in the latter. Whereas a national park is set aside for preservation and recreation, a national forest encompasses recreation, forestry, hunting, and various other uses of the land. National forests are often bigger than national parks, and islands of private land may exist within them.

Perhaps due to a lack of publicity, many travelers in search of natural beauty zoom through national forests on their way to national parks like the Great Smokies. In the parks they sometimes find clogged roads, crowded campgrounds and picnic areas, and just too many people. Many national forests offer the same wild beauty as the parks, hiking trails and campsites but with a lot less competition.

Such is the case with the Nantahala National Forest, which at 515 thousand acres is almost as large as the better-known Great Smoky Mountains National Park. Nantahala offers many more camping areas than the national park, and it includes the most rugged section of the entire Appalachian Trail—80 miles of it in all. Here also is the Joyce Kilmer Memorial Forest, an awe-inspiring thirty-eight-hundred-acre tract of virgin forest with trees that tower over a hundred feet high. Above the town of Sapphire you will find Whitewater Falls, where a river drops 411 vertical feet in a horizontal distance of five hundred feet. The national park has nothing like that.

There is a catch, though. Since it is far from the madding crowd, the Nantahala National Forest has few tourist towns—and this means few restaurants, shops, and other amenities for travelers. The campgrounds are simple; there are occasional pit toilets, no showers, and no electrical hookups for recreational vehicles. If you like roughing it this is fine, but those who fancy large camping trailers or motor homes may be less than happy with the situation.

Waterfalls

If you do nothing else in the Nantahala National Forest, visit the waterfalls. They are a delight for all ages, especially after several hours of riding in a car. Be careful, though, for every year needless accidents happen at the falls because of the slippery rocks and long drops.

The town of Highlands is the center of the waterfall country. From west to east, here are the falls: From Franklin to Highlands U.S. 64 follows the Cullasaja River, which has several sets of waterfalls. The first is **Lower Cullasaja Falls**, which is more of a cascade—the river falls over three hundred feet in a quarter mile. Next is **Dry Falls**, so named because visitors can walk behind the torrent of water and look out, never getting wet. Then comes **Bridal Veil Falls**, which splash down 120 feet, partly onto the road. You can get a free car wash here.

Once you get to Highlands, you can take North Carolina 106 south for two miles to the **Glen Falls Scenic Area**, where the water falls 50 feet. Or you can continue east on U.S. 64 until you come to Cashiers. Continue east and turn right on State Road 1149. From here it is ten miles to **Whitewater Falls Scenic Area**. Along the way you can see four other falls: **Horsepasture**, **John's Jump**, **Thompson's**, and **Rainbow Falls**.

Although you are now getting into the Pisgah National Forest, there are more waterfalls to come. U.S. 64 crosses the Toxaway River over **Toxaway Falls**, which are 123 feet high. See BREVARD for more falling water.

Ranger Districts

As a whole, the Nantahala National Forest is administered from an office in Asheville, but there are four separate districts within the forest. All of the districts contain camping and picnic facilities, and by writing to the respective offices or the central one you can get maps and further information. The headquarters of the Nantahala National Forest can be reached by writing Forest Supervisor, National Forests in North Carolina, 50 South French Broad Avenue, Asheville 28802. Call (704) 258-2850. The four districts, their features, and their office addresses are listed here.

Cheoah Ranger District. Just south of the Great Smokies, this section contains the Joyce Kilmer Memorial Forest. No camping is permitted in the Kilmer area, but other campgrounds are close by. The headquarters is on U.S. 129 north of Robbinsville. Write District Ranger, U.S. Forest Service, Route 1, Box 16-A, Robbinsville 28771. Call (704) 479-6431.

Highlands Ranger District. This is the section with the waterfalls, and it is an excellent place for picnicking. It runs from the Sylva area to the southern border of the state. The headquarters is on U.S. 64 in Highlands. Write District Ranger, U.S. Forest Service, P.O. Box 749, Highlands 28741. Call (704) 526-2562.

Tusquitee Ranger District. Extending all the way to the western tip of North Carolina, this district includes small TVA lakes nestled in the mountains. It is a good place for fishing and camping. The office is on U.S. 19 south of Murphy. Write District Ranger, U.S. Forest Service, 201 Woodland Drive, Murphy 28906. Call (704) 837-5152.

Wayah Ranger District. Reaching from the Cowee Bald to the Georgia border, this district includes the Wayah Bald, a mountaintop covered with wild azaleas that bloom spectacularly in May and June. The headquarters is on U.S. 64 west of Franklin. Write District Ranger,

U.S. Forest Service, Route 2, Box 194-B, Franklin 28734. Call (704) 524-6441.

ROBBINSVILLE. This is the seat of Graham County. Sixty percent of the land in the county is in the Nantahala National Forest.

This area was the home of the Snowbird Indians, Cherokees who lived in the Snowbird Mountains. The greatest of these was Chief Junaluska, who commanded his warriors in an alliance with Gen. Andrew Jackson against the Creek Indians in the 1814 Battle of Horseshoe Bend. Tradition says Chief Junaluska saved Jackson's life in an attack by a Creek warrior. Had the chief known of Jackson's hatred for Indians—a hatred that would lead to the "Trail of Tears" in 1834—he might not have bothered.

Joyce Kilmer Memorial Forest. "I think that I shall never see a poem as lovely as a tree." Thus begins Kilmer's most famous rhyme, and visitors will likely never see more lovely trees than those in the virgin forest named for this young writer who died in World War I in France.

Despite its primeval appearance, most of the forest in western North Carolina has been logged at least once; virtually all the trees that visitors see are second growth. The Joyce Kilmer Memorial Forest is one of the few tracts of virgin timber left. Totaling 3,840 acres, this untouched area is a part of the Joyce Kilmer–Slickrock Wilderness. To get to the forest take U.S. 129 north of Robbinsville, turn left on State Road 1116, then turn left on Forest Service Road 416.

Nantahala Gorge. The Nantahala River flows parallel to U.S. 19 from Topton to Wesser, about ten miles from Robbinsville. The gorge varies from five hundred to fifteen hundred feet deep, and offers excellent opportunities for white-water canoeing and rafting. Along the road are several picnic areas and places with access to the rushing water. White-water trips are offered by:

Nantahala Outdoor Center
U.S. 19W, P.O. Box 41
Bryson City 28713
(704) 488-2175.

High Country Outfitters
P.O. Drawer J
Bryson City 28713
(704) 438-1507

Nantahala Rafts
P.O. Box 45
Bryson City 28713
(704) 488-3627

Rolling Thunder River
   Company
P.O. Box 8
Almond 28702
(704) 488-2030

Events

Great Smoky Mountains Heritage Festival. Held around
the Fourth of July, this annual festival offers square
dancing, cake walks, lumberjack contests, country and
gospel music, an Indian stickball game, and fireworks.
There are displays of locally crafted goods, homesteading methods, and mountain artifacts.

Lodging and Dining

Blue Boar Lodge. Perhaps expecting a more rustic-look-
ing structure, visitors sometimes drive past the Blue
Boar without realizing it is a lodge. Open only in the
summer, it features rooms with modern furniture—
king-sized beds are available—and family-style meals.
Write the lodge at Route 1, 46A, Robbinsville 28771;
or call (704) 479-8126.

Snowbird Mountain Lodge. High above Robbinsville in
the Snowbird Mountains, this is more what visitors
expect in a mountain inn. The lodge is built of chestnut
logs and native stone, and from its flagstone terrace
there is a good view of the Snowbird Range. Guest
rooms are paneled in native woods with furniture to
match. Swimming is available in a nearby pool fed by
a cold spring. There are accommodations for 44 people.
Write the Snowbird Lodge at Robbinsville 28771; or
call (704) 479-3433.

Thunderbird Mountain Resort. There's nothing rustic here. The rooms, all of which face Lake Santeetlah, have modern furnishings. A swimming pool and tennis courts are offered, and guests can rent boats at a nearby marina. The resort is north of Robbinsville off U.S. 129. Write Star Route T1, Robbinsville 28771; or call (704) 479-6442.

ROSMAN. According to local lore, this town was a stop for escaping slaves on the Underground Railroad.

Rosman Satellite Tracking Station. Because the mountainous environment is relatively free of electronic interference, the National Aeronautics and Space Administration built two dish-shaped antennas, 85 feet in diameter, near the town of Rosman. Now they are operated by a private firm, but are impressive nonetheless. Located off North Carolina 215 on State Road 1326.

SAPPHIRE. This town is named for the gemstone, which is found in the area.

Youngbloods of Sapphire. This firm, which sells mostly by mail order, specializes in jams and jellies. The usual apple and grape are provided, but the real eyebrow raisers are jars of onion, garlic, and red-pepper jelly. You can also buy pickled pumpkin balls and zucchini relish. There are 49 kinds of preserve in all, and most of them are prepared on the premises. Regulars like to pull up in the parking lot, take a sniff, and guess what's cooking. Located at the corner of U.S. 62 and North Carolina 281. For a catalog write P.O. Box 100, Sapphire 28774; or call (704) 966-4466.

Lodging and Dining

Fairfield Inn. This beautiful white inn looks out over Fairfield Lake and onto Bald Rock Mountain. Three stories high, it was built in 1896, but is now a part of a condominium resort. Sadly enough, guests can no longer stay in the inn, although the dining rooms are still operating. You can rent a condo and enjoy golfing, tennis, a swimming pool, and various modern amenities, but it's just not the same. Write to the Fairfield Inn at 4000 Highway 64 West, Sapphire 28774. Call (704) 743-3441.

SYLVA. The seat of Jackson County, this town features a courthouse that must be the least wheelchair-accessible in the entire country. The Jackson County Courthouse is at the top of a 108-step staircase.

WAYNESVILLE. Located west of Asheville, this town was named after "Mad" Anthony Wayne, a general in the Revolutionary War. As is common with many towns named for heroes, Wayne never laid eyes on the place. The downtown area has been spruced up with brick sidewalks, and small shops have opened in several of the old brick buildings.

Museum of North Carolina Handicrafts. This museum is in the Shelton House, a two-story house built between 1876 and 1880 and now listed on the National Register of Historic Places. The museum contains Civil War artifacts, and displays of handcrafted goods such as wood carvings, quilts, pottery, and weavings. Located at the corner of Shelton and Pigeon Streets, it is open from May through October, from 10:00 to 5:00 Wednesday through Saturday and on Sunday from 2:00 to 5:00. No admission is charged. Call (704) 452-1551.

Lodging and Dining

Antipastos. This small restaurant is noted for its antipasto, but what follows it isn't always pasta. Diners can choose from barbecued ribs, steaks, and rainbow trout. There are a few Italian dishes, but strictly speaking this is not an Italian restaurant. It is located off U.S. 19A; take the exit for Waynesville 276 south and drive a short distance to the Waynesville Plaza shopping center. No reservations are taken.

Piedmont Inn and Motor Lodge. The original 15-room inn has been in operation since 1880, but since then cottages and a motor lodge have been added. The cottages and lodge rooms have modern furnishings, kitchenettes, TVs, and telephones, but the original building has more of what people expect in an inn—old furniture, wide porches, and a quiet atmosphere. No meals are served. Piedmont Inn and Motor Lodge is located on Eagle's Nest Mountain at Waynesville. The inn is open only from May through October, but the lodge and cottages are open year-round. Write P.O. Box 419, Waynesville 28786. Call (704) 456-8636.

The Swag. Constructed of hand-hewn logs, this inn sits on 250 acres bordering the Great Smoky Mountains National Park, and is very popular with hikers and honeymooners. The 12 guest rooms are furnished with antiques and patchwork quilts. Six of the rooms have fireplaces, and all have private baths. This is one of the few inns in the region to offer a racquetball court. The dining room serves three meals a day to guests and the public. Open from Memorial Day to the end of October, the Swag is located off I-40 at Exit 20; head 2.8 miles south on U.S. 276 to Hemphill Road and follow the signs. Write the Swag at P.O. Box 280-A, Route 2, Waynesville 28786; or call (704) 926-0430. Out of season call (404) 875-1632.

EIGHT

North Georgia

THIS IS DELIVERANCE AND FOXFIRE COUNTRY, and both works have done a lot to shape outside perceptions of mountain life. The former was poet James Dickey's first novel, and subsequently a very successful motion picture starring Burt Reynolds. This gripping tale, which revolves around four white-water canoeists from Atlanta who are attacked by two sadistic mountaineers, accomplished two things: it almost singlehandedly launched widespread interest in running north Georgia rapids, and it vividly depicted to thousands of readers and millions of moviegoers the dark side of the hillbilly force. The two screen villains who assaulted actors Ned Beatty and John Voight bore little resemblance to Jed Clampett of the "The Beverly Hillbillies."

The *Foxfire* books, conversely, sold millions of copies to people who were intrigued with the old ways of doing things, means and methods adapted by a people who for decades were largely cut off from the rest of civilization. These books, all of them written by local high school students, depict a way of life that is steadily vanishing.

The visitor who comes to north Georgia packing a copy

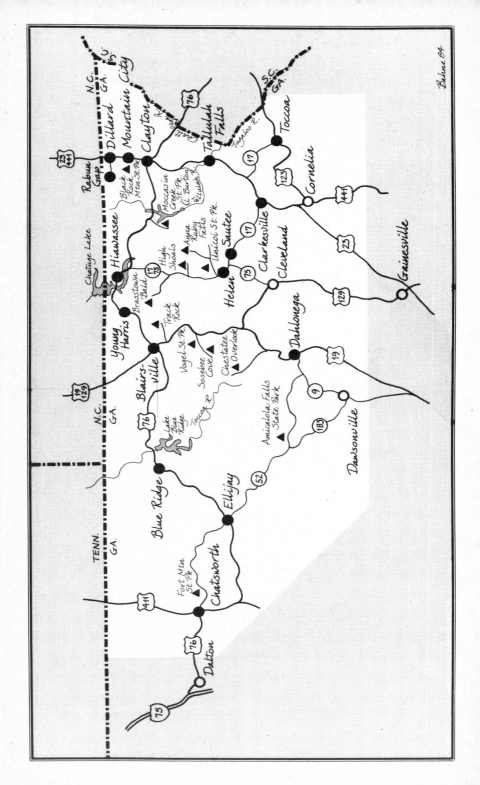

of *Deliverance* or *Foxfire* and expecting to step into its pages
is in for a let-down. Whereas the characters in Dickey's
story had to hunt for the edge of the river, present-day
adventure seekers will find white-water rafting services
that offer toll-free numbers and complete guided trips. The
Foxfire fancier, driving slowly along so as not to miss anyone making soap or tanning hides in the front yard, is
bound to be disappointed.

What will a visitor find in north Georgia? How is it
different from Tennessee or North Carolina? Sometimes a
state boundary marks more than a slight change in the
pavement; sometimes it marks a difference in culture, in
outlook, or in habits. Even if there were no signs to indicate
a person was in Georgia, the visitor could tell when the
line had been crossed by looking for one thing—boiled
peanuts.

This southern delicacy is usually prepared on the side
of a highway in a kettle or tub that sits atop a fire. If the
setup is fancy there is a gas fire, but more often than not
it is a wood fire under an iron kettle tended by someone
with time on his hands. When a customer appears and
requests an order of peanuts, the proprietor slowly gets to
his feet, reaches for a dipper, and plunges it into the dark
water. Out comes a mess of peanuts, boiled in their shells,
which are allowed to drain for a few seconds. Then they
are poured into a bag, and the dipper returned to dry in
the sun and await the next transaction.

If the customer takes some time to talk with the peanut
vendor, he hears an accent that is softer than those further
north, with less of the Appalachian twang and more of the
deep Southern drawl. The closer to Atlanta one goes, the
less and less the *r*'s are pronounced. The mountains are
softer, too, as the Appalachians gently come to an end. The
highest peak in Georgia is only 4,784 feet.

Perhaps this is a blessing, for north Georgia is spared
the large tourist attractions that mark sections of Tennessee and North Carolina. Visitors won't see many signs pro-

claiming "Complete Set of Dishes—$9.95." They will find a friendly people who are seldom so preoccupied with their business that they won't talk with an outlander. The people of north Georgia aren't all well educated, and to some their speech may seem quaint, but they are keen judges of character, and can smell condescension at a hundred paces. The tourists who try to have a little fun at some old codger's expense may afterward think they got away with it, only to find that the directions they received lead nowhere, or that the tales they heard are laughed at by anyone who knows anything about the area.

North Georgia is not like the rest of the southern Appalachians, though the difference is hard to explain. The best way to experience it is with one hand on the wheel and the other rooting around in a bag of warm boiled peanuts.

HOW TO GET THERE

BY AIR. The Atlanta airport, approximately two and a half hours from North Georgia, is the biggest air traffic center in the region. Delta Airlines is headquartered there, and the airport is served by most major carriers.

FROM ATLANTA. The weekend exodus from Atlanta takes place on two main roads—U.S. 19 and U.S. 23. U.S. 19 has four lanes as far as Dahlonega, and U.S. 23 has four lanes as far as Cornelia.

FROM TENNESSEE AND NORTH CAROLINA. Travelers interested in seeing the mountains should enter north Georgia through North Carolina. U.S. 19 and U.S. 129 swing around the edges of the Great Smoky Mountains National Park and funnel into the two main roads into Georgia—U.S. 441 and U.S. 19/129. Of the two, U.S. 441 is the most heavily traveled, especially on weekends in the fall.

ONCE YOU'RE THERE

North Georgia is much less commercialized than either Tennessee or North Carolina, although local merchants and entrepreneurs are working hard to rectify this situation. The big tourist center is Helen, with its Bavarian architecture and Oktoberfests, although a survivor of Gatlinburg, Tennessee, will find Helen pale in comparison.

The terrain of the Georgia mountains is easy on those who travel by means other than auto. Bicyclists will appreciate the relatively gentle hills and valleys, and hikers will find trails less steep than their northern counterparts. White-water enthusiasts will revel on the Chattooga River or the Chattahoochee, and fanciers of quieter water can paddle a canoe or use a power boat on one of the various lakes.

One of the best ways to see the area is to center on the excellent state parks. All have camping facilities, and all but one listed in this chapter—Moccasin Creek—have cabins for rent. These are good places from which to explore sections of the Chattahoochee National Forest, an area larger than the Great Smokies park.

One especially nice thing about the Georgia mountains is the high quality of the handcrafted goods sold here. The lack of a big tourist attraction cuts down on the gimcrack, although another positive influence may be the proximity of a big city, Atlanta, and the high standards demanded by its weekend refugees. The bad side of having weekend people is they stimulate condominium and cabin construction in otherwise pristine areas.

TOWNS AND ATTRACTIONS

AMICALOLA FALLS STATE PARK. The centerpiece of this park is the 729-foot Amicalola Falls, which are worth a side trip to see. The park also offers 17 tent and trailer sites, 15 cottages, and opportunities for fishing and hiking. It is located 16 miles northwest of Dawsonville via Georgia 52.

Write the park at Star Route, Dawsonville 30534. Call (404) 265-2885.

Events

Indian Lore and Legends. This one-day gathering, held in late April, celebrates the earliest inhabitants of the area. For further information contact the park officials.

BLACK ROCK MOUNTAIN STATE PARK. Located three miles north of Clayton on U.S. 441, this park is the highest in the state. It offers 54 tent and trailer sites, 10 cottages, fishing, and hiking. For further information write the park in Mountain City 30562. Call (404) 746-2141.

Events

Bloomin' Wild Flower Fair. Held in early May, this fair focuses on the wildflowers of the mountains, which at this time of the year grow in profusion. For further information write the park.

BLUE RIDGE. The seat of Fannin County, this small town lies in the area that was the Cherokees' last stronghold before they were shipped west to Oklahoma.
Blue Ridge Lake. This TVA lake extends ten miles upstream on the Toccoa River and offers opportunities for swimming, boating, fishing, and camping.

Events

Fannin County Fair. Traditional exhibits of livestock, local produce, and prepared foods mark this country fair, which is held in mid-August at the Kiwanis Fairgrounds. For further information contact Joe Clement at (404) 374-6526.

BLAIRSVILLE. Gold was commercially mined in this small town, the seat of Union County, until 1910.

Lodging and Dining

Goose Creek. Noted equally for its homemade soups and breads, this restaurant makes mountain trout its specialty. Dinner is served Wednesday through Saturday in the summers, and on weekends in October, November, and May. The restaurant is closed from December through April. Cabins and camping spaces are available. Located on U.S. 19 and U.S. 129 near Vogel State Park. Call (404) 745-5111.

Events

Blairsville Sorghum Festival. When mountain people talk about raising cane, they may be referring to either of two things. The first is making a fuss. The second is growing sorghum, which is crushed to obtain the juice. The juice is then boiled and reduced to sorghum molasses. This early October festival centers on producing the molasses, but also includes mountain arts and crafts, country music, square dancing, rock throwing, and greased-pole climbing. For further information write Louise Sprayberry, P.O. Box 701, Blairsville 30512. Call (404) 745-5789.

BRASSTOWN BALD. The Cherokee Indians tell a story much like the Bible's account of Noah. According to their version, Brasstown Bald was the place where the survivors of the flood brought their giant canoe to rest. It is the highest place in Georgia—4,784 feet—and from the top visitors can see into four states.

To reach the Bald take Georgia 66 off Georgia 75. You can drive almost to the top of the peak, where you'll find a picnic area, a visitors' center, and an observation tower. To get to the tower you can take a shuttle bus or walk less than a mile. It is open from dawn to dusk. No admission is charged.

CHATSWORTH. The Cherokees came to this area to find soapstone, which they carved into ceremonial pipes, beads, and pots. Nowadays talc is mined here for use in talcum powder, among other things.

Vann House. The son of a white trader and an Indian woman, James Vann was made a chief by the Cherokees. He owned over a hundred slaves, and in 1804 he built a two-and-a-half-story brick house that was described as "the only mansion in America built by an American Indian." When the Cherokees were banished to Tennessee in 1834 he abandoned the house, and later he was sent to Oklahoma on the "Trail of Tears." The home was restored in the 1950s, and is now maintained by the state of Georgia. Visitors can see period furniture—1780–1830—and a cantilevered stairway that has been studied by engineers and carpenters. The house is open year-round, Tuesday through Saturday from 9:00 to 5:00 and on Sunday from 2:00 to 5:30. It is located three miles west of Chatsworth at the intersection of Alternate U.S. 52 and Georgia 225. A small admission is charged. Call (404) 695-2598.

Events

Vann House Days. Held in mid-July, this annual event features demonstrations and displays of Indian crafts and tours of the Vann House. Indian finger weaving, carding, and spinning are among the crafts performed. Admission is free. For further information call (404) 695-2598.

Lodging and Dining

Cohutta Lodge and Restaurant. Located 10 miles east of Chatsworth atop Fort Mountain, this lodge contains 60 rooms, all of which have color TV, telephones, and private baths. The lodge also offers tennis, a heated pool, an archery range, horseshoe pits, and, in the winter, ice skating and tobogganing.

The restaurant serves three meals a day and is open to the public. It specializes in mountain trout, steak, and prime rib.

For further information write the lodge at 5000 Cochise Trail, Chatsworth 30705. Call (404) 695-9601.

CHATTAHOOCHEE-OCONEE NATIONAL FOREST. Once separately administered, the Chattahoochee and the Oconee have been combined to cut costs. The 854 thousand acres of the forest contain five hundred developed campsites, over two hundred picnic sites, two wilderness areas, the Chattooga Wild and Scenic River, six swimming beaches, thousands of acres of lakes and streams, and over three hundred miles of hiking trails. The last (or the first, depending on where you start) 83 miles of the Appalachian Trail is here.

Since the Oconee, the smaller of the two parts of the forest, is beyond the mountains to the south, it is not covered in this book. Discussed here is the Chattahoochee, which lies in the northeast corner of the state. Its seven districts are described separately. For further information about the entire forest write the Forest Supervisor, U.S. Forest Service, 601 Broad Street Southeast, Gainesville 30501. Call (404) 536-0541.

Armuchee Ranger District. The westernmost part of the national forest, this district lies outside of the area covered by this book. Further information and maps can be picked up or ordered from the district office. Drop by or write Armuchee District, 706 Foster Boulevard, LaFayette 30723. Call (404) 638-1085.

Brasstown Ranger District. Besides Brasstown Bald, the highest mountain in Georgia (listed separately in this chapter), travelers to this district should visit High Shoals, a 170-acre scenic area containing five waterfalls within 350 feet of one another. To get there take Georgia 75 north of Cleveland for 17 miles. Turn right on Forest Service Road 283, and drive one and a half miles to the start of the trail at Blue Hole Falls.

Also worth a visit is Sosebee Cove, which contains a tract of virgin hardwood timber with some of the largest trees in the eastern United States. It includes tulip poplars that are over 100 feet tall and 17½ feet in circumference. The cove is located off Georgia 180 between Lake Winfield Scott and Vogel State Park.

The final place to see in this district is Track Rock Archeological Area. On this 52-acre site prehistoric Indians created petroglyphs resembling animal and bird tracks. To get there take U.S. 19/129 south from Blairsville for three miles. Turn left on Georgia 2322 (Town Creek Road) and follow the signs for five miles.

Further information and maps can be picked up or ordered from the district office. Drop by or write Brasstown Ranger District, Highway 19/129 South, Blairsville 30512. Call (404) 745-6928.

Chattooga Ranger District. The biggest attraction here is Anna Ruby Falls, twin waterfalls that drop from Tray Mountain. A half-mile hike along a paved path leads the visitor to the base of the falls, one of which drops 153 feet and the other 50 feet. In the summertime the approach to the falls is always cool and inviting, and in the winter the ice formations in the stream and at the falls are worth a side trip. A picnic area and restrooms (closed during winter months) are located near the parking area.

To reach the falls take Georgia 75 north of Helen for one mile. Turn right on Georgia 356 for one and a half miles, then left at the entrance to the falls. Follow this road for three and a half miles to the parking area. Further information and maps can be ordered from the district office. Write Chattooga Ranger District, Burton Road, Highway 197, Clarksville 30523. Call (404) 754-6221.

Chestatee Ranger District. For those who like to see scenery without having to hike, the Chestatee Overlook provides a good view of the Blood Mountain Cove. To get to the overlook take Georgia 60 for 12 miles north of Dahlonega. Further information and maps of the district can be picked up or ordered from the District office. Drop by or write 200 West Main Street, Dahlonega 30533. Call (404) 864-6173.

Cohutta Ranger District. Located north of Chatsworth and bordering North Carolina, the 34,100-acre Cohutta Wilderness is the site of two of the best trout streams in Georgia. Deer, wild hogs, and bears inhabit the area, too. The Cohutta Scenic Overlook, with a good view of the Blue Ridge Mountains, lies just off Georgia 52 near Fort Mountain State Park. Further information and maps of the district can be ordered from the district office. Write 401 Old Ellijay Road, Chatsworth, 30705. Call (404) 695-6736.

Tallulah Ranger District. The northeastern corner of the national forest and the state, this district offers hiking on the Appalachian Trail, white-water canoeing on the Chattooga River, and beautiful mountain scenery. One hundred eighty-one acres of the Ellicot Rock Wilderness Area (most of which is located in South Carolina) lie in this district. Further information and maps can be picked up or ordered from the district office. Drop by or write Tallulah Ranger District, North Main Street, Clayton 30525. Call (404) 782-3320.

Toccoa Ranger District. Its name is misleading, for this district centers on the Toccoa River, not the town of Toccoa. The focal point of the district is Lake Blue Ridge, an impoundment of the Toccoa River. Morganton Point on this lake is a good place to camp, swim, and launch boats. Information and maps can be ordered from the district office. Write Route 2, Box 508-B, Blue Ridge 30513. Call (404) 623-3031.

CLARKESVILLE. In the 1800s flatlanders liked to visit this small town, the seat of Habersham county. They brought money and taste with them, and they built many vacation homes and at least one church. Today Clarkesville still attracts vacationers, a good number of whom decide to stay. In a survey taken in 1983 for a retirement guide, Clarkesville had the lowest crime rate of 107 towns, and was determined to be the third best place in the United States to retire. Habersham County produces lots of apples and peaches.

Habersham Plantation. In the display rooms of this furniture factory visitors can peruse colonial reproductions, usually in pine. Quilts, pottery, braided rugs, and baskets are also for sale. Located on Beaver Dam Road west of Clarkesville off Georgia 255. Call (404) 754-6225.

Grace Calvary Church. Built in 1842 by well-to-do summer people from Savannah, this is the second oldest church still in use in the state. It was completely restored in 1975, and contains the original slave balcony and large sheets of early glass in the windows. Located near U.S. 441 and U.S. 23, the church sits in a grove of cedar trees on the corner of Green Street and Wilson Street. No admission is charged.

Lake Burton Trout Hatchery. This place is misnamed, for trout are not hatched here. Instead they arrive as four-inch long fingerlings and are kept until they are at least nine inches long, when they are stocked in streams across the northern part of the state. This facility raises over 350 thousand fish per year. Visitors are invited to watch personnel feed the fish, some of which take their meals three times daily. The hatchery is located across from LaPrade's on Georgia 197. It is open daily from 9:00 to 5:00, and no admission is charged.

Mark of the Potter. Located in an old mill along Georgia 197 on the Soque River, this shop features pottery, which is thrown, fired, and glazed on the premises, often when visitors drop in. Also for sale are handmade works in wood, metal, and fabric. Children like to feed the trout that gather below the mill in the river's waters. The shop is open Monday through Saturday from 10:00 to 6:00 and on Sunday from 1:00 to 6:00. In January, February, and March the shop is closed on Tuesdays and Wednesdays. Call (404) 947-3440.

Serendipity. Upstream from the Mark of the Potter on Highway 197 is this stained glass studio and shop. Customers can choose from available items or special-order lamps, terrariums, or complete windows. Open Monday through Saturday from 10:00 to 6:00. The glaziers occasionally take a day off, so call (404) 947-3643 if you are making a special trip.

Upside-down Bridge. Eight miles north of Clarkesville lies a ford in Georgia 197. Once a common feature of roads, this stream flowing across the pavement is called an "upside-down bridge" by some of the locals.

Events

Chattahoochee Mountain Fair. Held on the Habersham County Fairgrounds in August, this fair offers agricultural exhibits, carnival rides, handcrafted goods, and a typing contest. For further information write the Habersham County Chamber of Commerce, P.O. Box 366, Cornelia 30531. Call (404) 778-4654.

Lodging and Dining

Adam's Rib. One of the few mountain restaurants that offer fresh seafood, this place is worth a detour. It is located on U.S. 441 South in Clarkesville, and serves three meals a day. Try country ham and biscuits in the morning, the lunchtime buffet, and seafood or steak at night. The lounge area features a giant TV. Phone (404) 754-4568.

The Charm House Inn. Built in 1848, this rambling white house with tall columns is located on a hill alongside U.S. 441 in Clarkesville. Inside is a combined bed-and-breakfast inn and antique store. Six rooms are available to guests; and all are furnished with antiques; this is one place where you can buy the bed you sleep in. In the mornings a buffet breakfast is served. The inn is on the National Register of Historic Places, and is open all year long. For reservations write P. O. Box 392, Clarkesville 30523. Call (404) 754-9347.

LaPrade's. Much like Fontana Village to the north, this camp was built in 1916 for workers who were constructing Lake Burton Dam for the Georgia Power Company. When the work was completed and the men were gone, the cabins and dining hall were converted to a fishing camp on the new lake. The facilities are very rustic; the cabins sleep as many as 12 people. Visitors may prefer to spend the night elsewhere and come to LaPrade's just to belly up to the groaning tables in the dining hall. The food is Southern style, and this means country ham and red-eye gravy for breakfast, and tempting items such as fried chicken, corn bread, and fresh vegetables for lunch and dinner. The dining room is closed on Wednesdays.

Open from April through November, LaPrade's is located 18 miles north of Clarkesville on Georgia 197. Write to Route 1, Clarkesville 30523. Call (404) 947-3312.

CLAYTON. This is the seat of Rabun County, the county with the most precipitation in Georgia. The Chattahoochee National Forest occupies 62 percent of the county's land, and much of the rest is owned by outsiders, primarily the Georgia Power Company and wealthy Atlanta people who have second homes in the area. Though a source of consternation to the tax assessor, all this open territory is a delight to visitors.

A welcome center in the middle of Clayton offers a map with directions to thirteen local waterfalls. You can drop by and pick up a map or request one by mail from the Rabun County Chamber of Commerce, P.O. Box 761, Clayton 30525. Call (404) 782-4812.

Bartram Trail. The Quaker naturalist William Bartram passed through this area over two hundred years ago. The midpoint of the trail named after him is three miles east of Clayton in Warwoman Dell on Warwoman Road. It extends for almost forty miles, marked by yellow and black signs.

Carne's Nectars of the Wild. This shop features jellies, jams, preserves, conserves, pickles, marmalades, and relishes. Located one mile north of Clayton on the North Main Street Extension, it is open from mid-May through mid-November from 9:00 to 6:00 daily.

Granny's Hilltop Crafts. Offering handmade toys, yarn creations, ceramics, water-ground grits and corn meal, all-natural jams and jellies (several with no sugar added), syrup, honey, chow-chows, and country antiques. Located on U.S. 441 three and one half miles south of Clayton. Open 9:00 to 6:00 seven days a week during the spring, summer, and fall, and weekdays only in the winter. Call (404) 782-3624.

DAHLONEGA. Visitors stand out less if they give this town's name the correct pronunciation—Duh-LON-eh-guh, which comes from the Cherokee word for yellow metal. What may have been just yellow metal to the Cherokees was gold, and it drove the white men crazy with greed. Even though these were Indian lands by treaty, white prospectors poured in during 1828 and 1829. This was the first important gold strike in the United States, and the model for countless Western boom towns was established here.

Unlike in many later boom towns, however, there was a lot of gold in Dahlonega. The federal government built a mint here, and from 1838 to 1861 struck 1,378,710 pieces of gold. The Civil War ended the mint, but gold has been mined from the area in varying amounts ever since. From 1930 through 1933 Georgia produced almost 18 million dollars worth of gold, and 16 million of that (in 1930s' prices) came from the Dahlonega area.

Nowadays there's gold in them thar tourists, and Dahlonega works those who pass through it as carefully as its miners once worked the ore.

Appalachian Adventures. These outfitters offer rock climbing, hikes, and guided raft trips on the Chestatee River. The headquarters is next to the Smith House Hotel in downtown Dahlonega. Write P.O. Box 2057, Dahlonega 30533; or call (404) 864-3562.

Crisson's Gold Mine. Much like the North Carolina gemstone mines to the north, this place offers visitors the opportunity to pan for gold. Anything you find you can keep. Located three miles north of town on Wimpy Mill Road off U.S. 19, the mine is open from early spring through late fall daily from 10:00 to 6:00. Call (404) 864-6353.

Dahlonega Gold Museum. This renovated 1836 courthouse contains exhibits relating the nation's first big gold strike. Some people claim that the building sits atop the town's largest vein of gold. Close observation will reveal gold flecks in the mortar that holds the bricks together. Located on the town square, the museum is open Tuesday through Saturday from 9:00 to 5:00, and on Sunday from 2:00 to 5:30. A small admission is charged.

Events

Gold Rush Days. Held in mid-October. For further information write the Dahlonega Chamber of Commerce, Dahlonega 30533. Call (404) 864-3711.

Fall Bluegrass Festival. Held in early September, this event features local groups and individual pickers and grinners. For further information contact Norman Adams at (404) 864-7203.

Lodging and Dining

Forrest Hills Mountain Resort. Consisting of small lodges and cabins, this resort is in the country outside of Dahlonega. All cabins and lodges have working fireplaces and porches complete with rocking chairs. The restaurant on the premises is open on weekends, and a crafts shop, an ice cream shop, and resort offices are close by in a hundred-year-old house. Guests may also pan for gold in a nearby stream. Forrest Hills is located off Georgia 52 near Amicalola Falls State Park. For further information write Route 3, Box 510, Dahlonega 30533. Call (404) 864-6456.

Smith House. Local lore has it that when the foundations for this hotel were being dug a large gold vein was struck. The city fathers did not want a mine in the middle of town, so they covered up the gold and built the Smith House anyway. The hotel now features 16 rooms, 4 suites, and a swimming pool. No digging is allowed in the basement.

The restaurant, located beside the hotel, offers a choice of 3 meats for dinner and 12 to 14 fresh vegetables. It is so popular that no reservations are taken. Sunday is the big day here, when as many as thirteen hundred people pass through a dining room with a seating capacity of two hundred. Open year-round, the Smith House is located in downtown Dahlonega. Write 202 Chestatee Street, Dahlonega 30533; or call (404) 864-2348.

Yahoola Creek Farm. A two-hundred-acre working farm is the site of this resort, which consists of six two-room cottages on the banks of Yahoola Creek. Country pastimes such as trout fishing, swimming in a swimming hole, and hayrides are a part of the action. Each cottage comes with a kitchen. Located five miles north of Dahlonega off U.S. 19. For further information write the farm at Route 4, Box 129, Dahlonega 30533. Call (404) 864-6735.

DILLARD. Just one mile south of the North Carolina line, this town was settled by the Dillard family. They claim to have bought all the land in this valley for one muzzle-loading rifle, a jug of apple brandy, and three dollars cash. They were the first to realize the tourist potential of the area when they started renting rooms to guests. Their establishment is still in business, operating as the Dillard House.

Dillard State Farmer's Market. Load up on fresh produce here. Located on U.S. 23/441.

Sky Valley Resort. Offering the southernmost ski trails in the United States, this twenty-four-hundred-acre resort is open to the public when the snow falls, whether natural or artificial. There are three ski slopes, a double chair lift and rope tow, and a ski school. During the spring, summer, and fall visitors can play golf and tennis, swim, ride horses, and fish. Accommodations are available in privately owned condominiums and resort homes. The lodge has two dining rooms and a ski shop or golf shop, depending on the season. For further information write Sky Valley Resort, Dillard 30537. Call (404) 746-5301. Visitors in surrounding states can call (800) 241-6941.

Vintage Auto Museum. A Lincoln-Continental that once carried Elvis Presley to and fro is the centerpiece of this museum, which also includes a 1909 Interstate and a 1937 Terraplane. Located on U.S. 23/441, the museum is open daily from 8:00 A.M. to 8:30 P.M. Admission is charged. Call (404) 746-2626.

Events

Top of Georgia Jamboree. Country music punctuated by the stamps of cloggers pours forth from the Rabun Gap Elementary School, adjacent to the Dillard House, every Saturday night in the summertime. Designed for family entertainment, the show runs Saturdays 8:00 to 10:00 P.M. from June through August. For further information write Fred Huff, Box 68, Eastanolee 30538. Call (404) 779-2263.

Lodging and Dining

Andy's Trout Farm and Copecrest Square Dance Resort. These lively places are adjacent to each other in Dillard. The trout farm consists of a stream stocked with rainbow trout. The visitor is invited to catch his or her own fish, which is then cleaned and cooked on the premises.

The dance resort offers a package deal made up of lodging, breakfast and dinner, daytime workshops, and evening square dance parties. Visitors can stay in the

Copecrest Inn, a cabin, or a 48-person dormitory. Accommodations are available year-round, but the square dance program operates from March through mid-November only.

The trout farm and dance resort are located on Betty's Creek Road outside of Dillard. Write the Copecrest Dance Resort at P.O. Box 129, Dillard 30537; or call (404) 746-2134.

Dillard House. The oldest place to eat and sleep in town, the Dillard House is famous for country ham. It also offers 60 guest rooms in two buildings, tennis courts, a swimming pool, a farm zoo, and horseback riding. Located on U.S. 441, it is open all year. For further information write P.O. Box 10, Dillard 30537. Call (404) 746-5348.

ELLIJAY. In 1540 Hernando DeSoto, having missed the turnoff to Dahlonega, came through this area looking for gold. The name of the town comes from a Cherokee word which is usually translated as "place of green things." Some of the green things here now are apple and peach trees. Gilmer County, of which Ellijay is the seat, produces Granny Smith, Red Delicious, Golden Delicious, and about 22 other varieties of apples. The most famous summer resident of the area is President Jimmy Carter, who enjoys fishing the many trout streams in the county.

Possum Hollar Country Store. This store offers locally handcrafted goods and antiques. Located east of Ellijay on Georgia 52. Call (404) 635-7255.

Events

Apple Festival. Held on the second weekend in October, this fair celebrates the large apple crop produced in the area. The fair includes arts and crafts demonstrations, a road race, clogging, and a band concert. For further details write to the Ellijay Chamber of Commerce, P.O. Box 818, Ellijay 30540. Call (404) 635-7400.

Lodging and Dining

Circle L-J Dude Ranch. This adults-only resort enables visitors to escape the little buckaroos and enjoy tennis, horseback riding, rafting, clogging, square dancing and, when it's all over, a sauna and whirlpool. The price includes all meals, trail riding, and live music on Saturday nights. Guests stay in relatively new rustic cabins. Located on Highway 5 about two miles north of Ellijay. Write to P.O. Box 897, Ellijay 30540 for further details, or call (404) 635-7717.

FORT MOUNTAIN STATE PARK. Located seven miles west of Chatsworth on Georgia 52, this park is considered the southern terminus of the Appalachian mountains. The park offers 77 tent and trailer campsites, 15 cottages, hiking trails, and a 17-acre lake for swimming and boating. Boats are available for rent. For further information write the park at Chatsworth 30705. Call (404) 695-2621.

HELEN. This is the Gatlinburg of North Georgia. In the 1960s Helen was an ugly little town that was bypassed by tourists heading into the mountains. Three local businessmen decided to change all this. They hit on the idea of transforming the town into a Bavarian village, and talked the local shopowners into going along.

And it worked. The result is a town that looks totally different from any other place in the region. It has more hotel rooms than it does citizens, and on weekends "you can't stir the tourists with a stick," as one observer put it. The shops specialize in high-roller arts and crafts from Europe, and on the streets one can buy leather goods and jewelry along with souvenir T-shirts and other tourist paraphernalia.

Mountain Madness. Bicycle rentals and guided tours are the specialties here. Visitors can rent high-tech 18-speed bikes or rugged "stump jumpers." Located four miles north of Helen and one mile northeast of Unicoi State Park. Call (404) 878-2851.

Museum of the Hills. The wax figures in this museum were once displayed in Underground Atlanta, where the usual collection of famous people stood stiffly as the patrons walked by. Now the likes of Mark Twain, Albert Einstein, and Gerald Ford can be found in mountain garb posed in idealized hillbilly settings. Mark Twain stands as a village barber, and looks singularly disgusted with his newfound position. Located on Main Street in Helen. Call (404) 878-3140.

Tekawitha. A member of the Indian Arts and Crafts Association, this shop features the work of over fifty tribes. Included are pottery, jewelry, beadwork, moccasins, pipes, Kachinas, wall hangings, carved gourds, and much more. Located next to Fain's Antiques on South Main Street in Helen. Call (404) 878-2938.

The Wildewood Shop. This outfitter offers whitewater trips, backpacking expeditions, and leaf excursions. Equipment is available for rent. Located on River Street in Helen. Call (404) 878-2541.

Events

Fasching Karnival. A German version of Mardis Gras, this six-week celebration rolls on every weekend at various restaurants in town from January through February for local and out-of-town revelers. Participants—adults only—are asked to come costumed and masked. At 12:16 A.M. the masks come off. For further information on this and all the following events write the Helen Chamber of Commerce, P.O. Box 192, Helen 30545. Call (404) 878-2181.

Helen Arts Council Craft Show. Held in the last weekend in October, this event brings in craftspeople for demonstrations and sales. Held in the Helen Pavilion.

Hot Air Balloon Festival. This festival marks the start of a balloon race from Helen to the Atlantic Ocean. Visitors can take rides in tethered balloons, eat, and generally celebrate lighter than air flight. Held at the end of May and beginning of June.

May Fest. Held weekends in May, this event features Maypole dancing with the Alpine Village Cloggers (how's that for a cultural mix?), polka bands, and German bands.

Oktoberfest. What would a German village be without an Oktoberfest? Helen's features various German bands, a parade, singers, and the ubiquitous cloggers. Held in October.

Lodging and Dining

Alpenhof Motel. Open all year, this motel has two locations and features a heated pool, kitchenettes, facilities for the handicapped, and a bridal suite. Write Box 396, Helen 30545. Call (404) 878-2191.

The Castle Inn. Located on the edge of town, this motel features cable color TV and private balconies overlooking the Chattahoochee River. Write Box 258, Helen 30545. Call (404) 878-3140.

Derdenhof Inn. The 26 rooms here are furnished with nineteenth-century antiques. All rooms have cable color TV, and the inn includes a swimming pool. Write Box 405, Helen 30545. Call (404) 878-2141.

Helendorf Inn. Cable color TV, dining facility, and balconies overlooking the Chattahoochee River are featured here. Write the inn at Box 305, Helen 30545. Call (404) 878-2271.

Hofbrauhaus Inn. Located on the outskirts of Helen, this hotel features a restaurant offering German food and a beer garden overlooking the Chattahoochee River. The rooms offer cable color TV and private balconies. Write 1 Main Street, Helen 30545. Call (404) 878-2248.

Links. This is Helen's oldest and largest German-American restaurant. The specialty is Wiener schnitzel. Visitors can dance to the Heidelberger Dance Band every weekend. Located in downtown Helen. Call (404) 878-2986.

Wurst Haus Restaurant and Biergarten. A good selection of German beers is featured here along with imported

Schaller and Weber sausages. There is live German music on some nights. Located on Main Street in Helen. Call (404) 878-2647.

HIAWASSEE. This small mountain town just below the Tennessee border is the scene of the Georgia Mountain Fair, the largest event of its kind in the state. A three-thousand-seat auditorium is the scene of six country music concerts per year with big-name entertainers.

Lake Chatuge. This is sometimes called "the crown jewel of the TVA system." It offers boating and fishing.

Towns County Park. Located on the edge of town and on the shores of Lake Chatuge, this park features camping (220 sites), boating, water skiing, swimming, and tennis. More sedentary visitors can enjoy the rhododendron garden.

Events

Georgia Mountain Fair. One hundred seventy thousand people and more descend on Hiawassee during this 12-day fair, which commences on the first Wednesday in August at the town's fairgrounds. Visitors find demonstrations of soap making, blacksmithing, quilting, and board splitting. Approximately sixty craftspeople make and sell items such as apple-head dolls, pottery, weavings, and jewelry. A three-thousand-seat music hall is the scene of country, bluegrass, and gospel music. Children enjoy the carnival rides. For further information write the Georgia Mountain Fair, P.O. Box 444, Hiawassee 30546. Call (404) 896-4191.

Spring Country Music Festival. Held on the third weekend in May, this event dusts off the seats of the auditorium for the summer months. For further information write P.O. Box 444, Hiawassee 30546.

MOCCASIN CREEK STATE PARK. Located 25 miles north of Clarkesville on the shores of Lake Burton, this park emphasizes water sports such as skiing, fishing, and swimming. It has 53 tent and trailer sites and boat rentals. For further information write Route 1, Clarkesville 30523. Call (404) 947-3194.

MOUNTAIN CITY. Originally called Passover, this town was a main stop on the early railroad through the mountains.

Heritage Gallery. Nostalgia is the theme here, with a special emphasis on Norman Rockwell. Housed in a 1928 general store building, the gallery offers almost all of Rockwell's 323 *Saturday Evening Post* covers, as well as twentieth-century sheet music, books, and cards, signed and numbered prints, and vintage clothing, linens, and china. Not everything in the place is old: local artists' paintings, sculpture, and pottery is also for sale. Located on U.S. 23/441 in Mountain City, the gallery is open seven days a week all year, except on bitterly cold days. Write the galley at P.O. Box 423-D, Mountain City 30562. Call (404) 746-2933.

Lodging and Dining

York House. The 15 guest quarters in this 1870s clapboard house are furnished with antiques. A continental breakfast is brought to each room on a silver tray. No dinner is served. Guests like to sit on the rocking chairs on the two-story veranda and take in the view of the mountains. The York House is located between Mountain City and Dillard, one-quarter mile off U.S. 23/441. For further information write P.O. Box 126, Mountain City 30562. Call (404) 746-2068.

RABUN GAP. This town is famous for the *Foxfire* books, which originally came out of the Rabun Gap-Nacoochee School. The school itself has an interesting history: founded in 1903 as the Nacoochee Institute, it merged with the Rabun Gap Industrial School in 1926, and for a period it operated as a junior college in which male and female students paid for their education by working on farms owned by the school. Another program admitted entire families for five-year periods, in which they learned modern agricultural methods while working 40-acre tracts on the sharecrop system. There was also a day school for local children. Now the school is private; it includes boarding and day students in grades eight through twelve.

The Foxfire phenomenon came about when Eliot Wigginton, a young English teacher fresh out of Cornell, realized he was not getting anything across to his young charges. He threw out the textbook and asked the students if they would like to produce a magazine. This idea captivated them, and they set out to interview older relatives and neighbors in an effort to learn about planting by the signs, hog killing, and various other mountain activities. The first edition of the magazine *Foxfire* sold out six hundred copies. Subsequent issues were gathered into a book, and it sold thousands of copies. Other volumes followed, and the program attracted national attention from educators and folklorists alike.

Visitors are often disappointed to learn that Rabun Gap offers almost nothing to see that is specifically related to Foxfire. There is no Foxfire World, no Foxfire Souvenir Stand, and no Foxfire Mountain Village. Perhaps this is a good thing.

Hambidge Center. Established in 1934, this community center for the arts is situated on six hundred acres. It was incorporated in 1944 for the purpose of "perpetuating the knowledge of handweaving and the value of handicrafts as a way of developing one's inner life." Individuals are invited to participate in weekend or week-long workshops centering on photography, dance, music, creative writing, and painting, as well as handweaving, pottery, and other crafts.

There is a residence program for qualified artists, composers, and writers. Visitors are welcome; the center is open May through October from 10:00 to 5:00 daily. It includes a grist mill that operates on Fridays, and a gift shop. The Hambidge Center is located on Betty's Creek Road in Rabun Gap, three miles west of

U.S. 23/441 in Dillard. For further information write the center at P.O. Box 33, Rabun Gap 30568. Call (404) 746-5718.

Rabun Gap Crafts. Operated by the Rabun Gap-Nacoo-chee School, which is across the highway, this shop features weavings, wood carvings, pottery, handmade dolls and toys, and other locally crafted goods. Located on U.S. 23/441, the shop is open Monday through Saturday 8:30 to 5:00 from March through December.

Lodging and Dining

Moon Valley. A group of cabins hidden away at the foot of a mountain, Moon Valley is special in that it offers food to please a gourmet. Trout is raised in lakes in sight of the cabins, so it's always fresh. Other dinner items include rack of lamb and Chateaubriand. The cabins, which come with kitchenettes, are furnished in a country chic style. Moon Valley is open all year and located off Betty's Creek Road. For further information write Box 235, Rabun Gap 30568. Call (404) 746-2466.

SAUTEE. Four miles from the Germanic bustle of Helen, this small town offers a good selection of crafts stores. Though there is little indication today, the area was once the center of the Cherokee Nation.

Country Store at Sautee. This restored drugstore, ice cream parlor, and soda fountain, built in the 1890s, contains period antiques and goods made by local artisans. Located on the Skylake Road off Georgia 255.

Nora Mill Granary and Store. Operating since 1876, this mill continues to grind corn and wheat the old-time way with water power and stone wheels. Not only is the process interesting to watch, but because the grains are not subjected to the heat of modern milling methods the result is healthier and better-tasting whole wheat flour, rye flour, buckwheat flour, white and yellow grits, corn meal, and self-rising cornmeal. All of these products are sold on the premises. Lifelong grits eaters, especially, are surprised at how much better the stone-ground kind is. The mill is on the Chattahoochee River on Georgia 75, just north of the Georgia 17 intersection. For information on mail orders write Nora Mill, P.O. Box 41, Sautee 30571. Call (404) 878-2375.

Old Sautee Store. Listed on the National Register of Historic Places, this country store—museum was built over a hundred years ago. It contains antique jars, display cases, and coin-operated musical instruments. In the back of the store is **The Norwegian Import Shop**, featuring Scandinavian sweaters, hand-carved trolls, and Norwegian pewter. Open all year, the Old Sautee Store is located at the intersection of Georgia 17 and 255. No admission is charged. Phone (404) 878-2281.

Trollstua. This shop, attached to the front of the owner's home, features hand-knitted sweaters. Woolen yarns and needlepoint supplies are also available. Located on Georgia 17 one and a half miles south of the Old Sautee Store. Phone (404) 878-2505.

Lodging and Dining

Sautee Inn. Situated in a turn-of-the-century home, this restaurant features buffets of fried chicken and other Southern specialties, but also serves up more imaginative dishes such as squash with mushrooms, cheese, and almonds; ginger carrots; Creole hominy; and beets Norway. The owner of the restaurant, a former Lockheed engineer who now calculates good meals, lives overhead. The inn is small, and reservations are a good idea. Located four miles west of Helen on Georgia 17, Sautee Inn serves lunch and dinner on a schedule that varies seasonally. Call (404) 878-2940.

Stovall House. Now an inn, this house was built in 1837 by Moses Harshaw, who was reputed to be "the meanest man who ever lived." He was an attorney. The five guest rooms are all furnished with antiques, and some have working fireplaces. The restaurant, which is open to the public, specializes in home-cooked meals presented in an intimate, informal atmosphere. Reservations are a good idea. The inn is located on Georgia 255—Lake Burton Road—five miles east of Helen off Georgia 17. For further information write the inn at Route 1, Box 103-A, Sautee 30571. Call (404) 878-3355.

TALLULAH FALLS. The meaning of this Indian word has been lost, but is assumed to be "terrible"; perhaps the name came about after someone paddled a canoe down the river and went over the waterfall. Whatever its meaning, the name served Tallulah Bankhead well; it's said she was called after this place. Karl Wallenda once walked a tightrope across Tallulah Gorge in 1970, and *Deliverance* was filmed here.

The famous falls leading into Tallulah Gorge are no longer there; the Georgia Power Company dammed the river, creating Tallulah Lake. Today visitors must imagine what the falls looked like as they watch water spill over the dam. The gorge, whose extremely steep sides range from six hundred to a thousand feet deep, is owned by the power company. Though the company does its best to keep people out, every year one or two trespassers slip on the moss-covered rocks and fall to their death.

Tallulah Falls School. Having opened in 1909 with 21 pupils and one teacher, this private school now has about 140 students in grades six through twelve and a student-teacher ratio of 12 to 1. Owned and operated by the Georgia Federation of Women's Clubs, the school is not affiliated with any particular religious group, although chapel attendance is required. All students share in the tasks necessary to run the school; they work on the school farm, cook, clean, and wash dishes. The school owns the Tallulah Gallery.

Visitors are invited to tour the school museum and the grounds, which total six hundred acres; call (404) 754-3171 to make sure the museum is open. No admission is charged. To reach the school, turn off U.S. 23/441 on the road just north of the Tallulah Gallery.

Tallulah Gallery. Located on the east side of U.S. 23/441, this gallery features paintings, jewelry, pottery, and locally crafted goods. It is open every day from 10:00 to 5:00 and in October from 10:00 to 8:00. Call (404) 754-6020.

Terrora Park. Located near the dam that backs up Tallulah Lake, this park offers camping, picnicking, tennis courts, hiking trails, and a visitors' center with exhibits on Georgia Power's control of the water. The campground has 51 sites with full hookups, and hot showers. The park is open year-round. For further information write P.O. Box 9, Tallulah Falls 30573. Call (404) 754-3276.

Whitewater Rafting. Many people want to do more than look at the rushing water. Though rafting is not permitted in Tallulah Gorge, it is offered on the Chattooga River. Most of the rafting companies are headquartered out of state, but they have Georgia facilities. Here are some that offer trips on the Chattooga:

Nantahala Outdoor Center
U.S. 19W, Box 41
Bryson City, North Carolina 28713
(704) 488-2175

Southeastern Expeditions
1955 Cliff Valley Way Northeast, Suite 220
Atlanta, Georgia 30029
(404) 329-0433

Whitewater, Ltd.
Long Creek, South Carolina 29658
(803) 647-9587

TOCCOA. The seat of Stephens County, this town is known to thousands of children as the site of Camp Toccoa, a first-rate facility owned and operated by Camp Fire, Inc. It is also the site of Toccoa Falls College, a fundamentalist four-year Bible college that was the scene of a tragic dam break that led to the death of 39 people in 1977.

Toccoa Falls. Located off Georgia 17 north of the downtown area, these 186-foot-high falls are on the campus of Toccoa Falls College. There is a small admission charge. The falls are open daily from 8:00 A.M. till dusk. **Traveler's Rest State Historical Park.** Once a stagecoach inn, Traveler's Rest was built in 1815 and added on to in 1830. Among the notables who stayed here are John C. Calhoun and Georgia's Confederate governor, Joseph E. Brown, who spent his wedding night in the building.

The combined house and inn has been restored to its 1850 appearance, complete with two slave cabins out back. All of the furniture is original, and all but one piece was made by hand specifically for this house. Traveler's Rest is listed on the National Register of Historic Places. Located on U.S. 123 six miles east of Toccoa, it is open Tuesday through Saturday from 9:00 to 5:00, and on Sunday from 2:00 to 5:30. A small admission is charged. Phone (404) 886-2256.

Events

Currahee Arts and Crafts Festival. Usually held in April, this festival brings together local craftspeople for demonstrations and sales. For further information write the Toccoa Chamber of Commerce, P.O. Box 577, Toccoa 30577. Call (404) 886-2132.

Harvest Festival. Held at the outdoor mall in Toccoa, this festival takes place in late October or early November.

UNICOI STATE PARK. This is one of the finer state parks in the area, offering 96 tent and trailer sites, 25 cottages, a beach for swimming, and boat rentals. It is located two miles north of Helen via Georgia 356. For further information write P.O. Box 256, Helen 30545. Call (404) 878-2201.

Events

Appalachian Music Festival. Held in mid-July, this festival brings together bluegrass, folk, and old-time players for a weekend of concerts, workshops, and mountain round dancing. For further information contact the park.

Fabric Creations from the Mountains. A part of National Spinning and Weaving Week, this is a gathering of weavers and spinners who demonstrate, exhibit, and sell their work. For further information write the park.

Fall Harvest Music and Dance. Held in late October, this event features live Appalachian music and round dancing. Admission is charged. For further information contact the park.

Fireside Arts and Crafts. Held in mid-February, this show brings together local craftspeople for demonstrations, workshops, and sales. For further information write the park.

Gardening Workshop. Held in mid-March, this event brings together the green-thumb crowd, and those who would like to join. Covers all aspects of gardening. For further information contact the park.

Georgia Mountains Eatin's and Squeezin's. Local people demonstrate how to make apple cider, churn butter, cook on a wood stove, and other old-time kitchen skills at this festival, which is held in mid-August. For further information contact the park.

Mountain Living. Here's a chance to try your hand at making baskets, quilting, making soap, riving shingles, dipping candles, and other traditional mountain arts. Held in mid-June. Contact the park for further information.

Native Americans of the Southeast. Displays of Indian artifacts and demonstrations of Indian skills mark this gathering, which is held in late September. Contact the park for further information.

Spring Wildflower Weekend. This late-April event provides walks and lectures on wildflowers, which proliferate in the mountains at winter's end. For further information write the park.

Turkey Hunter's Workshop. If you think you can call turkeys pretty well, here is a chance to find out how good you really are. This event features calling contests, movies, workshops, banquets, and sales of turkey-hunting paraphernalia. Held in late January. For further information write the park.

VOGEL STATE PARK. Located 11 miles south of Blairsville on U.S. 19/129 at Vogel Lake, this park is one of the oldest in the state. It has 85 tent and trailer campsites, 36 cottages, and a beach for swimming, and the Appalachian Trail runs through it. For further information write Route 1, Box 97, Blairsville 30512. Call (404) 745-2628.

Events

Along the Wildflower Trail. Late April is the time for this celebration of wildflowers. For further information contact the park.

Lake Trahyta Arts and Crafts Show. Artists and craftspeople demonstrate their work and sell toys, baskets, pottery, paintings, woodwork, and other items. Held in late July. Contact the park for further information.

Old Timers' Day. Storytelling, fiddling, banjo playing and an old-fashioned hoedown mark this happy event, which is held in mid-August. Contact the park for further information.

YOUNG HARRIS. This mountain town is the home of Young Harris College, a two-year school whose graduates have included Oliver Hardy, of Laurel and Hardy fame; Ronnie Milsaps, a country music singer; and Wayland Flowers, manipulator of a risqué puppet named Madam.

NINE

Southwest Virginia

OF ALL THE REGIONS covered in this book, Southwest Virginia has the most contrasts. The visitor to Abingdon, for example, will find the State Theater of Virginia and the nineteenth-century elegance of the Martha Washington Inn only a few miles from the bleak grit of a coal mining town. Breaks Interstate Park, the "Grand Canyon of the East," lies a few ridges away from mountains covered with the scars of strip mining. And accounts of violent coal strikes, both long-past and recent, will contrast with perhaps the warmest welcome you'll receive in the entire region.

Southwest Virginia is the place most likely to fulfill the visitor's stereotype of Appalachia—those who look for it will find poverty, tin-roofed shacks, and bleak towns. Paradoxically, however, the traveler may see more newly constructed mansions, some with swimming pools and helicopter landing pads, than anywhere else in he region.

Much of this is due to the region's history. The last part of the state to be settled, the mountains and "hollers" were populated by a proud and independent people who were all but ignored by those in eastern Virginia. The discovery

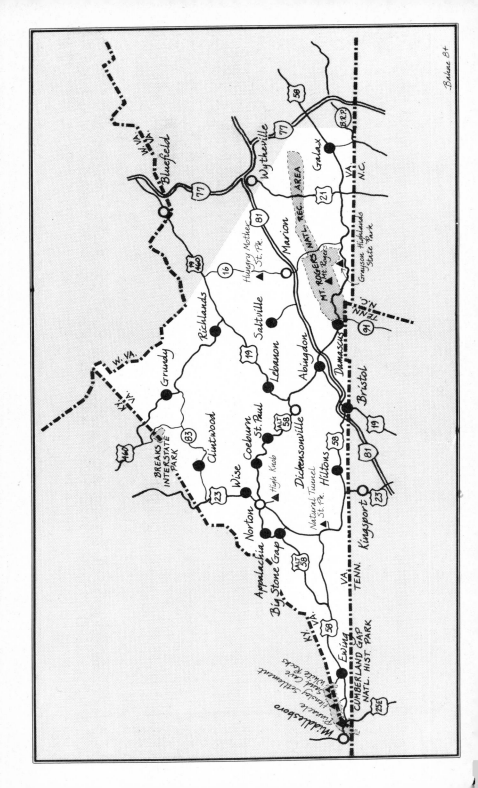

of coal, while not provoking a California-style gold rush, led in the 1880s to an influx of capital and the buying of land and mineral rights by large companies, some of them foreign. Many of the towns in Southwest Virginia received their charters at this time, and the long coal trains that are such a common sight in the region began to roll.

The people who had formerly scratched out a living on farms got jobs in the mines. Immigrants from Europe who spoke no English found themselves living in company housing and buying all their goods at the company store. "Saint Peter don't you call me, cause I can't go / I owe my soul to the company store" sang Tennessee Ernie Ford, and for some people it was true. When the unions and strikes came to the mines, the violence on both sides was appalling.

In the late fifties and sixties low oil prices caused coal mining to lag, and the people suffered. Stories about the region's poverty were published nationally. Then came the Arab oil boycott, and the nation discovered coal again. Men who had been truck drivers or small businessmen got in on the new coal boom, and they are today well represented among the millionaires who have built the mansions with the swimming pools. The region's new wealth is reflected in spruced up towns such as Big Stone Gap and Wise.

As in most booms, there was a bad side. Earlier in the century many an illiterate family had sold the mineral rights to their land for a pittance—sometimes as little as a dollar an acre. In the 1970s these families stood numbly by while coal operators with massive bulldozers and strings of trucks stripped the coal from what had been their family farms.

The mountains of Virginia are not usually on the itinerary of most out-of-state travelers. They either barrel down I-81, stopping only for gas or something to eat, or motor down the Blue Ridge Parkway further east. While the region is certainly not the Smoky Mountains, it has a beauty that is worth a journey to see. The Cumberland Gap National Historical Park is one of the gems of the national park system, on both historical and natural accounts. Breaks Interstate Park is equal to any park in North Carolina.

And best of all—despite the efforts of brochure writers and chambers of commerce—Southwest Virginia isn't crowded with tourists. Drama lovers can often get tickets to the Barter Theatre on the night of the performance, and backcountry permits are much more easily come by at Cumberland Gap than in the Smokies. The people in the museums and shops are delighted to see out-of-towners, and will go out of their way to make them welcome.

A swing through southwestern Virginia will give the traveler a look at a colorful way of life and a lovely piece of nature, and an experience that most visitors to the southern Appalachians never have.

HOW TO GET THERE

BY AIR. The closest commercial airport is Tri-Cities, near Bristol, Virginia. It is served by Piedmont, USAir, and Eastern airlines. The Knoxville, Tennessee, airport, about fifty miles away, is served by Delta, Eastern, Republic, United, and USAir, as well as smaller carriers.

FROM TENNESSEE. I-81 stretches from Tennessee through the eastern portion of the area discussed in this chapter. U.S. 11, the highway that preceded the interstate, runs parallel to it. U.S. 23 runs from Kingsport through the heart of Southwest Virginia, and connects to I-75 coming through Kentucky from the Midwest. From Knoxville, take I-75 or U.S. 25E north and join U.S. 58 near Cumberland Gap National Historical Park.

FROM NORTH CAROLINA. The Blue Ridge Parkway crosses the eastern extreme of the area discussed in this chapter. It may be more convenient to cut across Tennessee and connect to U.S. Alternate 58 in Abingdon or U.S. 23 in Kingsport.

ONCE YOU'RE THERE

The widest choices of restaurants and lodging places lie along the Tennessee border—in Abingdon, Bristol, and Kingsport, Tennessee, and in Middlesboro, Kentucky, near Cumberland Gap. These towns are all connected by U.S. 58, making an easy drive across the region.

If you are camping the possibilities widen, for the Jefferson National Forest, Breaks Interstate Park, and the park at Cumberland Gap offer plenty of spaces.

If you come in the summer, try to visit Big Stone Gap and see *The Trail of the Lonesome Pine*, an adaptation of a best-selling novel that was written in the town. Big Stone Gap is a nice place to walk around, as is Abingdon, Virginia, home of the all-round best festival in the area, the Virginia Highlands Festival.

As for natural beauty, try to see Breaks Interstate Park, and don't miss the Sand Cave and White Rocks at Cumberland Gap. Natural Tunnel State Park is worth a stop, and the Grayson Highlands State Park near the Blue Ridge Parkway is another good place to go.

TOWNS AND ATTRACTIONS

ABINGDON. Wolf Hills was the original name of this town. It seems that Daniel Boone, in passing through the area, tied his dogs up near a cave. While he was away some wolves came out of the cave and frightened the dogs. Today Abingdon is perhaps the most charming town in Southwest Virginia. Surrounding the Barter Theatre and the Martha Washington Inn is a small town with brick sidewalks, Federal-style houses, and tall trees.

Barter Theatre. The story of the State Theater of Virginia begins in the Depression, when local boy Robert Porterfield was a starving actor—literally—in New York. He knew that the folks back home in Abingdon had hard times, too, but at least they were eating well. Porterfield convinced a group of actors and actresses to come to Virginia with him, and together they opened the Barter Theatre. In those early days the box office accepted produce and canned goods in exchange for tickets, and playwrights' royalties were paid with country hams.

The theater flourished, and with a bettering economy was able to gently phase out the barter policy. The name remained, however, and under its aegis worked such thespians as Patricia Neal, Hume Cronyn, Gregory Peck, Ernest Borgnine, and Ned Beatty. In 1953 Robert Porterfield learned that the vintage Empire Theater in New York was to be demolished. He asked for and received the furnishings, including seats, curtains, and equipment, at no charge.

Serious drama and comedy are performed all year long by professional actors at the Barter Theatre, and children's productions and new plays are presented at the Barter Playhouse across the street. News of upcoming plays and ticket information can be obtained by writing the theater at Abingdon 24210. Call (703) 628-3991.

Cave House Craft Shop. The cave from which came the wolves that scared Daniel Boone's dogs is on the property of this cooperative crafts shop. The shop features a wide range of handmade goods, including quilts, baskets, baby clothing, pottery, dulcimers, stuffed animals, weavings, rugs, metalwork, small furniture, and wheat weavings. It is located at 279 East Main Street in Abingdon. Call (703) 628-7721.

Dixie Pottery. This warehouse of crockery is a good place to pick up an inexpensive set of dishes, glasses, or baskets. There are no potters on the premises, and virtually all of the goods are mass-produced. Located on U.S. 11 between exits 5 and 6. Open all year, Monday through Saturday from 9:30 to 6:00 and on Sunday from 1:00 to 6:00.

Dulcimer and Weave Shop. The Old Abingdon Weavers are headquartered here; products include handwoven cotton and wool coverlets. They also sell dulcimers, complete and in kits; wooden folk toys; and pottery. Located at 380 East Main Street in Abingdon. Open daily. Call (703) 628-4233.

Events

Virginia Highlands Festival. This is one of the better festivals in the region. Held in downtown Abingdon, it includes art shows; lectures and workshops by well-known writers; classical, folk, and bluegrass music; antique shows; old car shows; theater; and lots to eat. Held in the first two weeks of August. Write the Virginia Highlands Festival, Box 801, Abingdon 24210.

Lodging and Dining

The Martha Washington Inn. George Washington never slept here, and neither did Martha. The name comes from a women's college that was housed in this building from 1860 through 1932. The large, rambling wooden inn has 65 guest rooms furnished with antiques. It is open all year.

The inn is widely known for its dining room, a favorite stop for patrons of the Barter Theater before the performance. Breakfast as well as dinner is served, and the food is Southern style. The inn is located at 150 West Main Street in Abingdon. Write P.O. Box 1037, Abingdon 24210. Call (703) 628-3161.

APPALACHIA. Three railroads converge on Appalachia, which lies in the center of the coal-producing region of Virginia. For an idea of how much coal comes from this area, take a look at the Westmoreland Coal Company's Transloader, a device that loads railroad cars with four to five million tons of bituminous coal per year. It is not open to the public, but can be seen from U.S. 23 and Virginia 68.

Events

Railroad/Coal Days. This summer weekend celebrates the town's coal and railroad heritage with a gathering of retired miners, country and gospel music, a tennis tournament, a road race, local craftspeople, and plenty of home-cooked food. The activity revolves around Island Park in downtown Appalachia, and the centerpiece of the weekend is a ride on a steam train. The date of the festival varies from year to year, depending on the availability of the train. For further information contact the Wise County Chamber of Commerce, P.O. Box 226, Norton 24273; or call (703) 679-0961.

BIG STONE GAP. As might be guessed from the name, this town is in a gap in the mountains, and this location, with the confluence of three forks of the Powell River, led to a settlement. The discovery of coal in the region and the coming of the railroad put the town on the map; it received a charter as Mineral City in 1888 and became known as Big Stone Gap in 1890.

The popular image of mountaineers as feudin' and fightin' hillbillies was helped along by the writings of John Fox, Jr., a Harvard-educated Kentuckian who contracted tuberculosis and came home in 1884, more or less to die. He joined his family in developing timber and coal in the Big Stone Gap area, and became very close to many of the mountain people.

While his family exploited the mountain resources by day, at night Fox appropriated local tales and characters and put them on paper. The results were several books about southwestern Virginia, among them the best-selling *Little Shepard of Kingdom Come* and *Trail of the Lonesome Pine*. His vision of the mountaineer can be described as luridly romantic.

Fox traveled to Bar Harbor, Maine, and other fashionable watering holes to hang around his old Harvard chums, including the occupant of the White House, Theodore Roosevelt. By this time a best-selling author, Fox set his sights on Mme. Fritzi Scheff, a young opera singer, and married her after a courtship of 24 hours. He brought her in triumph to Big Stone Gap; old-timers used to claim she had 80 trunks and servants with her. Somehow the area wasn't quite what she had in mind; she soon left. Fox lived until 1919, when he died of pneumonia.

Harry W. Meador, Jr., Coal Museum. Owned by the Westmoreland Coal Company and operated by the Big Stone Gap Department of Recreation, this museum reflects the transition of the coal industry from the pick-and-shovel days to the mechanization of mining. It contains a replica of a coal company's dentist office, original chandeliers from company houses, equipment from company stores, a shuttle car, and various other period items. Located at East Third Street and Shawnee Avenue, the museum is open Wednesday through Saturday from 10:00 to 5:00. No admission is charged. Call (703) 523-4950.

John Fox, Jr., House. The man who put Big Stone Gap on the literary map wrote in this two-story house. Built in 1888 and now included on the National Register of Historic Places, it contains original Fox family furniture, including the pieces in the study where Fox did most of his writing. The house is now owned by the Lonesome Pine Arts and Crafts Association, and is located at 117 East Shawnee Avenue. It is open Tuesday through Saturday from 1:00 to 5:00 and Sunday from 2:00 to 6:00. A small admission is charged.

June Tolliver Craft House. John Fox, Jr., based the character of June Tolliver, the heroine of *The Trail of the Lonesome Pine,* on a young woman who boarded in this house while attending the Duff Academy. The house was built in 1890 and is on the National Register of Historic Places. It now contains a crafts shop that features locally made articles, including weavings, corn husk dolls, coal jewelry, and coal figurines. It is adjacent to the June Tolliver Playhouse, where *The Trail of* *the Lonesome Pine* is performed in the summer. The June Tolliver Craft House is open year-round from 10:00 to 5:00 on weekdays and from 2:00 to 6:00 on Sundays. **Southwest Virginia Museum.** Located in a house built in 1893 by an early developer of the area, this museum began with the donation of the Slemp Collection, an eclectic mix of mountain crafts, some Minton china originally presented to Benjamin Disraeli by Queen Victoria, quilts, Indian artifacts, pioneer relics, and early firearms. The museum is at the corner of West First Street and Wood Avenue in Big Stone Gap. It is open in the summer months Tuesday and Wednesday from 9:00 to 5:00, Thursday through Saturday from 9:00 to 6:00, and Sunday from 12:00 to 6:00. The rest of the year it is open Tuesday through Saturday from 9:00 to 5:00 and Sunday from 12:00 to 5:00. A small admission is charged. Call (703) 523-1322.

Trail of the Lonesome Pine. This adaptation of a novel by John Fox, Jr., has been performed every summer since 1963, making it the longest-running outdoor drama in the state. Acted by local people, the tale centers on a mountain girl and her beau, a young mining engineer from the East. Assorted characters such as Bad Rufe Tolliver and Devil Judd Tolliver add adventure to the love story. The drama is performed from the end of June through August on Thursday, Friday, and Saturday nights. Held in the June Tolliver Playhouse at Jerome Street and Clinton Avenue. For ticket information write June Tolliver Playhouse, Drawer 1976, Big Stone Gap 24219; or call (703) 523-2060.

Events

Christmas in the Mountains. On the first weekend in December local garden clubs decorate the John Fox, Jr., Museum, the June Tolliver House, and the Southwest Virginia Museum, all of which are open to the public. There are also flower shows and a concert. Write Garden Clubs of Big Stone Gap, Drawer 1976, Big Stone Gap 24319; or call (703) 523-0983.

Home Crafts Day. Held in mid-October, this gathering features mountain arts and crafts. For further information write the Gap Corporation Tourist and Information Center, P.O. Box 236, Big Stone Gap 24219.

Lonesome Pine Arts and Crafts Festival. Begun in 1964, this festival in early May features demonstrations of wood carving, quilting, and weaving, and sales of the products. Also provided are music, displays of antiques, and plenty to eat. Write Ruth McClanahan, P.O. Box 285, Big Stone Gap 24219. Call (703) 523-0846.

BREAKS INTERSTATE PARK. Often called the "Grand Canyon of the East," this park is the result of 250 million years of work by the Russell Fork River, which has carved the largest canyon this side of the Mississippi River. Located on the Kentucky-Virginia border, the canyon is five miles long and, in places, over sixteen hundred feet deep. The area of the park is rich in history: the Shawnees conducted powwows in a cave nearby, Englishman John Swift reportedly hid a fortune in silver somewhere in the vicinity, and the Hatfields and McCoys settled disputes here in their unique manner.

The park covers forty-six hundred acres. It features a modern lodge with 34 units, fully-equipped family cottages, and camping. From April through October an Olympic-sized pool, an ampitheater, and a visitors' center with a museum are open. Write to the park at Breaks 24607; or call (703) 865-4413.

BRISTOL. See BRISTOL in Chapter 1.

CLINTWOOD. This is the seat of Dickenson County.

Cumberland Museum. This museum depicts the lives and livelihoods of Appalachian people, ranging from Indians to miners. It includes a blacksmith shop and household items and farm tools, and a still for making moonshine. A log cabin on the property was used as a workshop by Big Stone Gap author John Fox, Jr. One interesting exhibit is the replica of a coal mine. Located three blocks south of the Dickenson County Courthouse, the museum is open from April through September, on Saturdays and Sundays from 1:00 to 4:00. There is a small admission fee. Call (703) 926-6632.

COEBURN. Supposedly named for a railroad engineer named Coe and a judge called Burn, this town was originally chartered in 1894. It is a railroad junction through which a lot of coal trains roll.

Events

Ralph Stanley Bluegrass Festival. The Stanley Brothers are in the pantheon of bluegrass music, and this festival, held in late May, brings together pickers, singers, dancers, and people who just enjoy a good time. Write for further information to Ralph Stanley, Stanley Ridge, Coeburn 24230. Call (703) 395-6318.

CUMBERLAND GAP NATIONAL HISTORICAL PARK. Whether you're interested in its historical significance or its natural beauty, you shouldn't miss this park. It ranks high on both accounts.

Cumberland Gap is one of the more historically significant sites in the region. Animals used it first; herds of buffalo stamped through it as they moved north and south. The Indians had traversed the gap for years, but the first white man to publicize it was Dr. Thomas Walker, an English land surveyor who passed through in 1750. He came at the right time. For decades, the increasing number of people in the East lacked a passage to the land beyond the Appalachian mountains. Explorers returned with tales of rich and fertile land beyond, but the long mountain ridges proved a formidable barrier.

A war with the French and continuing Indian troubles prevented much migration before 1775. Following the Treaty of Sycamore Shoals, however, Daniel Boone and a crew of 30 men set off from what is now Kingsport, Tennessee, and marked a trail—the Wilderness Road—into Kentucky. The land rush was on. By the end of the Revolutionary War some twelve thousand people had gone through the gap, and by 1800 over three hundred thousand people had crossed it, including Abraham Lincoln's parents. As the people prospered in Kentucky, they began to send goods and livestock back through the gap to the markets in the East.

By the 1820s and 1830s, however, the mountains had been breached further north, and traffic through Cumberland Gap slowed to a trickle. During the Civil War it became strategically important, and was occupied at various times by both Confederate and Union soldiers. The late 1800s witnessed an infusion of English capital into the iron and coal reserves in the area, and for a brief time the area around the gap prospered.

In our own century the Cumberland Gap was crossed by a modern highway, and it experienced a migration of a different sort. As economic opportunities opened in the cities of the North, many Southern black families passed through on their way to a better life. Now the gap is pierced by a railroad tunnel, and coal trucks thunder on the road. There is talk of building a highway tunnel underneath the gap, but nothing substantial has been done about this proposal.

Amid all this, a few remaining portions of the Wilderness Road still lie beneath the trees that grow in the gap. Visitors can stand there and ponder the words of Frederick Jackson Turner, who in 1893 wrote: "Stand at Cumberland Gap and watch the procession of civilization, marching single file—the buffalo following the trail to the salt springs, the Indian, the fur-trader and hunter, the cattle-raiser, the pioneer farmer—and the frontier has passed by."

The gap offers a lot to backpackers, day hikers, and naturalists as well. The park covers over twenty thousand acres, which can best be viewed from the Pinnacle, an overlook from which one can see into three states.

Activities in the Park

Camping. A 160-site campground is located on the Virginia side of the park. It can accommodate anything from pup tents to large recreational vehicles, but has no showers or hookups for RVs. There are four primitive campgrounds on the Ridge Trail; permits for these must be obtained at the Visitor Center. At certain times during the year fires in the backcountry are prohibited.

Hiking. The Ridge Trail, which runs along the top of Cumberland Mountain, is the main trail in the park. It extends 20 miles, from the Pinnacle to the parking lot at Sand Cave. There are three points along the trail that can be reached by driving along the bottom of Cumberland Mountain and hiking straight up.

Sights in the Park

Hensley Settlement. In 1904 a man named Sherman Hensley led his family to the top of Cumberland Mountain and established Hensley Settlement, which remained a largely self-sufficient community for nearly fifty years. Hensley's band of twentieth-century pioneers built their own houses, rail fences, and outbuildings. If they couldn't make or grow something, they rode horses down the mountain to get it.

The Hensleys began to leave their mountain home in the 1940s, and when the park was established in 1955 the farmsteads were dilapidated. Since then three farms, a small schoolhouse, and a cemetery have been restored. During the summer months young people stay at the settlement and demonstrate early farming techniques.

To get to Hensley Settlement drive along U.S. 58 in Virginia to Virginia 690. Stop at a small parking area, and walk up the trail. About three miles long, it goes right up Cumberland Mountain. The trail is steep, but the settlement is never crowded once you get there. Children—if they can make the hike—usually like this outing.

Sand Cave. The truly astonishing natural feature of Cumberland Gap National Historical Park is Sand Cave. Located on the Kentucky side of the park, it is accessible only by hiking about four miles, but it is well worth the trip. The cave is one enormous room—almost an acre and a quarter in size. The entrance alone is imposing; it is 80 feet high. The cave floor is made up of dry sand—tons and tons of it. Children of all ages will like climbing to the top of the sand bank and running down. Outside is a waterfall, whose volume fluctuates according to the amount of rainfall. And best of all, since it's a good hike to Sand Cave, there are never many people there. To get to the cave drive east on U.S. 58 to Ewing, Virginia. Turn left at the People's Bank, and drive a short way to the Civitan Club Parking lot. Lock the car and start hiking.

White Rocks. The land that makes up the park was once under the sea, and this is nowhere more apparent than at White Rocks. Rising at the east end of Cumberland Mountain, these sheer cliffs are made of huge hunks of conglomerate, a combination of sandstone and pebbles. To pioneer travelers the cliffs were fearsome symbols of the hazards they would soon face, but modern day explorers—including children, if they are adventuresome—will enjoy the view from the top. Again, you have to hike up the side of Cumberland Mountain for about three miles to get there. The cliffs are only a one-mile hike from Sand Cave, so you can see both in one trip. To get to the trailhead drive east on U.S. 58 to Ewing, Virginia. Turn left at the People's Bank and drive a short way to the Civitan Club Parking lot.

Further information on the park can be obtained by writing the Superintendent at Cumberland Gap National Historical Park, Box 840, Middlesboro, Kentucky 40965, or by calling (606) 248-2817.

DAMASCUS. This town lies on U.S. 58, the best route to Backbone Rock and the Iron Mountain Stoneware pottery in Tennessee. See Chapter 1 for details.

EWING. The trailhead for White Rocks and Sand Cave in the Cumberland Gap National Historical Park, this town lies on U.S. 58.

Karlan. Visitors can tour this privately owned ante-bellum home and see a guest house and garage that were formerly slave quarters, a carriage house, three barns, a machinery shed, and various barnyard out-buildings. A gift shop and concession stand are on the premises. Located on U.S. 58 just east of the Elydale School. Open May through October, Tuesday through Saturday from 1:00 to 4:30 and Sunday from 1:00 to 5:00.

GALAX. Although in music circles it is synonymous with old-time fiddling, the name of this town actually comes from a mountain evergreen herb with small white flowers.

Jeff Matthews Memorial Museum. Since local museums generally take whatever is given to them, their collec-tions are limited only by the taste and efforts of the donors, and are therefore almost always unconven-tional. This museum is a good example: it has—take a deep breath—eighty-five hundred arrowheads and other Indian artifacts; over a thousand knives; over forty mounted animal heads from Alaska, British Columbia, Alberta, Mexico, and the Yukon; an African collection of musical instruments and other items; a 1931 fire truck; and an exhibit on the 1979 Miss America. There are also two restored log cabins.

Museum professionals may sniff at the lack of a unifying theme, but few museums in places like Boston or New York can approach the scope of this one. It is open Wednesday, Thursday, and Friday from 1:00 to 5:00, Saturday from 11:00 to 4:00, and Sunday from 1:00 to 4:00. No admission is charged. The museum is located at 606 West Stuart Drive, adjacent to the Vaughan Memorial Library. Call (703) 236-2402.

Rooftop of Virginia. This crafts shop features work by low-income people who are struggling to be self-sufficient. Located at 206 North Main Street, it is open on Monday through Friday from 9:00 to 5:00.

Events

Old Fiddlers' Convention. Old-time musicians have convened here since 1935 in this oldest and largest such gathering in the country. Beginning musicians, established bands, and "sources" in today's folk music renaissance park their cars and camp in Felts Park, where impromptu ensembles play all day and all night while contestants perform on stage. Music literally fills the air. In recent years more and more bluegrass players have come to Galax, and their fast licks on banjo and soaring fiddle solos have attracted crowds of spectators who counter hot bluegrass music with cold beer. They can get pretty obnoxious in the process.

Camping is virtually the only way to go at the Old Fiddlers' Convention—the few motels in the area are booked long ahead. Contestants can park for free inside the park; noncontestants can park for free outside. For further information write Oscar Hall, P.O. Box 655, Galax 24333; or call (703) 236-6355.

GRAYSON HIGHLANDS STATE PARK. Located on U.S. 58 midway between Independence and Damascus, this out-of-the-way park is a pleasant surprise for the first-time visitor. Located near Mount Rogers, at 5,729 feet the highest point in the state, this park has several peaks jutting above the five-thousand-foot level.

The flame azaleas and rhododendron bloom in late May and early June, and a visitors' center that is open in the summer contains displays of pioneer items and mountain crafts. The park also has excellent camping and picnicking facilities and hiking trails. For further information write Superintendent, Grayson Highlands State Park, Route 2, Box 141, Mouth of Wilson 24363. Call (703) 579-7092.

GRUNDY. This is coal country. Buchanan County, of which Grundy is the seat, has extensive deep mines and strip mines—or "surface mines," as the industry euphemistically calls them. Some of the mine shafts penetrate thirteen hundred feet into coal seams, making them among the deepest in America. The money from all this coal is evident in the number of large homes and private aircraft in the area, and especially to those just passing through on the way to Breaks Interstate Park, in the number of huge coal trucks that fill the roads.

Events

Big K Raft Race. The Levisa River provides the setting for a ten-mile race with rafts, canoes, kayaks, and other watercraft. Held in mid-April. Write Curtis Mullins, Grundy 24614; or call (703) 935-2181.

Buchanan County Fair. The fair features displays of agricultural produce and handicrafts as well as mountain music and plenty to eat. Held in the first week in August. Write the Grundy Chamber of Commerce, P.O. Box 672, Grundy 24614; or call (703) 935-4147.

HILTONS. Situated on U.S. 58, this town sits at the foot of Clinch Mountain, the first barrier encountered by early pioneers.

Carter Family Fold. A. P. Carter, his wife Sarah, and her cousin Maybelle made up the Carter Family, one of the earliest country music groups. Between 1927 and 1942 they recorded over three hundred songs, one hundred of which were penned by A. P. Some have become classics in country and folk music: "Wildwood Flower," "I'm Thinking Tonight of My Blue Eyes," and "Keep on the Sunny Side."

None of the Carter Family trio is alive today, but the tradition of simple music without the rhinestones is kept alive at the Carter Family Fold by Janette and Joe Carter, two of A. P. and Sarah's children. The fold, which consists of a museum and a rustic shed seating a thousand on the side of a hill, features a live concert every Saturday night. Only acoustic instruments are played, and the music ranges from soulful ballads to frenetic bluegrass. Members of the audience are invited to clog on a concrete floor in front of the stage, and on most nights the dust is raised by a colorful conglomeration of young and old, fat and thin, some with braces and some without teeth.

Unlike at many gatherings of bluegrass fans, no drinking (or "drankin," as Janette Carter pronounces it) is tolerated. Offenders are rapidly shown the door.

The Carter Family Fold is off U.S. 58 on Virginia 614. Admission is charged. Call (703) 386-9480.

Carter Family Museum. After the Carter Family retired from performing, A. P. ran a store from 1945 to 1950. The building now houses a museum, which contains, among other things, the original pressings of Carter Family 78-rpm records, photographs and books, musical instruments, show clothes, and other memorabilia. It is open only from 5:00 to 7:00 on Saturday nights, before the weekly concert begins.

Events

August Festival. The Carter Family made their first record in August of 1927, and to commemorate this a festival is held in early August each year. Shows run continuously from early afternoon until almost midnight. Local craftspeople and artists display their wares in tents. For information write the Carter Family Fold, P.O. Box 111, Hiltons 24258. Call (703) 386-9480.

HUNGRY MOTHER STATE PARK. This park gets its name from a legend concerning a pioneer woman and her toddler who were captured by raiding Shawnee Indians. The woman escaped, carrying the child, and got as far as the peak known as Molly's Knob before collapsing. The child waded down a shallow creek to a group of houses crying "Hungry—Mother! Hungry—Mother!"

The park features a 108-acre lake set amid 2,180 acres of gentle mountains. It also offers swimming, camping, cabins, hiking, horseback riding, pleasure boats, a visitors' center, and a restaurant. The cabins are isolated and inexpensive. The park is three miles north of Marion on Route 16. For further information write Superintendent, Route 5, Box 109, Marion 24354. Call (703) 783-3422.

JEFFERSON NATIONAL FOREST. There are no national parks in this part of Virginia, but this national forest offers many opportunities for outdoor adventure. Much of the three hundred miles of the Appalachian Trail in Virginia is located here, as are various camping sites and a total of 950 miles of trails. Jefferson National Forest also includes the Mount Rogers National Recreation Area, which is listed separately.

The camping areas, like others that are federally administered, are simple. All have tent pads, cooking grills, tables, and toilets. Some have warm-water showers and special attractions such as fishing lakes and beaches. Unless otherwise posted, backcountry camping is encouraged all over the forest.

Big game is hunted in this forest, and the quiet hiker may get a chance to see black bears, deer, and wild turkeys. More than 160 types of birds either live in the forest or migrate through it.

Two districts of the Jefferson National Forest lie within the region covered by this book.

Clinch Ranger District. This westernmost section of the forest contains five campgrounds. Of particular interest is the High Knob Recreation Area, which is 3.7 miles south of Norton on Virginia 619; turn left on Forest Service Road 238. This peak rises 4,162 feet for a panoramic view of the surrounding area. For more information and a map of the district write: District Ranger, U.S. Forest Service, Route 1, P.O. Box 320-H, Wise 24293. The district office is across from Clinch Mountain Community College on State Route 646. Call (703) 328-2931.

Wythe Ranger District. Few recreation areas in this district lie in the range of this book. For a map and information on the area, write: District Ranger, U.S. Forest Service, Route 4, Wytheville 24382. The office is located on U.S. 11 west of Wytheville. Call (703) 228-5551.

The headquarters of the Jefferson National Forest can be reached by writing: Forest Supervisor, Jefferson National Forest, 210 Franklin Road, Roanoke 24011. Call (703) 982-6270.

LEBANON. The seat of Russell County was named for its tall cedar trees, which suggested the Biblical Cedars of Lebanon.

Old Russell Courthouse and Museum. From 1799 to 1818 this small brick structure was the courthouse for Russell County. It now houses artifacts from the country's history. Located nine miles from Lebanon on Virginia 71 in the village of Dickensonville. Hours vary. For further information write E. S. Fugate, Jr., Box 62, Lebanon 24210; or call (703) 889-2757.

MOUNT ROGERS NATIONAL RECREATION AREA. Covering one hundred thousand acres, this section of the Jefferson National Forest is one-fifth the size of the Great Smoky Mountains National Park, but has far fewer than one-fifth the visitors. Because the area is less heavily promoted than scenic parts of North Carolina, travelers often pass it by in their race to the Smokies, which suits its regular users just fine.

At the southern end of the recreation area is Mount Rogers, which at 5,729 feet is the highest peak in Virginia. Wildlife present include black bear, deer, wild turkey, and smaller creatures such as ruffed grouse, flying squirrel, and various hawks. The only species of tree on the U.S. endangered list, the Virginia round-leaf birch, grows here in small numbers. The hiking here ranges from short nature walks to the 38½-mile trail from Whitetop Mountain to Iron

Mountain. The area includes ten campgrounds and the Buller Bass Fish Hatchery.

Additional information and maps of the area can be obtained by writing: Area Ranger, U.S. Forest Service, Route 1, P.O. Box 303, Marion 24354. Call (703) 783-5196. The office is seven miles south of Marion on State Route 16.

NATURAL TUNNEL STATE PARK. William Jennings Bryan once pronounced Natural Tunnel the Eighth Wonder of the World. This accolade may have been meant for local consumption, but the tunnel and adjacent natural ampitheater are definitely worth seeing.

The tunnel is estimated to be over one million years old, and has been shared by a stream and a railroad since 1890. It is 850 feet long, with an opening as high as a ten-story building. Its southern end leads into a deep, semi-circular basin known as the Amphitheater. The nearly vertical walls of this limestone basin rise to a height of four hundred feet. Long a gathering place for mountain people, the Amphitheater has served as the site for gospel singings, Sunday afternoon picnics, and political meetings.

A state park since 1967, Natural Tunnel offers a small museum and attractive facilities for picnicking, camping, swimming, and hiking. Drive 13 miles north of Gate City on U.S. 23 and one-half mile to the right on State Route 871. No admission is charged. For further information write Natural Tunnel State Park, Route 3, P.O. Box 250, Clinchport 24244. Call (703) 940-2674.

RICHLANDS. This small town in the coal country has a vital arts program. A year-round series of performances includes classical musicians, mountain musicians, and theater. For details write Richlands Area Citizens for the Arts, P.O. Box 1558, Richlands 24641; or call (703) 963-3385.

Events

Arts and Crafts in the Heart of the Coalfields Festival.
Held in the first week of October, this festival features
locally handcrafted weavings, pottery, paintings, rugs,
and quilts. Gospel, choral, and bluegrass music is performed. Write Richlands Area Citizens for the Arts, P.O.
Box 1558, Richlands 24641. Call (703) 963-3385.

SAINT PAUL. The coming of the railroad to this area prompted
quite a few money-making schemes. A promotion company
in this town, anticipating wonderful things, proposed
building twin cities named Minneapolis and St. Paul. The
boosters paid $100 to the postmaster of another village
named St. Paul for exclusive rights to the name, and streets
were laid out. Then the financing for the railroad failed,
and the village of Minneapolis never saw the light of day.

SALTVILLE. Long before coal was discovered in southwestern Virginia, this town was known for its salt deposits. In
prehistoric times mastodons, ground sloths, bison, and
other animals came to the salt licks. Migrating birds de-
posited the seeds of saltwater plants, providing coastal vegetation hundreds of miles from the seashore.

The first commercial salt mine was dug in 1799. In the
days before refrigeration, salt was vital for preserving meat,
and production increased as the population of the colonies
grew. In the 1800s huge furnaces were used to reduce brine
to salt, and the area was contested in the Civil War, since
it was the South's chief source of salt.

In modern times, as the need for salt diminished, the
town began to produce crushed stone and chemicals. A
seven-mile tramway was constructed to carry limestone
overhead to a processing plant.

Saltville has more historic buildings and houses, in
proportion to its size, than any other town in southwestern
Virginia. The Smythe County Chamber of Commerce has
prepared a brochure listing the old houses, the Civil War

fortifications, and the historic salt works. See the address below.

Saltville Museum Park. This museum is housed in what was the office of a salt company over a hundred years ago. The park includes two steam locomotives that were used by local industries, tramway buckets, and huge iron kettles that were used to boil brine in the nineteenth century. Located on Palmer Avenue in Saltville, the museum is open from 9:00 to 5:00 during the summer months, and other times by appointment. For further information contact the Smythe County Chamber of Commerce, 200 East Main Street, Marion 24354; or call (703) 783-3161.

WISE. The first recorded venture into this neighborhood was in 1750, when Capt. Christopher Gist came back with a lump of coal in his knapsack and reported to Gen. George Washington. Wise County was established in 1856; the town that was to become Wise had only 250 inhabitants at the time. The area boomed when the railroads came at the end of the nineteenth century, and again during the energy crisis of the 1970s.

Lodging and Dining

The Inn at Wise Courthouse. Long a stop for circuit-riding judges and attorneys who were arguing cases, this inn, located next to the courthouse in Wise, has 44 new motel units, six dining rooms, and a taproom. Write the Inn at Wise, Main Street, Wise 24293; or call (703) 328-2241.

Index

Folk Art Center, 166
Folk Life Center of the Smokies, 36, 37
Folk Life Festival, 37
Fontana, 90, 185–86
Foothills Parkway, 89–90
Forbidden Caverns, 62
Ford, Tennessee Ernie, 6
Forges, 150, 186
Fort Loudon State Historical Area, 82–83
Fort Mountain State Park, 221
Fort Patrick Henry Dam, 21
Fort Watauga, 11, 13
Fox, John Jr.: *Little Shepard of Kingdom Come*, 244–45
"Trail of the Lonesome Pine," 246
Foxfire, 205, 228–29
Franklin, 186–87
French Broad River, 5, 10, 141, 145
Frozen Head State Natural Area, 37–38
Fruit crops, 190–91, 223

Galax, 252–53
Gatlinburg, 38–42, 87
Gems, 186, 202
  festival of, 187
  museum, 48, 150
  See also Minerals
Georgia Mountain Fair, 227
Glass-staining, 217
Gold mining, 210, 219, 220
Goodwin Guild Weavers, 133
Graham, Rev. Billy, 132
Grandfather Mountain, 118, 143–44, 164
Grand Guitar, the (museum), 7
Graphite Reactor, 35, 57
Grayson Highlands State Park, 253–54
Greasy Cove Racetrack, 14
Great Smoky Mountains National Park, 8, 41, 85–87
  areas of interest, 93–98
  entries and scenic roads, 87–93
  recreational activities, 100–14
  wildlife, 98–100

Great Warpath, 63, 73
Greeneville, Tennessee, 3, 5, 15–17
Gregory Bald, 98, 107–108
Gregory Ridge Trail, 108
Grotto Falls, 97, 110
Grove, E. W., 120, 125
  Grove Park Inn, 120, 129
Grundy, 254

Hambidge Center, 229–30
Hang gliding, 71–72, 143, 144
Harps. *See* Dulcimers and harps
Harrison, Mount, 39
Harrogate, 35, 36, 42–43
Hayesville, 188
Health Adventure, 124–25
Helen (town), 209, 224–27
Hendersonville, 188–92
Hensley Settlement, 250
Henson and Courtner, 8
Henwallow Falls, 110
Hiawassee, 227
High Knob Recreation Area, 256
Highland Games, 42, 144
Highlands, 192–95
High Shoals, 213
Hiker's Guide to the Smokies (Sierra Club), 106
Hiking
  Bartram Trail, 218
  along Blue Ridge Parkway, 159, 161, 164
  in Cumberland National Park, 250
  in Great Smoky Mountains National Park, 103–108
  in Pisgah National Forest, 148
  in Mount Rogers National Area, 257–58
  in Nantahala National Forest, 188
Hiking, backcountry, 99
Hiltons, 254–55
Hiwassee Dam and Lake, 196
Holmes State Forest, 189
Holston River, 22
Hope, Thomas, 46
"Horn in the West," 137
Horseback riding, 111–12, 224

Meat, smoked, 8
Meigs Falls, 96
Metcalf Bottoms, 91, 95
Middlesboro, Kentucky, 10, 241
Mills, grain, 59, 94, 95, 229, 230
Minerals, 150, 186
   festival, 151
   museums, 48, 123, 164
   See also Gems
Mingus Creek, 111
Mingus Mill, 95–96
Mining, 79–80, 82, 150, 186, 259
   See also Coal; Gold mining
Missionary Ridge, 65, 67
Mitchell, Dr. Elisha, 165–66
Moccasin Creek State Park, 227–
   28
Morristown, 6, 24–25
Moses H. Cone Memorial Park,
   133, 159, 161, 163
Mountain City (Georgia), 228
Mountain City (Tennessee), 6, 25
Mountain climbing, 149, 219
Mountain Heritage Center, 182
Mount Jefferson State Park, 141–
   42
Mount Mitchell State Park, 165–
   66
Mount Rogers National Recre-
   ation Area, 257–58
Murphy, 195–97
Muscle Shoals, 31–32
Museum of Appalachia, 35, 55
Museums
   antique autos, 126, 222
   gold, 220
   handicrafts, 203
   historical, 11, 15, 24, 35, 41,
      68–69, 81, 123, 257
   of Indian life, 180, 195–96
   Jeff Matthews Memorial Mu-
      seum, 249
   Knoxville Academy of Medi-
      cine, 48
   McClung Museum, 48
   music, 17, 255
   National Knife Museum, 70
   pioneer and mountain life, 55,
      79, 146, 182, 231, 246, 247–
      48

Saltville, 260
Scopes Museum, 81
Southwest Virginia Museum,
   243
   See also Art museums; Chil-
      dren; Coal; Gems; Minerals;
      Railroads; Wax Museums
Music
   country, 6–7, 222, 253
   gospel, 26, 144
   mountain, 37
   See also Music concerts; Music
      festivals
Music concerts, 139, 174–75, 193
Music festivals
   bluegrass, 27, 42, 142, 187, 220,
      227, 234–35, 248, 253
   mountain music, 55, 59, 61,
      129, 147
Mystery Hill, 133–34

Nantahala Gorge, 200
Nantahala National Forest, 197–
   200
   Cheoah Ranger District, 199
   Highlands Ranger District, 199
   Tusquitee Ranger District, 199
   waterfalls in, 198
   Wayah Ranger District, 199–
      200
National Cemetery, Chattanooga,
   68
National Climatic Center and Na-
   tional Weather Records Cen-
   ter, 125
National Knife Museum, 70
National Storytelling Festival, 19
Natural Tunnel State Park, 258
Nature roads in Great Smoky
   Mountains, 91–92
Netherland Inn, 22
Newfound Gap Road, 88–89
Newport, 5, 25
New River Outfitters, 142
New River State Park, 142
Nolan, Dr. John, 20
Norris, 54–55
Norris Dam, 35, 55
   State Park, 35, 55
Norris Lake, 36

For Your Information

The Harvard Common Press is located in Boston, Massachusetts. We specialize in practical guides to small business, careers, travel, family matters, and cooking. We also have an imprint, Gambit Books, which includes illustrated children's books and literary titles. If you'd like to see a copy of our complete catalog, please write to us at: The Harvard Common Press, 535 Albany Street, Boston, Massachusetts 02118. Our books are available at bookstores or, if you'd like to order directly from us, please send a check for the cost of the book plus $2 postage and handling.

We have listed a few of our titles below that we thought might interest readers of this book.

***Exploring Our
National Parks and Monuments***
Revised Eighth Edition
By Devereux Butcher
$10.95 paperback, ISBN 0–87645–122–9
$19.95 cloth, ISBN 0–87645–124–5
"This is very possibly the best available collection of photographs of our national parks. Schools and libraries will find it an admirable guide and sourcebook as will the traveler."—*Library Journal*
"This book is informed by the passionate belief that there is a better way to save this national heritage."—*The Atlantic Monthly*
Completely revised and updated, this classic guide has 140,000 copies in print and includes over 400 black and white photographs. *374 pages.*

How to Take Great Trips
With Your Kids
By Sanford and Joan Portnoy
$8.95 paperback, ISBN 0–916782–51–4
$14.95 cloth, ISBN 0–916782–52–2
"The Portnoys write with professional and parental au-
thority, having traveled extensively with their two chil-
dren. Their guidelines for a successful trip cover all bases
and will be valuable to those without children as well.
Especially useful are the games to play and the list of names
and addresses of travel organizations. Recommended."—
Library Journal. 196 pages.

The Portable Pet
How to Travel Anywhere
With Your Dog or Cat
By Barbara Nicholas
$5.95 paperback, ISBN 0–916782–49–2
$10.95 cloth, ISBN 0–916782–50–6
A lively and pragmatic guide to travel with dogs and cats.
The author guides readers through travel situations in the
U.S. and abroad, and addresses all problems in a simple,
questions-and-answer format. Whether you're planning a
Sunday drive or a long-distance flight, *The Portable Pet* will
help you insure the comfort and safety of your dog or cat.
96 pages.